T0284550

PONDER ANEW

PONDER ANEW

CONVERSATIONS IN 21ST CENTURY CHURCH MUSIC

EDITED BY JESSICA NELSON

Foreword by William Bradley Roberts

Contributors include: Jennifer Melnyk Deaton, Deon Johnson, C. Ellis Reyes Montes, Rita Teschner Powell, David Sinden, Michael Smith, Keith Tan

CHURCH
PUBLISHING
INCORPORATED

Copyright © 2022 by Jessica Nelson

All rights reserved. No part of this book may be reproduced, stored in a retrieval system, or transmitted in any form or by any means, electronic or mechanical, including photocopying, recording, or otherwise, without the written permission of the publisher.

Unless otherwise noted, the Scripture quotations are from New Revised Standard Version Bible, copyright © 1989 National Council of the Churches of Christ in the United States of America. Used by permission. All rights reserved worldwide.

Scripture quotations marked (NIV) are taken from the Holy Bible, New International Version®, NIV®. Copyright © 1973, 1978, 1984, 2011 by Biblica, Inc.™ Used by permission of Zondervan. All rights reserved worldwide. www.zondervan.com The "NIV" and "New International Version" are trademarks registered in the United States Patent and Trademark Office by Biblica, Inc.™

Scripture quotations marked (KJV) are taken from the KING JAMES VERSION (KJV): KING JAMES VERSION, public domain.

Church Publishing
19 East 34th Street
New York, NY 10016

Cover design by Dylan Marcus McConnell, Tiny Little Hammers
Typeset by Denise Hoff

Library of Congress Cataloging-in-Publication Data

Names: Nelson, Jessica, editor. | Roberts, William Bradley, writer of foreword.
Title: Ponder anew : conversations in 21st century church music / edited by Jessica Nelson ; foreword by William Bradley Roberts.
Description: New York : Church Publishing, 2022.
Identifiers: LCCN 2022004773 (print) | LCCN 2022004774 (ebook) | ISBN 9781640654440 (paperback) | ISBN 9781640654457 (epub)
Subjects: LCSH: Church music--21st century. | Music in churches. | Public worship.
Classification: LCC ML3000 .P67 2022 (print) | LCC ML3000 (ebook) | DDC 781.71--dc23
LC record available at https://lccn.loc.gov/2022004773
LC ebook record available at https://lccn.loc.gov/2022004774

In thanksgiving for the Mississippi Conference
on Church Music and Liturgy

Contents

II ▪ CONVERSATIONS IN VOCATION

III ▪ SERMONS

Foreword

The title of this collection of essays celebrates both the wisdom of legacy and the fresh insights of new thinking. *Ponder Anew* is accessible and richly layered. *Ponder* suggests looking deeply at an idea, turning it like a prism to see multiple facets. *Anew* implies that the readers have thought about the matters at hand and are now ready to think about them again in a new way. *Ponder Anew* is not only an invitation, but also an imperative.

To be invited to ponder anew is a profound honor, because the authors thus imply that the reader not only knows something of our worship's legacy—in this case the practice of liturgical music—but also has the capacity to rethink issues with a storied past so that they sparkle with contemporary energy. What an exciting journey on which to embark, especially in the company of the present authors, companions who will shine their searchlights on the subject matter.

The authors—priests, bishops, church musicians, composers, professors—are variously practitioners of not only traditional church music, but also of popular religious song[1] and proponents of diverse worship practices from low church to high. They are just the kind of people whose company you want to share while marveling over a collection of rare jewels.

Church music, like the rest of our culture, is changing and developing at a dizzying pace. Even the most observant practitioners find themselves inundated with a flood of new information and repertoire. To be sure, some will react to this challenge with a stern digging in of heels. For them, earlier visions of church music are adequate and must be defended at all costs. In doing so, they inadvertently imply that the Anglican musical legacy is fragile and must be protected. This book is probably not for them (unless they are courageous enough to read with a perspective other than their own, a daring act for any of us). This is not to suggest that anything new must be good, any more than everything old must be good. It is to suggest instead that both old and new deserve a fresh look.

Who will delight in *Ponder Anew*? Both professional church musicians and amateur (in its best and original meaning) aficionados of the art, who vigorously support the rich heritage of the composition, preparation, and performance of

---

1. *Popular religious song* is a term created by Carol Doran to denote music that appeals to a broad spectrum of people, informal music, what musicologist Wiley Hitchcock refers to as "music of the vernacular tradition." For a fuller discussion, see *Music and Vital Congregations* by William Bradley Roberts (New York: Church Publishing), 45ff.

great sacred music and who also are interested in new directions, fresh thoughts, and new composition. These are the advocates of church music who wonder about the culture around us and how our worship and music might engage with it. They concern themselves with demographic shifts inside and outside the church, knowing that welcoming the stranger is not a mere nicety, but a life-giving mandate from our Lord.[2]

Music is a profound cultural marker. Learn the songs of a culture, and you will quickly learn insights that otherwise might have required a much longer time. A friend of mine says that if she has a date with a person who doesn't like the music of J. S. Bach, that date is the last one. "That tells me all I need to know," she says. Music speaks to our identity.

Sometimes our own cultural markers are so integral to our identity that we don't recognize those that are just as engrained in others. When English-speaking missionaries first traveled to Africa, they took with them a large dose of their own culture, which in many instances was entwined with the gospel they preached. If natives of the mission field were to become Christianized, it was thought, they must learn the hymns and songs the missionaries knew. Gospel hymns of the late nineteenth century became the worship music of the new Christians. Contemporary missionaries, on the other hand, are more likely to affirm the culture of the people they serve. That includes music for worship, which nowadays is likely to be fashioned from local folk tunes (or else composed in that style).

Traveling around Africa and listening to the music of worship, one can easily determine when and by whom native people were missionized. In some areas, the worship music repertoire still consists of nineteenth-century gospel hymns from the United States and the British Isles. In other areas one hears music in church that has a distinctively local feel to it. In both Davies, South Africa, and Guayaquil, Ecuador, I was delighted to hear passionate singing by parishioners whose repertoire was totally Indigenous music.

As our cultural comprehension broadens, we hear the same gospel in a new light. For example, the last few decades have seen a rise in the public role of women in the church. (Some recognize that women have always guided the church but weren't acknowledged for it.) Racial reconciliation has become a front-burner issue, and many churches have committed themselves to making huge changes in church and culture to correct the demeaning injustices endured by People of Color.

LGBTQIA+ parishioners and citizens have moved "beyond inclusion" (to borrow the name of an effective conference on the subject[3]) to full, robust participation at every level. Tolerance is no longer enough. Those who have felt the

---

2. "Be not forgetful to entertain strangers: for thereby some have entertained angels unawares" (Heb 13:2, KJV).

3. This influential conference was first offered in April 1998 by All Saints Episcopal Church, Pasadena, California.

sting of exclusion are now unsatisfied by tolerance and rightly expect instead to be fully embraced for who they are. God has no stepchildren. Every member of the human race is a child of God.

These relatively rapid changes (though they feel distressingly slow to those who have suffered and endured) have enormous implications for the practice of church music. Much of sacred music is sung and, therefore, has texts. Any linguist, amateur or professional, will attest to the nature of language to change, to incorporate new words, even to embrace intentionally created words. One cannot notice the shifts in culture and pretend they have no ramifications for worship. When and how is worship language changed to relate to contemporary people? In my experience, language changes are best made (1) using the aid of experts— poets, theologians, liturgists, musicians; (2) altering words deliberatively, not spontaneously; (3) avoiding trendy words that might seem dated in five years; and (4) listening for the beauty of language as well as its accuracy.

Sometimes new movements arise to fill a gap or respond to a need. Worship with the Book of Common Prayer is the enduring treasure of Anglicanism. Many of us were attracted to liturgical worship by the beauty of its language and the rich understanding of prayer it offers. From the original Book of Common Prayer, created largely by Archbishop of Canterbury Thomas Cranmer (1489–1556), to subsequent editions in many countries, Christianity has greatly benefited from "common prayer," the prayers of all the people.

As wonderful as the Book of Common Prayer is, some have sensed the need for silence as a balance for continual wordiness. This silence is manifest in the surge of interest in contemplative prayer, in worship derived from the monastic life. This way of praying involves large amounts of silence, a rare commodity in much liturgical worship. Some worshippers sense the need to retreat from the noisy clamor of the culture to a dark, quiet, meditative place where God's voice is easily heard. When human chatter ceases, practitioners of contemplative worship discover that God's "still small voice" (1 Kings 19:12, KJV) is heard in stark contrast. To be sure, there are opportunities for silence in liturgical worship (even mandated by the Prayer Book after the breaking of the bread), but often we tramp right through those silences to get out of church earlier. Nor is expediency the only rationalization for eschewing silence in church. There is an even more substantive reason: because silence is intimate, it causes fear to arise in many people, and intimacy can be frightening, at least at first. When one leans into that discomfort until finding quiet and stillness, that intimacy turns to resting on the bosom of Jesus as did the beloved disciple (John 13:25).

The service of Compline (pronounced "COM-plin") is called the "goodnight prayer of the church," because it is the last service of the day in a monastery or convent. It is a quiet service, and, in strict monastic practice, there is no speaking allowed during the Great Silence after Compline until the first office of the next morning. The quiet simplicity of that service appeals to many contemporary worshippers. Silence is, in a sense, fasting from the noise, chaos, confusion, and distractions of daily life.

Of course, silence is not antithetical to liturgical worship. Indeed, silence can amplify a note of mystery in worship that might otherwise have gone unnoticed. The Holy Spirit is always present. What is needed is for us to slow down and quiet down so that we can notice her presence. To invoke the Holy Spirit, then, is really a matter of invoking our own attention to her ubiquitous existence.

This practice should not be confined to monastic communities. A glorious example of incorporating silence into worship can be experienced at St. Stephen's Episcopal Church, a large parish in Richmond, Virginia. The parish began a Sunday evening service of Celtic evensong with Eucharist. I confess that, though I had heard of this service for many years, I assumed Celtic referred to its music, and I was not particularly drawn to attend. (I'm all for Celtic music; I just never felt in the mood to hear it in worship—my oversight and a cautionary tale for those resisting "new" music.) In fact, "Celtic" refers to the spirituality of the liturgy, not its music.

When I finally did attend the Celtic evensong, I was completely disarmed by its style and content. The forces are simple compared with festive evensong services: a piano, a cantor, and a solo orchestral instrument—sometimes oboe, other times cello or flute. The service follows the basic form of evensong except that all the language is inclusive and expansive, and there are moments of copious silence. The church has ample candles, scattered around the chancel and altar, with dimmed artificial light. Instead of a sermon by a clergyperson, a layperson offers a reflection, usually focused on the speaker's personal story of spiritual revelation. It is a powerful service.

Following Celtic evensong with Eucharist, there is a community supper, then a service of Compline. The whole evening is sometimes called "the three acts." Compline consists of a superb choir, sitting behind the congregation and singing plainsong and polyphony with prayers and the gospel. Like the Celtic service, there are numerous candles, only this time there is no artificial light. The service is filled with silence and opportunities for meditation, and the congregation is freed from any verbal participation, allowing worshippers to focus on the presence of the Holy Spirit.

As beautiful as the music is, it is not the primary content. The primary content is the movement of the Holy Spirit and our response to her action among us. To say that this is a powerful service is simply naming the obvious, because the Spirit is palpable. People leave blessed and transformed and, perhaps most significant, as vessels filled with the Holy Spirit, prepared to pour out that blessing on others.

One indicator of the richness of this worship is the attendance. Of the several services offered on Sunday, the Celtic service is by far the largest, surpassing the usual principal service on Sunday morning. Contemplative worship has become the norm for this congregation.

This is not the only congregation experiencing the quiet, powerful bliss of contemplative worship. Such a phenomenon is starting to appear across the country.

Because our society is impressed by polls and statistics, some of us have come to believe that our church is on an unavoidable downward trend. Some of the rest of us, however, will have none of that. Whatever trends might appear from myriad studies, people of faith will attest that these trends are not inexorable. Responding to the leadership of the Holy Spirit, God's people are empowered to march boldly, filled with the promise that God will never leave us. *Ponder Anew* is witness to the Spirit's abundance.

Used thoughtfully, *Ponder Anew* spotlights worship in the Spirit and illuminates the role music plays in preparing us to be "true worshippers . . . in spirit and in truth" (John 4:23). Listen attentively as these imaginative essayists invite us into a rich environment of sacred music that sensitizes us to the movement of the Spirit and, therefore, to deep worship. The results will be just what the church needs right now: the life-giving transformation of a direct encounter with God.

To this end, may God be praised.

The Rev. William Bradley Roberts, DMA
Professor Emeritus of Church Music, Virginia Theological Seminary
Richmond, Virginia
All Saints Day, 2021

Introduction

The idea for this volume bubbled up nearly simultaneously in two different places: in an editorial consulting group for Church Publishing and in a group text involving me and a handful of church musician colleagues. This ongoing group text has been a go-to resource for me for all sorts of things—the mundane and unglamorous (repertoire suggestions, troubleshooting an aging and temperamental organ, the care and feeding of choristers) as well as a sounding board and source for productive advice on trickier topics (delicate pastoral care issues, negotiating complicated professional relationships, running music programs in the age of coronavirus, and other esoterica). At least a few of the topics discussed here were inspired by conversations with a small professional cohort convened by Ellen Johnston, a mentor and colleague who has worn many hats over the course of her service to the church—parish musician, conference director, consultant. This cohort has been a wonderful resource. It was formed in response to the coronavirus pandemic and has been meeting about once a month via Zoom. These are all musicians actively working in parish ministry, and though our contexts are a little different, the issues we all grapple with are remarkably similar. I am grateful for all of the above-mentioned friends. Would that all of us were surrounded with a like constellation of knowledge, wit, and faithfulness.

The title for this collection, *Ponder Anew*, is borrowed from a hymn treasured by many. Catherine Winkworth's 19th-century translation of Joachim Neander's 17th-century amalgamation of bits and pieces of psalms is set to *Lobe den herren*, a bright and buoyant tune that, when supported with a sense of forward movement and judicious articulation, is a total jam, an exhilarating waltz that leaves you slightly out of breath. "Ponder anew" comes at the highest point pitch-wise in the tune—the peak of the antecedent clause to which the remainder of the tune responds. Now, I am prone to neurotically overanalyze, and this could just be an inconsequential occurrence not worth the musing, but to me, this is a magical moment in the hymn. The confluence of the shape of the phrase with the text detonates an explosion in every place I've sung this hymn—a burst of energy that could shatter (stained) glass. Perhaps this is the Holy Spirit?

Inspired by the thousand or so sermons I've heard over the years that have deployed the same device, I found the original German text to see what, if anything, had been lost or gained in translation. I learned that Neander's "denke daran" became Winkworth's "ponder anew." Now, it's been nearly twenty years since my one semester of German in college, but in my limited understanding, this shakes out to something in English along the lines of "think about it." This is a fairly literal translation, and I'm sure the nuanced understanding of a native German speaker would reveal a shade of meaning that I'm unable to appreciate, but to my ears, this strikes me as amusing. "Think about it" is a casual admonition, something one might say in the course of a conversation about where to have dinner. "Do you want Applebee's or Red Lobster?" *Shrug.* "Well, think about it." In my ears, Winkworth's rendering of "ponder" is weightier. We're meant to consider, reflect, contemplate. *Marinate* on it, as I sometimes say.

As long as I'm torturing meaning out of words, I might as well address "anew." I'm sure the same has been true for every generation, but the nonstop feed of news via the breaking news alerts dinging on my phone every few minutes makes me deeply aware of how quickly the world is changing. In my twenty or so years as a church musician, the cultural and professional landscapes have changed immensely and are changing still. Although my perspective is understandably limited to that of a middle-class millennial woman in the Deep South, I can identify a number of issues that have profoundly affected the way I perceive the world and, consequently, the way I approach my work. In the past several years alone, the rise and ubiquity of social media (for better or for worse) has changed the way we live our lives in community and both the quantity and quality of interpersonal communication. Identity politics are at a fever pitch, and movements—Black Lives Matter, #MeToo, climate change reversal—all galvanized by the social media maligned not one sentence ago, have deeply affected both my personal and vocational lives. This was *not* going to be a book about the coronavirus pandemic, because as of this writing, we're still living through it and don't yet have the benefit of perspective and clarity that a little distance will eventually bring. I don't think that we can ignore it, though. It's changed so much and so quickly. The Rev. Susan Anderson-Smith is a founder of Imago Dei Middle School in Tucson, Arizona, a tuition-free Episcopal school exclusively serving students from low-income families. She is also a skilled musician and liturgist. In a conversation with Susan earlier this year, she opined that church musicians will be on the front lines of helping the church recover from the effects of the coronavirus pandemic, *if* we are to recover. Where do we even start?

The church's self-consciousness is at an all-time high—I'm unaware of another era in Christian history in which the church has been so prone to self-examination on so large a scale. Every month or so, a new article makes the rounds on social media—someone panicking about the imminent demise of the institutional church, in damning hyperbole, statistics, and pie charts in an effort to get page clicks. People wring their hands and share away, piling their own anxiety on top. I'm weary of panicking. I need to use that energy elsewhere. The church is changing and has been since the very beginning. My hypothesis is that the role of the church musician in parish ministry is changing along with it. I sense that our role is expanding—that the church needs us to wear hats on top of our musician hats. We'll have to be advocates, collaborators, ministry planters. Maybe this isn't as daunting as it sounds. Doesn't gathering people to sing on a regular basis mean we already know something about community organizing?

Advances in technology, especially in communication technology, have changed *how* we do our work. Social media has put our professional communities into more frequent contact than ever before. Friendships are formed, resources and ideas are exchanged, all without ever actually meeting each other in person. Thanks to video meeting platforms, it's no longer necessary to be in the same building (or even in the same area code) to do ministry together. And with the advent of tools like desktop publishing and especially the little recording/photography/movie studios we carry around in our pockets, we can create nearly nonstop and communicate ideas as quickly as they occur to us. Widely available notation software has turned our offices into engraving desks. We can have an idea at breakfast, commit it to the page by lunch, and have copies printed and bound by the evening choir rehearsal. If you had asked me two years ago what came to mind when I heard the phrase *virtual choir*, I would've looked at you blankly. In the earliest weeks of the coronavirus pandemic, when the first virtual choir videos began to circulate on social media, I turned my nose up. "Yeah, I'm not doing that," I may have said out loud to my boss. But at this point, I estimate I've assembled a hundred or so of these remotely recorded pieces to be used in prerecorded and livestreamed liturgies. It wasn't the thing we so desperately missed, and I'm not sure that I would jump at the opportunity to spend hours hunched over a MacBook again, but it wasn't nothing. It wasn't at all an adequate substitute for what we'd temporarily lost, but it wasn't *nothing*. Are these things good? Well, maybe they are and maybe they aren't, but at this point, we cannot unknow what we know.

This is not a how-to guide or a textbook. If you're looking for registration suggestions for a Bach trio sonata or perhaps hymn suggestions for the Feast of Saint Ludwig the Least, I do have lots of thoughts about those things, but I'll offer them on another occasion. Contained within are essays addressing specific issues about which I think church musicians need to be especially mindful. These essays seek to answer the questions that I've encountered the most often over the past several years, including, What does it mean to be Anglican? What is the role of music and the musician in pastoral care? How do we negotiate new technologies in our work? There are also a handful of conversations and interviews, that we might learn from the life experiences of others. Although sermons are a medium best delivered live and in person, a small number of sermon transcripts have been included—not just because they're beautiful pieces of prose, which they certainly are, but mainly in the interest of providing a good and encouraging word to us on our way. These sermons include funeral homilies for two giants in our field: Ray Glover and Gerre Hancock. They've been included not as tributes, but because these peoples' lives have provided us with enduring models of vocation.

At its heart, this is a book about vocation—about who we are and what, exactly, it is that we mean to be doing. I think it's empirically observable that the *how* is changing, but is the *what* changing as well? What do we need to be equipped to negotiate this roller coaster, other than several giant cups of coffee and a relentlessly positive (if occasionally somewhat grating) attitude? I am not prone to false modesty, so please know that what follows is not that: I know that I am not the smartest person in the room, nor the best organist, composer, or choirmaster. What I do excel at, however, is surrounding myself with very smart and talented people. The content of the following pages represents the collective wisdom of a group of people that spans hundreds—if not a thousand—years of experience, training, and wisdom, and with facets of perspective too numerous to count, high church, low church, and every conceivable gradient thereof. These contributors have been chosen specifically for their thoughtfulness and intentionally skew toward people in the late-early to middle stages of their career. Perhaps one day my friends and colleagues will forgive me for giving them homework assignments and for responding to most any comment with, "Can you say more about that?"

Some of these writings may prove to be more helpful to you than others. It also occurs to me that you may not like or agree with everything each contributor has put forth, because neither do I. In fact, some of the perspectives contained within may contradict others. I've always found, though, that tangling up with and butting against a position counter to my own is the quickest and most complete way to clarify my own understanding. After all, we're capable of holding two ideas in our heads at once. Isn't holding things in tension the Anglican way? This volume is intentionally designed to be cafeteria style, to be consumed a bit at a time and not necessarily in order. It is, by design, incomplete. I don't know all the questions that need to be asked, and besides, even if I did, there are limits to what you can put in a book. I hope that somebody comes along after me and puts together a second, third, fourth volume. More than anything, I hope that what we have done here, at the very least, is to begin to raise the questions, challenge the assumptions, and ponder the issues that we need to consider as we live into the next millennium of making music to the glory of God and in the service of the church's worship.

I

ESSAYS

1

How Can I Keep from Singing?

On Music as Pastoral Care

The Rev. Jennifer M. Deaton

"I would rather preach a gospel sermon to an appreciative, receptive congregation than write a hymn," insisted Robert Wadsworth Lowry, an American minister in the late nineteenth century.[1] But there was more melody and poetry in his proclamation than could be contained in a pulpit. Appreciative, receptive congregations today don't remember Lowry's gospel sermons, but they do still sing his gospel hymns, of which there are hundreds, including "Shall we gather at the river?," "All the way my Savior leads me," and this one:

> My life flows on in endless song above earth's lamentations.
> I hear the sweet, though far-off hymn that hails a new creation.
> No storm can shake my inmost calm while to that Rock I'm clinging.
> Since love is Lord of heav'n and earth, how can I keep from singing?[2]

Lowry considered music an avocation, secondary to his preaching and pastoral ministry. Music, though, has a vocation all its own in the life of a worshipping congregation, providing pastoral care to those who are gathered, echoing the endless and ever-modulating song of creation, a song of life and death and life again, a song of praise and lament. Musicians, then, and all who participate in planning and leading a liturgy that includes music, have the opportunity to render pastoral care to individuals, families, congregations, and entire communities. How, then, can we keep from singing?

---

1. Jacob Henry Hall, *Biography of Gospel Song and Hymn Writers* (New York: Fleming H. Revell, 1914), 76.

2. "How Can I Keep from Singing," *The Upper Room Worship Book: Music and Liturgies for Spiritual Formation*, ed. Elise S. Eslinger (Nashville: Upper Room Books, 2006), hymn 170.

An Endless Song: Singing in Scripture

The story of our faith is filled with song, glorifying God who made all things and who makes all things new. In the first chapter of Genesis, creation itself comes into being through the sound of God's voice: "Then God said, 'Let there be light'; and there was light" (Gen. 1:3). Over and over again, God says, "let there be," and there is—light, dark, night, day, land, water, air, animals, and humankind. Reading the story, we learn its several refrains—"let there be," "and there was," "and it was good"—and we say them along with the text. Christian writer and theologian Clive Staples Lewis, in *The Magician's Nephew*, transposed the language of God's creation from speech into song, so that the land of Narnia, a magical copy of our own world, is created through music. "In the darkness," Lewis wrote, "something was happening at last. A voice had begun to sing."[3] It is the voice of the great lion, Aslan, the Christ-figure in Narnia. As the melody rises, light appears first as stars and then in a sunrise. The song rumbles low, and valleys form, filled with water and green grass. When the tune grows more animated, "it made you want to run and jump and climb. It made you want to shout. It made you want to rush at people and either hug them or fight them."[4] Animals of every shape and size begin appearing, adding their voices to the song of creation.

In our Holy Scriptures, everything in creation is capable of making music. God invites those exiled in Babylon to repent and return to a life of abundance, promising them, "You shall go out in joy, and be led back in peace; the mountains and the hills before you shall burst into song, and all the trees of the field shall clap their hands" (Isa. 55:12). The book of Psalms is filled with human voices and instruments; the sea and its creatures, the land and its beasts, and the sky and its sparrows and stars also make music and participate in praising God. A psalmist writes, "The pastures of the wilderness overflow, the hills gird themselves with joy, the meadows clothe themselves with flocks, the valleys deck themselves with grain, they shout and sing together for joy" (Ps. 65:12–13). Borrowing from King David's celebration when the ark of God was brought into the tent (1 Chronicles 16), another psalmist writes, "Let the heavens be glad, and let the earth rejoice; let the sea roar, and all that fills it; let the field exult, and everything in it. Then shall all the trees of the forest sing for joy before the Lord" (Ps. 96:11–13). In yet another psalm, we read, "Let the floods clap their hands; let the hills sing together for joy at the presence of the Lord" (98:8–9).

"Let heaven and nature sing,"[5] declares a beloved Christmas hymn, and indeed in scripture we often hear the music of angels and of earth. It is human-kind, though, who makes music most often in scripture—songs of victory, songs of thanksgiving, songs of mourning, songs of consolation, songs of praise, and

---

3. Clive Staples Lewis, *The Magician's Nephew* (New York: Collier Books, 1955), 98.
4. Lewis, *The Magician's Nephew*, 113.
5. "Joy To the World," *The Hymnal 1982* (New York: Church Hymnal, 1982), hymn 100.

songs of longing, expressing the fullness of human experience and emotion. "The motivation to express the depths of our feelings in song is basic to almost all human beings,"[6] observes Raymond Glover, general editor of *The Hymnal 1982*, and we certainly witness it in the stories of our ancestors in faith. Moses and Miriam rejoice as the waters of the Red Sea rush back on the Egyptians and God's people are finally free: "Then Moses and the Israelites sang this song to the Lord: 'I will sing to the Lord, for he has triumphed' . . . Then the prophet Miriam, Aaron's sister, took a tambourine in her hand; and all the women went out after her with tambourines and with dancing" (Exod. 15:1, 20). In the wilderness, the Hebrew people give thanks for God's gift of water at "the well of which the Lord said to Moses, 'Gather the people together, and I will give them water.' Then Israel sang this song: 'Spring up, O well!—Sing to it!" (Num. 21:16–17). In his final lament, Job grieves his misfortunes and says, "My lyre is tuned to mourning, and my pipe to the voice of those who weep" (Job 30:31). When Saul begins to suffer a mental illness, his servants suggest music might help, so they bring young David to console him with song: "Whenever the evil spirit from God came upon Saul, David took the lyre and played it with his hand, and Saul would be relieved and feel better, and the evil spirit would depart from him" (1 Sam. 16:23). Solomon brings musicians and instruments to the temple to sound the people's praise as the ark is brought inside: "It was the duty of the trumpeters and singers to make themselves heard in unison in praise and thanksgiving to the Lord, and when the song was raised . . . 'for he is good, for his steadfast love endures forever,' the house, the house of the Lord, was filled with a cloud" (2 Chron. 5:13). The Song of Solomon collects fragments of poetry such as would have been sung of the love between a bridegroom and his bride, often understood as the relationship between God and God's people.

In Luke's Gospel, Mary cannot keep from singing as she and her cousin, Elizabeth, rejoice in the favor God has shown them, and the child in Elizabeth's womb leaps when Mary comes near. "My soul magnifies the Lord," Mary sings, "and my spirit rejoices in God my Savior" (Luke 1:46–47). Her song is filled with wonder that so powerful a God would choose so lowly a servant, and with hope that the new work God is doing through the child in her womb will transform suffering into joy. Zechariah sings a similar song after his son, John, is born (Luke 1:68–79). With the Christ child in his arms, Simeon sings in wonder and relief, "Now you are dismissing your servant in peace, according to your word; for my eyes have seen your salvation, which you have prepared in the presence of all peoples" (Luke 2:29–31). In a prison cell at midnight, their bodies bruised and beaten, Paul and Silas pray and sing hymns to God as the other prisoners listen (Acts 16:25). Letters to early Christian communities urge congregations to "sing

---

6. Raymond Glover, "What Is Congregational Song," in *The Hymnal 1982 Companion*, vol. 1, *Essays in Church Music* (New York: Church Hymnal, 1990), 3.

psalms and hymns and spiritual songs among yourselves, singing and making melody to the Lord in your hearts, giving thanks to God the Father at all times and for everything in the name of our Lord Jesus Christ" (Eph. 5:19–20; see also Col. 3:15–17 and James 5:13).

These songs, along with many others, appear in the narratives of the story of salvation, sung by specific individuals or communities in their specific circumstances. The book of Psalms contains songs many people sang in worship in the temple—it is a hymnal of sorts, as well as a music textbook, inviting and instructing God's people in praying and responding to God through song in such familiar keys as joy, sorrow, fear, gratitude, bitterness, grief, anger, hope, and praise. There are instructions to choirmasters, suggestions for accompaniment, and notes about composers. Nearly one-third of the psalms make reference to music, and many allude to other liturgical practices such as pilgrimage, entering the temple, approaching the altar, or offering a sacrifice. Fragments of psalms and other ancient hymns appear throughout the Old and New Testaments, familiar enough through repeated use that the faithful across many generations would recognize them from having sung them often in worship and prayer.

Through All the Tumult and the Strife: Liturgy as Pastoral Care

We still sing in worship and prayer—except, of course, at the early service on Sunday mornings. Our prayer book liturgy itself, though, is almost musical since we pray so much of it aloud together. Even what is spoken has rhythm and cadence as our voices rise and fall, tripping over certain syllables and sounds and lingering over others, and we move our bodies in unison as we pray—stand, sit, kneel, reach out our hands at the rail. When in any worship service some combination of hymns, canticles, service music, chanting, preludes, postludes, and anthems *are* included, we often sing more of our liturgy than we speak. We held a weekday service of Holy Eucharist at noon in the chapel at St. Andrew's Cathedral in Jackson, Mississippi, a brief spoken liturgy attended by only a handful of worshippers. One gentleman, every time we prayed the Lord's Prayer, would say, "Thy kiiiiiiingdom come, thy wiiiiiiiiill be done," crescendoing and ascending the scale on "kingdom" and "will" before dropping back down to "come" and "be done." There was no music in that service, but he certainly sang that phrase of the prayer.

The Pastoral Offices, liturgies that mark rites of passage or threshold moments in human lives (such as Confirmation, Marriage, Sickness, and Burial), form a small section toward the end of the Book of Common Prayer. Supplemental liturgical resources have introduced additional rites to help us respond to the changes and chances of life, trusting "the divine Love to embrace us through all the joys and pains of transition" and affirming that "we are so interconnected

by the Holy Spirit that a transition in one member's life affects the whole Christian community."[7] We bring to our regular Sunday morning celebrations of Holy
Eucharist, however, the same anxieties, hopes, and hurts that these liturgies and
rites address along with all the joys and sorrows of our daily lives, so that in our
primary experience of corporate worship we are a congregation filled with every
imaginable emotion from all that has happened to us during the week. All liturgy,
then, has the potential to offer us pastoral care.

Liturgy is the ordering of our expressions of praise and thanksgiving to God.
It is rightly directed toward God. Pastoral theologian Elaine Ramshaw explains
that liturgy can also comfort the human heart.[8] It provides order and familiarity
in the midst of chaos. It reaffirms and re-engages our connection to a larger community and a larger story. Liturgy helps us acknowledge the ambivalence inherent
in times of transition, when we might feel both fear and hope, grief and gratitude,
pain and joy. The dissonance may not be resolved, but the presence of a praying
congregation and the reminder through scripture and sacrament of God's promise to remain steadfast adds a sustaining note that augments the chord. In liturgy
we bear witness to God; who is both beyond us and within us; who is mystery,
and who is found in such knowable acts as breaking bread, drinking wine, and in
the laying on of hands.

The ministry of pastoral care is most often made up of hospital visits, home
communion, sympathy cards, chicken spaghetti casseroles, and flower arrangements taken from the altar. There is talking and listening, and sometimes there is
silence. There are smiles, tears, and tissues. Many definitions of pastoral care reference tending troubled souls and comforting emotional distress. But the practice
of pastoral care is profoundly incarnate and personal, even sacramental. Delivering a plate of cookies, holding a hand in prayer, humming a beloved hymn by a
hospice bedside—surely these are "outward and visible signs of inward and spiritual grace,"[9] means by which God's loving and healing presence is made known
within individuals, families, and entire congregations in need. We literally feed
the bodies of those whose lives are unsettled. We offer to run errands or sit by
a bedside so that a primary caregiver can rest. We anoint the forehead of a sick
person with oil. We send, in the form of a notecard or a flower or a prayer shawl, a
tangible reminder that a faith community is holding them in prayer, loving them
as we have all been loved by God in Christ. Like good liturgy, and within good
liturgy, good pastoral care provides a moment of order (now we pray, now we eat,
now we rest). It reconnects us *to* and *as* a community of shared faith, and it makes
space for conflicting thoughts and feelings to exist together in the presence of
God. The second verse of Lowry's hymn sings of this kind of care that does not

7. *Changes: Prayers and Services Honoring Rites of Passage* (New York: Church Publishing, 2007), 4.
8. Elaine Ramshaw, *Ritual and Pastoral Care* (Philadelphia: Augsburg Fortress, 1987), 22–33.
9. *The Book of Common Prayer* (New York: Church Publishing, 1979), 857.

necessarily diminish the darkness or still the storm, but that provides a source of strength within it, something to which we can both literally and spiritually cling.

> Through all the tumult and the strife, I hear that music ringing.
> It finds an echo in my soul. How can I keep from singing?
> No storm can shake my inmost calm while to that Rock I'm clinging;
> Since love is Lord of heav'n and earth, how can I keep from singing?

In the midst of all that threatens our peace, liturgy as pastoral care through scripture and sacraments, through prayer and community, and through song, fastens us to that Rock.

Within a worship service, music can reinforce the scripture readings or the liturgical or theological theme of the season or day. It provides an opportunity for choirs and church musicians to celebrate their God-given gifts of creativity and artistry by offering them back to God in the context of worship. Music can assist us in prayer as we sing service music, or chant a litany, or use a brief refrain with our intercessions. Music can be devotional, leading us in meditation following a scripture reading or sermon, and it can be purely functional, engaging the congregation while worship leaders are performing a necessary task. "One of the most important parts of planning and preparation for any service is the choice of hymns," wrote the Rev. Dr. Marion Hatchett, for reasons such as those listed above, but also because we respond to music, in body, mind, and spirit, differently than we do to the spoken word alone: "People's theology is probably influenced more by the hymns they sing than by the lessons and sermons they hear or the prayers they pray."[10]

Music as Pastoral Care for the Body

Liturgical singing, even more than liturgical speaking, is a bodily, physical act. In addition to holding a book in our hands, reading a page with our eyes, and moving our mouth to form words, we must be more aware of and intentional about our breathing when we sing. We take deeper breaths to make it through a verse, and the extra oxygen benefits our bodies in other ways, improving our lung function, our mood, and our heart and brain health.

Our bodies are naturally rhythmic and resonant, consisting of a beating heart, coursing blood, expanding and contracting lungs, and vocal cords and ear drums that vibrate. Even if we cannot manipulate the sounds we make to sing on key, our bodies hear and feel the music we make and the sounds we produce. There is evidence that singing reduces cortisol levels (a stress hormone made by

---

10. Marion J. Hatchett, *A Liturgical Index to The Hymnal 1982* (New York: Church Publishing, 1986), 1.

our bodies), increases endorphins (a neurochemical that produces a sense of well-being), and possibly stimulates our immune response.[11] Music can soothe us when we are agitated and help us to be still, or it can stir us when we are lethargic and create the urge to move. I have seen both happen at once when singing a simple gathering song with children at the beginning of a formation class. "Be still, and know that I am God" (Ps. 46:10), we sang quietly and slowly, with accompanying hand motions. The music and the movement focused the fidgety and drew in the disinterested until we were all singing and signing together and ready to start our lesson.

Music as Pastoral Care for the Mind

Music engages our minds, our thoughts, our beliefs, our memories, and our capacity to learn, and so can help us see patterns where there seems only confusion, make new meaning in the midst of uncertainty, and create connections we have not known or of which we have lost sight. Our attention is drawn toward patterns—musical phrases, rhythms, rhymes, refrains, and repetition make it easier for us to hear the good news when there is so much other noise around us and within us. Perhaps it is those same patterns that help us remember music even when other memories have begun to fade. A friend recalls visiting his grandfather at a memory care center. He was surprised that "Jesus Loves Me" was sung two weeks in a row at the worship service. The pastor explained that while it was sometimes difficult to tell how the residents were connecting with any spoken elements of the service, they had grown up with the song and were able to engage and participate when it was sung. The sentimentality and the sentiment of the song—how it was connected to a memory, even if the fullness of the memory was inaccessible, and the meaning expressed in the lyrics, that we are held in the love of Jesus Christ—were a gift of pastoral care.

Many of us can name hymns that, when we hear them or sing them, bring to mind significant people, places, or experiences. My mother was watching a movie when she recognized in the film score the tune "Melita," which accompanies the hymn "Eternal Father, strong to save." Memories of her own father, and of singing that hymn at his funeral, brought tears to her eyes, though she told me they were good tears—she was grateful for the moment of feeling connected to him. Whenever we sing "Love divine, all loves excelling" in worship, I am taken back to my wedding and can see as if I was there again the friends and family who gathered around my husband and me as we all sang, "lost in wonder, love, and praise."[12] In my former parish, at an annual service honoring first responders

---

11. Rebecca Joy Stanborough, "10 Ways That Singing Benefits Your Health," Healthline, November 10, 2020, https://www.healthline.com/health/benefits-of-singing#benefits.

12. "Love Divine, All Loves Excelling," *The Hymnal 1982* (New York: Church Hymnal, 1982), hymn 657.

held every September 11, we sang "O beautiful for spacious skies." Worshippers remembered singing that hymn in the wake of September 11, 2001, and shared how singing it every year allowed their grief from that tragic day to mingle with their gratitude for God's loving care both then and now.

Whether it is a joyful, sorrowful, anticipated, or unanticipated event that has triggered a change in our lives—a birth, a death, a diagnosis, a divorce, or a new job—we are faced with new realities that challenge how we perceive and make meaning of the world and our place in it, and how we make meaning of our faith and its place in our lives. Liturgical scholar Don Saliers and singer-songwriter Emily Saliers cite Rabbi Abraham Joshua Heschel, who writes, "Religious music is an attempt to convey that which is within our reach but beyond our grasp,"[13] which is to say, the mystery of God, who is the source of life. "Music thrives in the space created by the tension between what we can imagine and what we can put into words, in the vibrant space of possibility that exists in the gap between our longings and our present reality. Living in this gap can be painful at times; but if we inhabit it with openness and wonder, it can be a place of amazement."[14] A young woman with whom I spoke remembers being in church and singing "What wondrous love is this" not long after a close friend had died by suicide. She struggled with singing the hymn, wondering whether that love could be trusted in the wake of such a tragedy. The hymn's tune and slow tempo mirrored and magnified her grief, which returned in some measure whenever it was sung in worship. Years later, in another congregation, musicians pulled out tambourines to accompany the hymn at a livelier pace, and by the time the last verse began, the hymn for her was no longer about sorrow but, rather, joy: "And when from death I'm free, I'll sing on. And when from death I'm free, I'll sing and joyful be, and through eternity, I will sing, I will sing, and through eternity, I will sing."[15]

There are many words in our liturgy—scripture readings, prayers, a sermon, announcements. Whether we are speaking them or listening to them, they engage our rational minds first and then, if we allow our minds to wander, our imaginations. When we sing the same words, though, or hear them set to music, we move more quickly into imagination as the tune adds its own interpretation to the text, reinforcing the meaning of the words or giving them new meaning. Words by themselves try to *define* or *contain* mystery, a clergy colleague mused. Music taps into mystery in a different way, swelling around the boundaries, creeping through the cracks. "Holy Ghost, dispel our sadness," begins a hymn, never specifying

---

13. Abraham Joshua Heschel, *Man's Quest for God: Studies in Prayer and Symbolism* (New York: Scribner, 1954), quoted in Don Saliers and Emily Saliers, *A Song to Sing, a Life to Live: Reflections on Music as Spiritual Practice* (San Francisco: Jossey-Bass, 2005), 170.

14. Saliers and Saliers, *A Song to Sing, a Life to Live,* 171.

15. "What Wondrous Love Is This," *The Hymnal 1982* (New York: Church Hymnal, 1982), hymn 439.

what the source of that sorrow might be, so that it might be our own. "Pierce the clouds of nature's night; come, thou source of joy and gladness, breathe thy life, and spread thy light," the verse continues, all in a minor key. Shifting, then, into a major key in the middle of the verse, the hymn affirms the graciousness of God in providing for us far more than what we have asked. The mingling of minor and major keys in the melody helps us, also, hold fast to hope that God will "rest upon this congregation with the fullness of thy grace" even in the midst of our sadness.[16]

Pastoral care, whether it is directed at an individual, a group, or an entire congregation, is a ministry of connection. Liturgy, too—both individual prayer and corporate worship—connects us with one another and with God, especially in a tradition that practices common prayer, as we do in the Episcopal Church. The phrasing of the prayers we say together is almost musical, but once a hymn begins, the gathered body is connected as we inhale to sing, and we move our mouths and voices in the same direction, at least mostly—my son, himself a musician, notes that while not all singing is masterful, singing together is always beautiful, and in a guide for music leaders I once read that if enough people sing off key it sounds like harmony. A lay ministry colleague who is also a chorister suggested to me that singing takes us "inside the puzzle," showing us how we fit into a larger whole. He especially experiences this at choir rehearsals and when the choir is singing anthems or leading hymns in worship. A single vocal part, or a note in the accompaniment, will be what makes a chord major or minor or will be the part that resolves from dissonance into harmony. Higher vocal parts will lift the sound while lower voices deepen it, and the middle voices add richness and texture. It is gratifying, he said, to participate in creating something larger than your own contribution to it, and in rehearsal, when the vocal parts are broken down and presented separately as they are being learned, to appreciate the uniqueness of each person's part. An ordained deacon who leads a contemplative community evensong service studied music in college, where there was frequently competition between singers for recognition. In choral and congregational singing, however, she experiences creating a single sound from many voices, showing how things literally work together in harmony, an experience we can then take away with us and apply in our daily lives, understanding ourselves to be connected with one another at all times and in all places.[17]

---

16. "Holy Ghost, Dispel Our Sadness," *The Hymnal 1982* (New York: Church Hymnal, 1982), hymn 515.

17. I am grateful in this and following sections to Dr. Stephen Stray, Cathy Grooms, Edith Marie Green, the Rev. Melanie Lemburg, Charlie Deaton III, the Rev. Deacon Sarah Stripp, the Rev. Dr. Bryan Owen, the Rev. Jody Burnett, Dr. Susan Lee, Will Melnyk, the Rev. Glyn Ruppe-Melnyk, and the Rev. Charlie Deaton Jr. for various conversations we shared about their experiences of music as pastoral care.

Music as Pastoral Care for the Spirit

By the time we have considered how we respond to music in body and mind, we have already begun to consider how we respond to it in spirit. Music as pastoral care *inspires* us in every sense of the word as it fills our bodies with breath, our minds with understanding, and our hearts with not just connection but belonging. Saliers and Saliers write, "We sing out of who we have become as a people, yet that singing can take on new forms as our identity and sense of belonging expand over time. We sing what we belong to and feel at home in. But we also sing to become part of a larger social reality. What some call spirituality—a way of being fully alive—is shaped by both of these pulls."[18] When we sing together in church, even if we are singing with strangers, we are doing so not just as a choir or a collection of voices but as members of the body of Christ, "we the Lord's people, heart and voice uniting."[19] As a human life is one life with many changes and chances, and a worship service is one liturgy with many elements, and a song is one piece with many notes and words, Paul reminds us that "so it is with Christ" (1 Cor. 12:12), in whom we, who are many, are one body: "If one member suffers, all suffer together with it; if one member is honored, all rejoice together with it" (1 Cor. 12:26). Congregational singing, suggested the deacon with whom I spoke, is a metaphor for the ideal church—in singing together our psalms, hymns, spiritual songs, we offer up together our sorrows, suffering, hope, and praise. Sometimes we are the part of the congregation that carries on singing while someone has lost their breath or their voice or their faith because of grief or overwhelming gratitude; sometimes we are the one carried by the congregation while our own tears fall or while wonder washes over us and we, overcome, cannot sing.

Brené Brown, in a sermon preached at Washington National Cathedral, and in her research on belonging and loneliness, defined spirituality as "the deeply held belief that we are inextricably connected to each other by something greater than us, and something that is rooted in love and compassion. I call that God."[20] While that connection cannot be severed, she says, it can be forgotten. Singing together in church, Brown says—again, even singing with strangers—is a way to share in collective joy and pain and collective vulnerability, and to remember that we are always already in community.

We are in community not only with the people singing around us, but with all who have lifted up their voices before us, in praise or in lament. All these become one choir, notes the Rev. Dr. Bryan Owen, former chaplain and faculty

---

18. Saliers and Saliers, *A Song to Sing, a Life to Live*, 83.

19. "We the Lord's People, Heart and Voice Uniting," *The Hymnal 1982* (New York: Church Hymnal, 1982), hymn 51.

20. "Sunday Sermon by Dr. Brené Brown at Washington National Cathedral," January 21, 2018, video, 17:51, https://www.youtube.com/watch?v=ndP1XDskXHY.

member for the Mississippi Conference on Church Music and Liturgy. It is not unlike, he said, the *anamnesis* (the Greek word means "recollection") in our eucharistic celebration, the prayers in which we not only recall the saving acts of Christ's death and resurrection, but participate in them as they become a present reality. Music does something similar, moving through our bodies and minds and engaging our spirits, the deepest part of who we are, deeper than our defenses against any emotion or doubt, where our personal and communal identity abides in the love of God. It is for this reason that my mother has more than a hundred favorite hymns but loves singing the service music best—the *Gloria*, the *Sanctus*, and the Fraction. On a Sunday morning, her church and mine may choose to sing entirely different hymns, but we will all be singing the same service music "with Angels and Archangels and with all the company of heaven who for ever sing"[21] these words of praise. There is healing in belonging.

When We Were Kept from Singing

As I write this, we are slowly returning to singing after having been kept from it for some eighteen months. Businesses, theaters, schools, churches, and entire countries closed their doors to mitigate the spread of COVID-19. Many congregations, including the one in which I served, moved their worship services online, prerecording or livestreaming their liturgies while church members participated from home. Early research indicated that the virus is transmitted through aerosol particles that are projected in higher quantities and with more force when we sing. Following guidance from health officials and professional organizations of musicians, singing even in small groups was strongly discouraged. A clergy colleague, reflecting on the experience of worship in his congregation during this time, said he heard often from his parishioners that one of the things they longed for most in the midst of so much uncertainty and unrest was the comfort of singing together. At graveside funerals, with no more than ten people present, we were not able to weep while the congregation sang "The King of love my shepherd is" or cling to hope while singing "Joyful, joyful, we adore thee." When we finally returned to in-person worship in our congregation, wearing masks and sitting at least six feet apart, we still had not been given permission to sing other than using a quartet of choristers. But any time the organ played, we heard many more than four voices and saw indications of mouths moving behind their masks. "The sound of people singing creates a yearning to sing along," write Saliers and Saliers, because it is a shared language of the soul.[22]

---

21. *The Book of Common Prayer* (New York: Church Publishing, 1979), 362.
22. Saliers and Saliers, *A Song to Sing, a Life to Live*, 11.

Songs in the Night He Giveth:
Musicians as Pastoral Caregivers

> What though my joys and comforts die? The Lord, my Savior, liveth.
> What though the darkness round me close? Songs in the night he giveth.
> No storm can shake my inmost calm while to that Rock I'm clinging.
> Since love is Lord of heav'n and earth, how can I keep from singing?

How can we keep from singing? We cannot. Saliers and Saliers write, "Music recreates our sense of the world and who we are in it, right in the midst of the terrors and beauties, the pain and deep pleasures, of human existence. Coming alive to music, we are led on a double journey: into the mystery of God and into the depths of our humanity."[23] Music is already in us, already how we experience life in the rhythm of breath and heartbeats and the sound of voices. It is part of the created order in which we live, part of our cultural and community identities, and part of our identity as people of faith—there is singing in our story from the first day the morning stars sang together (Job 38:7), to the last when all creatures in heaven and on earth will sing around the throne of God (Rev. 5:13), and in countless songs of praise and lament on every day between. Clergy, lay worship leaders, and church musicians are more than liturgists as they prepare and lead worship containing music—they are ministers of pastoral care.

Whether a church has professional musicians, a trained choral director, and paid choir members, or a volunteer accompanist without a choir to direct, the musical selections—hymns, anthems, and instrumental offerings—should support the liturgy and not the performers. Worship should invite participation, insists Elaine Ramshaw. The more widely and actively people are able to engage, the more connected they will feel with other worshippers.[24] Because music enlists our whole selves—body, mind, and spirit—it can care for our whole selves; whether we are singing or playing an instrument or simply listening, music is a thin space in which our aching and our alleluias are encompassed by God. "It's not about my ability," says the musician in my current congregation, "it's about my availability." She understands her role to be part theologian, choosing hymn texts that augment our understanding of the nature of God, part liturgist, using her musical training to help create a cohesive worship experience, and part pastor, meeting the congregation in the places of shared and individual vulnerability by offering them the opportunity to sing their laments, their longings, and their praise. Playing a sufficient introduction to assure the congregation of a melody and setting a tempo that helps singers stay connected to the music, to their breath, and to one another are ways of caring for a congregation in worship. Because it so

---

23. Saliers and Saliers, *A Song to Sing, a Life to Live*, 1.

24. Ramshaw, 30.

easily accesses our hearts, music is the balm that soothes us and the impulse that energizes us—it is medicine, but it can also be used to manipulate emotions and ideas. The musician as pastor meets people where they are, not imposing feelings they do not feel, but offering opportunities both to express what is authentically in their hearts and to affirm, whether solemnly or joyfully, their faith (or at least their hope) in God, who transforms darkness into light, sadness into joy, loneliness into belonging, and even death into life.

The music that will accomplish this is as varied as we are, and it changes as we change and as the world changes around us. A familiar tune can pray for us when we are at a loss for words—for my husband, who is also an Episcopal priest, the tune "Old 100th" always reminds him of gratitude, regardless of the text being sung. A former organist-choirmaster in a congregation I served compiled a list of familiar hymns often chosen for funerals, which I would share with individuals and families planning a service. It was tender to watch as they read that list and one or another of the first lines caused them to smile, cry, or sing. When planning principal worship services, these same familiar favorites can both comfort and animate a congregation. New texts and tunes, though, can help expand the language and music that are then available when pastoral needs arise. In several congregations I have served, "The Tree of Life," a relatively new hymn not yet included in authorized hymnals of the Episcopal Church, is often requested for funerals—it is filled with language about the power of God in Christ to transform suffering and death into resurrection life. Many congregations incorporate chants from the Taizé and Iona communities, brief lines of scripture and prayer set to music and sung repeatedly like the refrains of gospel hymns, easily learned and accessible both in that moment of worship and when we are in the midst of our day-to-day lives. There is an endless supply of song for us to use in our liturgies, written and composed by women and men, people of color and other underrepresented communities, in other languages, and for every imaginable instrument and voice, demonstrating the universality of our impulse to sing our prayers.

How Can We Keep from Singing?

"When we sing," writes theologian Dr. Wendy Wright, "we heighten our praying. We gather up breath and body; we give form and flight to the keenest longings of our hearts. Our whole selves engage in what we pray. 'My whole being desires you like a dry, worn, waterless land,' we sing, and the notes take the shape of our desire; they trace our thirst and ache with our longing for God."[25] We are made *of* music, of bodies that contain rhythm and resonance. We are made *for* music, with the capacity to create and sustain sound—words, laughter, wailing,

---

25. Wendy Wright, "Praying the Daily Liturgies Together," in *Upper Room Worshipbook: Music and Liturgies for Spiritual Formation* (Nashville: Upper Room Books, 2006), 7.

whooping, whistling, and singing. In the Christian imagination of C. S. Lewis, we are made *by* music—in the beginning was the song, and the song was with God, and the song was God. Music has been an element of our worship of God for as long as we have worshipped God, for as long as we have lamented, for as long as we have rejoiced, for as long as we have asked God to help us in our weakness and woundedness, for as long as we have been grateful for God's healing and strength.

There was grief and there was gladness at a memorial service for Fran McKendree, whose gifts as a church musician created community from rhythms and refrains. The Rev. Barbara Brown Taylor, preaching at the memorial service, said, "He could sing about the saddest things and leave you reason to hope. He could sing about the happiest things and remind you of their cost." This is what music can do, making all who plan and lead music in worship not just liturgists but pastors. Robert Lowry may have had a way with words in the pulpit, but it was his way with a tune that still touches human hearts and turns them to the love of God in Christ. "The beauty of the song strengthens the soul to hear the truth in it, and maybe even sing along," said Taylor. "So dream on, you preachers—given a choice between a sermon and a song, who wouldn't choose the song?"[26]

> The peace of Christ makes fresh my heart, a fountain ever springing.
> All things are mine since I am his! How can I keep from singing?
> No storm can shake my inmost calm while to that Rock I'm clinging.
> Since love is Lord of heav'n and earth, how can I keep from singing?

---

26. Barbara Brown Taylor, "Fran McKendree Live Stream," September 11, 2021, video, beginning at 46:56, https://www.youtube.com/watch?v=EiOSfoSs6UA&t=3968s.

2

Tablets and Technology

Liturgy and Music in the Information Age

David Sinden

What role does technology play in our worship of the living God? What opportunities does the Information Age provide to churches in the first part of the 21st century? How do the products and techniques of digital technologies shape and disseminate our liturgy? Seen one way, the very existence of Israel was shaped around a God-given technological product: "The Lord said to Moses, 'Come up to me on the mountain, and wait there; and I will give you the tablets of stone, with the law and the commandment, which I have written for their instruction'" (Exod. 24:12).

At the Lord's invitation, Moses ascends Mount Sinai to receive two tablets of the covenant that the Lord has already written. But the Lord's summons to Moses doesn't include the full agenda for their meeting. Moses stayed on the mountain for forty days and forty nights and received, in detail, instructions for the liturgical life of Israel (Exod. 25–31). The Lord gives Moses detailed instruction about everything the Israelites will need for the worship of the living God in the tabernacle: materials, measurements, vestments, ceremonial actions, and so forth. Moses is told and "shown" all this information. But this seminal technological work of the Lord (engraving on stone) was destroyed shortly after its creation. And Moses returns again to the mountain to engrave two new stone tablets of the covenant himself, this time dictated by the Lord. In this case, the written word, one of the earliest forms of information technology, is received as a gift from the Lord. It is destroyed. It is re-created. And even in its destruction, the information endures. I wonder how much of a theology of information technology can be gleaned from these famous tablets. Here are some things to hold in mind:

- The God-given information is what defines the community.
- Both the information and the medium itself is a gift from God.
- The medium can be destroyed and remade, but the God-given information stays the same.

❖ ❖ ❖

The story of the tablets of the covenant is one of receiving more than just the written word, but simultaneously receiving detailed instructions for a liturgical life together. Since Moses and the Israelites first received the tablets of the covenant, many Jewish and Christian worshippers adopted new technologies in their liturgical lives. By the time of Jesus, worship in the synagogue included the reading of scripture, likely from scrolls. (It is the scroll of the prophet Isaiah that Jesus reads from in Luke 4:16–20.) Since the time of Jesus, various technologies have developed and found their way into worship. These technologies are so pervasive in the daily lives of most Episcopalians that their inclusion in the worship space is assumed and largely unnoticed. And yet, worship itself has changed over time because of them. The development of printing technology allowed for the printing of the written word in the codex and, eventually, the book. Scripture was translated into different languages and disseminated. The very notion of Anglican prayer books is surely contingent on printing technology. The composition of new Christian hymns also relied on their being distributed and sung from mass-produced books.

Before Thomas Edison installed a 30-bulb electrolier in First Presbyterian Church, Roselle, New Jersey, in 1883, no worship spaces benefited from electric light.[1] Today, it would be difficult to find a sacred space in the Episcopal Church that does not include artificial light of some kind. In the Episcopal Church, where candles are usually found on and around the altar, their ceremonial and symbolic role continues in the midst of an otherwise artificially lit church. On occasion, the electric lights may be intentionally lowered or turned off completely so that the use of candlelight may be more keenly observed (e.g., Christmas Eve, the Stripping of the Altar on Maundy Thursday, evensong, and the Office of Compline). For most of the church's existence, architecture and acoustics[2] have shaped the

---

1. Liv Meier, "First Lighted Church in Roselle Celebrates 150th Anniversary," *Union News Daily*, October 20, 2018, https://unionnewsdaily.com/news/roselle/41498.

2. Roman Mars, "Episode 236: Reverb: The Evolution of Architectural Acoustics," November 14, 2016, in 99% Invisible, podcast, MP3 audio, 22:35, https://99percentinvisible.org/episode/reverb-evolution-architectural-acoustics/. The scientific study of acoustics did not begin to develop until the early 20th century. Until then, the resulting acoustics of a new building were essentially a roll of the dice. When it was built in 1913, St. Thomas Church, Fifth Avenue, was intentionally deadened through the use of Rumford tiles. In the 1970s, "the Rumford tiles were painted over to seal off their sound-absorbing pores and let the reverb back into the space," a decision that surely went hand in hand with electronic amplification of the spoken word.

way the spoken word has been received by the gathered assembly. Pulpits served to raise preachers well above the ground and sometimes provided acoustical audio reinforcement in the form of a sounding board (a flat wooden surface placed directly over the pulpit).

The first loudspeaker prototype, invented in the late 19th century, was called a "bellowing telephone." Since then, microphones and loudspeakers have found their way into accepted liturgical use in spaces of all sizes. The electronic reinforcement of the human voice has also been a bane and blessing to modern liturgical worship. Present in many Episcopal churches is (1) a sound system and (2) some persistent level of dissatisfaction with it. But the use of a public address sound system within liturgy says certain things about worship: the words of the celebrant, officiant, preachers, lectors, and intercessors should be heard clearly by everyone gathered. There may be other unexamined impacts too. The inclusion of public address sound systems within the liturgy has had a gradual impact on the oratorical styles of celebrants and preachers generally. Depending on the style of the liturgical leaders or preachers, words need not be declaimed but can be merely spoken. The style of address to the assembly can take the form of a more personal style of conversation.

The impacts of the inclusion of the public address sound system on the congregation may be more subtle, but they are worth examining. If words are easily audible, congregations can focus on the meaning of what is being said rather than trying to decipher the content. In some places, the availability of assistive listening devices that are linked to the sound system may give some members the ability to hear the service more clearly. Were children previously excluded (either explicitly or implicitly) from the service in part or in whole because they were "too noisy?" The sound system may have answered the "I can't hear the priest" complaints and permitted children to attend.

The church, of course, existed for nearly two thousand years without electronic sound amplification, and its music evolved in a purely acoustic form. In the music of the Anglican church, the organ has played a central role: "The organ is, together with the clock, the most complex of all mechanical instruments developed before the Industrial Revolution. Among musical instruments its history is the most involved and wide-ranging, and its extant repertory the oldest and largest."[3]

The organ and choral model developed in the absence of electronic amplification. Most organs' technical design allows them to have a range of color and intensity of sound to suitably accompany a small choir to the largest congregation. In many architectural settings, multiple singers are more clearly audible than a single cantor. Electronic amplification changes these calculations. In many places,

---

3. Grove Music Online, s.v. "Organ," by Barbara Owen, Peter Williams, and Stephen Bicknell, accessed July 1, 2021, https://www.oxfordmusiconline.com/grovemusic/view/10.1093/gmo/9781561592630.001.0001/omo-9781561592630-e-0000044010

the tradition of singing parts of the liturgy has fallen out of favor as sound systems have improved. Musical forces have changed, and new instruments requiring amplification have been introduced. In 1939, Jerome Markowitz invented an electronic alternative to a pipe organ. If needed, acoustic instruments of all types can be suitably amplified to match the volume previously only achieved by the organ. Fully electronic instruments (e.g., guitars, keyboards, synthesizers) can be directly incorporated into the live sound design. And certain kinds of electronic composition (e.g., prerecorded media, live electronics) can commingle with live performance.[4]

Today, a variety of practices exist in the Episcopal Church in regard to the amplification of music, from a totally unamplified pipe organ and choir to a fully amplified praise band. With prayer books and hymnals in the pews, many congregations have little need for further printed material. Hymn numbers can even be communicated with a hymn board that can be updated with high-visibility numbers, the hymns appearing in the order they would be sung. The kinds of in-house typesetting and printing capabilities have evolved. A century ago, the service leaflet in my parish was created with a typewriter. The advent of desktop publishing has brought a new standard to the publication of church service sheets and booklets.

Finally, in some larger church buildings, video monitors have been installed to enable congregations to better see visual detail of, for example, the preacher's face, the manual acts at communion, and so on.[5] In some cases, video monitors allow congregants to see the action of the service from a seat that otherwise would have an obstructed view. Video feeds also can be viewed in other parts of the church campus for overflow seating or for parents and guardians who take young children out of the worship space for a time.

Before we examine new and emerging uses of technology, it's worth some reflection on the forms of technologies that have gradually found their way into accepted, regular use in our liturgies. In every case that we've examined these are deployments of internal technologies, designed to propagate text, light, and sound within the worship space itself; even in the case of video feeds to a neighboring room, these are intended for persons who are present on the church grounds and would be inside the nave with a slight change in circumstance.

But what happens when the audio and visual information from a liturgy reaches beyond the nave and the undercroft? Of particular interest to the Episcopal Church now, especially beginning with the coronavirus pandemic, is the increased prevalence of technology that disseminates liturgical worship beyond its particular space and time. Prior to the pandemic, many Episcopal churches were

---

4. Larry King, musician at Trinity Church Wall Street, New York, explored these possibilities beginning in the 1970s.

5. The National Cathedral in Washington, DC, and Trinity Church Wall Street, New York both have video monitors throughout the nave.

already webcasting services live. During the pandemic, these churches continued or upgraded their webcasting capability. St. Thomas, Fifth Avenue, New York, for instance, transitioned from audio-only webcasting to video webcasts. Other Episcopal churches that were not previously webcasting used free online platforms to begin live webcasting immediately. In the beginning of the pandemic, some churches decided to record the Sunday liturgies in advance (in the days or weeks leading up to the liturgy) and upload the video or audio recording to "premiere" or "go live" at a fixed time on the respective Sunday. And still other congregations opted for a "virtual meeting" model on Zoom or another video conferencing platform. Congregations were forced to gather outside of their traditional worship spaces. Many congregations, including my own, relied on a purely virtual model, not being permitted inside the church building for several months. For Episcopalians, however, the underlying technology of the book remained: the prayer book served as a resource for Episcopal worship as it always has. Seeing the difficulty in distributing the sacrament under strict social distancing rules, many churches opted to conduct a Morning Prayer service during the pandemic.

These three virtual modes—live, prerecorded, and virtual meeting—were also combined in various ways. For instance, a prerecorded virtual choir video could be played during a virtual meeting. Throughout this whole period, there were at least as many approaches to the virtual worship idea as there are congregations, if not more. In some places, the diocese was able regularly to produce a recording of a worship service for parishes to use. Sunday was still held as the Lord's Day, but clergy and laypeople found different modes of observing it and found new definitions for corporate worship.

Q. What is corporate worship?

A. In corporate worship, we unite ourselves with others to acknowledge the holiness of God, to hear God's Word, to offer prayer, and to celebrate the sacraments.

—from the Catechism, Book of Common Prayer, p. 857

In the first part of the prayer book's answer, the question of the physical gathering of the corporate body almost can be avoided. We can seemingly "unite ourselves with others to acknowledge the holiness of God, to hear God's Word," and "to offer prayer" using virtual means. The question of celebrating the sacraments becomes a bit trickier when the corporate assembly is physically dispersed and joined via virtual means. Do we truly unite ourselves with others if we merely view the service in isolation from different screens? All of the modes of transmitting worship digitally have their challenges here. In the prerecorded worship service, the viewer is separated not only by distance but also by time since the event taking place has already finished.

In my parish, as in many others, our prerecorded worship service was made up of various constituent elements submitted by clergy, staff, and laypeople, and edited into a single digital product. Though the final video may adhere to the liturgy of the Book of Common Prayer, this is not a recording of an actual liturgy. It only formed the semblance of one in the video editing software. As we continued this habit during the early stage of the pandemic, my thoughts often turned to St. Clare of Assisi. Once, when Clare was too ill to attend Mass, she was able to see and hear a kind of divine projection of the liturgy on the wall of her room. But woe betide any aspiring St. Clares expecting to magically eavesdrop on one of these collaborative liturgies. He or she might experience, without warning, the Prayers of the People on Tuesday evening, the lessons read midday on Wednesday, various pieces of music very late at night throughout the week, and a whole slew of different takes of the sermon on Friday and Saturday. Clare's miracle would be more of a nightmare, but with a restful day indeed on Sunday! The miracle of these collaborative services was that we produced something resembling a prayer book liturgy in a very disjointed way.

In the virtual meeting mode, at least it can be said that a worship gathering takes place simultaneously at an agreed-upon time. Worshippers in this mode saw many of their fellow worshippers but mainly just their faces. There's an added element of each worshipper being on display to everyone else in a way that doesn't occur in most churches (but, to be fair, an element of this does occur for those churches that gather in the round). Virtual meetings allow for the possibility of real-time participation from any one computer at any given time. Text chat and other annotation tools are also a possibility. For as much participation as the virtual meeting software (such as Zoom) allows, however, some of the primary mechanisms of corporate worship cannot take place. Corporate recitation or communal singing is not possible. As many churches quickly learned, the delay inherent in virtual meeting platforms makes unison speaking or singing an impossibility.

Many churches took the pandemic as an opportunity to add to their weekly worship schedule with various combinations of services from the Daily Office: Morning Prayer, Noonday Prayer, Evening Prayer, and Compline. The pattern of these virtual offices was often a virtual meeting that was then livestreamed to another platform (e.g., Facebook or YouTube). This instituted a kind of digital rood screen, where the officiant and lector were the only ones collaborating in a virtual meeting space. For practical reasons, the rest of the congregation was viewing a livestream of this virtual meeting.

In my own congregation, daily Morning Prayer was instituted online when no prepandemic pattern of Morning Prayer existed. After a period of months, the service was seen by some as a great success since Facebook analytics revealed that hundreds of people were seeing each service daily. A closer examination of the data, however, revealed that the majority of these were three-second views of the video, whether it was live or the video replay, likely someone scrolling by the muted video on their Facebook feed. It was a lesson that online technology does not provide a magic bullet. Cultivating a habit of praying the offices together is not something that can be achieved simply by making them available online. The Rt. Rev. George Wayne Smith has observed a "commitment *by the community* and not just by the priest can encourage a discipline of daily corporate prayer."[6] While technology potentially makes the commitment more convenient for the community, the commitment still must be made.

Whether worshipping by way of the virtual meeting or the prerecorded model, churches quickly implemented the technology and the skills necessary to disseminate familiar liturgical material to their congregations. The prerecorded mode of worship especially seems to have been a product of the early stage of the pandemic. The virtual meeting, too, has greatly declined in prevalence as time has gone on. What remains is the live weekly Sunday morning webcast, which is now present in many more Episcopal congregations than it was prior to the pandemic. The Sunday morning webcast seems to have value moving forward. Many congregations invested time and resources in hardware and software during the pandemic. Now, these congregations have a proven ability to webcast. Many parishioners in these congregations have been introduced and perhaps even grown accustomed to this resource being available. Assuming that the process of webcasting is sustainable at a given parish, what reason would there be to not continue webcasting in the future?

In the 1993 film *Jurassic Park*, the mathematician Ian Malcolm criticizes what he views as the rather unconsidered decision to recreate dinosaurs from fossilized DNA: "Your scientists were so preoccupied with whether or not they could, they didn't stop to think if they should."[7] All congregations were faced with a stark reality in and around March 2020 and had to determine what it was that they could still accomplish liturgically. But as the fog of the coronavirus pandemic lifts, perhaps we ought to heed Malcolm's advice and "stop to think if we should."

A digitally mediated experience of a liturgy is necessarily one of a forced perspective. What we see and hear is, by nature of the medium, limited. This is distinct from our experience in liturgy when we are physically present. Each of us has a slightly different visual and sonic experience of the liturgy depending on where we are located. And, to some degree, we can choose what it is that we see and hear. We make our own selections about what to look at, what to listen to, how to direct our attention. When we enter, exit, and move through the liturgical space and our perspective changes, we become keenly aware of the sights and

---

6. George Wayne Smith, *Admirable Simplicity: Principles for Worship Planning in the Anglican Tradition* (New York: Church Hymnal, 2000), 48.

7. *Jurassic Park*, directed by Steven Spielberg (1993; Universal City, CA: Universal Home Entertainment, 2012), DVD.

sounds around us. When we experience a digitally mediated liturgy, the immersive three-dimensional experience is flattened so that it can be disseminated. Not every element of the three-dimensional reality can be adequately captured by digital means. We all share the same curated perspective of the sights and sounds of what's going on. And that is to say nothing of the other senses we are able to employ when we are physically present: touch, taste, and smell. Like the data that make the webcast possible, our experience, too, is compressed. Webcasts of liturgy in and of themselves are not necessarily a bad thing; they enable greater access to the content of the liturgy (if not the full experience) for those members of a congregation who cannot attend. And webcasts also provide a window onto Episcopal liturgy for others, those who are tangentially connected to the worship life of a particular congregation, the curious, or those who may consider themselves church shoppers.

The commonly used phrase *church shopper* is, of course, problematic. It reflects the perspective of our hyperconsumerist culture. With the increased prevalence of liturgical webcasting, how much will we see a rise in online church shopping? Will prospective members of the community make their first visits online? Will they be able to glean enough about a local congregation to simply skip an in-person visit altogether? Does the new prevalence of webcasts in this denomination amount to a kind of Episcopal Church home shopping network? And can potential churchgoers really glean enough information from a webcast or two to decide whether to "buy in"? The typical questions (e.g., "What does this church have to offer me?") are even asked at a distance rather than explored in any kind of relationship or community. The church has no real opportunity to welcome or connect in a human way. The problem of the webcast church shopper is one of respect, as defined by philosopher Byung-Chul Han. Han breaks down the word's Latin root, *respectare*, to look back. He defines it as "a distanced look," one having "the pathos of distance."[8]

On the surface, one assumes that the live webcasting of a liturgy is a good thing: it makes the core act of the community more available to all. And this is true. Those members of the community who were prevented from attending for any reason still have access to the sights and sounds of the worship service. But in another sense, the medium is liable to change our interaction with the liturgy so it becomes one not of *respectare* but one of *spectare*. We are liable to become spectators, those who stare. With the physical separation from the acts of worship introduced by the technology, someone viewing the webcast is much more an observer only rather than an active participant. This is not how the Church or her liturgy was intended to function (merely as information for others). Liturgy is a communal act and requires the gathered assembly: "In all services, the entire

---

8. Byung-Chul Han, *In the Swarm: Digital Prospects (Untimely Meditations)*, trans. Erik Butler (Cambridge, MA: MIT Press, 2017), 1.

Christian assembly participates in such a way that the members of each order within the Church, lay persons, bishops, priests, and deacons, fulfill the functions proper to their respective orders, as set forth in the rubrical directions for each service."[9]

It is all orders of ministry that seek to unite themselves in worship. Cathedrals, churches, chapels, and other sacred spaces traditionally have been locations in which we do this. When gathered in a place appointed for worship, we are somehow made aware of the intangible presence of our shared attention to the liturgy and to each other. This shared attention begins even before we head for the location of the assembly. I would posit that most worshippers have private rituals of preparation. We bathe, eat, drink, and clothe ourselves in our Sunday best. Our route from our home to our worship site is also a kind of ritual pilgrimage. These things may seem trivial, but for many worshippers they likely represent, if not a time of outright prayer, then a time of mental preparation for and anticipation of the act of worship. The immediate availability of the webcast stands in stark opposition to our own individual rituals for a physical gathering. Without needing to travel outside the home or even be presentable in public, the ritual collapses into the pressing of a button, the tapping of a screen, the clicking of the mouse. And with so little invested in the beginning of the digitally mediated worship experience, is it any surprise that worshippers typically fall away in droves? In the video analytics that we see in my parish, most viewers of a live webcast turn it off in the first few minutes. But obviously, this is not how most congregations behave when they are present for a Sunday morning liturgy. And this raises an interesting question about how much we should be paying attention to webcast statistics at all. What constitutes a meaningful engagement with a digital presentation of a liturgical act, and is there an effect from this expected engagement on the liturgical act itself? Should worship leaders directly address those who are listening or watching the webcast? Notably, St. Thomas, Fifth Avenue has done this regularly for years, starting with their audio-only webcasts. They have continued the practice, now including a direct-to-camera address from the altar after the Breaking of the Bread.

The Rt. Rev. George Wayne Smith writes, "Our acts of worship do represent our beliefs, and a shift in the conduct of worship may also signal a shift in ways of believing."[10] Explicit acknowledgment or address of other worshippers who are not physically present in the room, or who may be listening or watching at a later time, does represent a shift in what we have traditionally assumed about what constitutes the gathered assembly. No longer is a miracle required for a projection of the Divine Mysteries; technology has opened a way for more observers to the Eucharist than St. Clare alone. But even if worship leaders explicitly acknowledge

---

9. *The Book of Common Prayer* (New York: Church Publishing, 1979), 13.

10. Smith, *Admirable Simplicity*, 146.

that others are viewing the webcast, those same viewers have little to no possibility of fulfilling the functions proper to their order. Viewers cannot participate in any of the ways prescribed by the rubrics of the prayer book, or if they do, they do so in the privacy of their own home. The collective attention and participation of the gathered assembly cannot be clearly perceived in the same way.

The Eucharist has always assumed the presence of more than those we can see. In the eucharistic prayer we are invited to "[join] our voices with Angels and Archangels and with all the company of heaven." But the intentional inclusion of living, earthly human beings who are not physically present is something new. A prayer called "An Act of Spiritual Communion" attributed to St. Alphonsus Liguori has enjoyed heightened popularity since March 2020, but there is also a feeling among some that technology can facilitate more than the Word only. The concept of digitally mediated sacraments is one that would imbue technology with more ecclesiastical authority than it has previously enjoyed. In Anglican liturgical practice, communion and baptism, as they have been understood, are conducted by a bishop or a priest. With the availability of virtual meeting platforms, the question has now arisen about the location of minister and people.

On Easter Monday, 2020, the Bishop of Western Louisiana, the Rt. Rev. Jake Owensby, allowed for a virtual Holy Eucharist in that diocese:

> Simply put, priests who have the technical know-how, the equipment, and the inclination will live-stream the Holy Eucharist on Sunday (or other appointed times). Instead, they may refer you to my weekly Eucharist. The people will attend from their own homes, maintaining physical distance as before. The people will provide for themselves bread and wine (bread alone is also permissible) and place it on a table in front of them.
>
> The priest's consecration of elements in front of her or him extends to the bread and wine in each of family's [sic] household. The people will consume the consecrated elements.[11]

The permission for this virtual Holy Eucharist was rescinded days after it was given,[12] but does Bishop Owensby's proposed scheme for virtual Holy Communion and the larger conversation about the potential for a technologically aided consecration of the elements of communion in the Anglican church represent a shift in what we believe? The prayer book catechism sidesteps the word

---

11. The Rt. Rev. Jake Owensby, "Home Based Worship and Resources: Keeping Connected amid Physical Distancing," email message from the Diocese of Western Louisiana, April 13, 2020, https://myemail.constantcontact.com/Home-Based-Worship-and-Community-Resources.html?soid=1111514195724&aid=nlM3_CQpxbM.

12. Mark Michael, "Western Louisiana Bishop Authorizes, Then Rescinds, Virtual Consecration," *The Living Church*, April 17, 2020, https://livingchurch.org/2020/04/17/western-louisiana-bishop-authorizes-then-rescinds-virtual-consecration/.

gathering in its definition of corporate worship, but most liturgical scholarship does not. The coming together of the assembly can delineate the bounds of the liturgical act itself.

> During the first eight or nine centuries of the church's life, when clerical dress did not differ substantially from that of the people, and even during the first three centuries, when the gathering place may have been indistinguishable from an ordinary house, the event of liturgical enactment could be marked or framed by this act of gathering and dispersal.[13]

Can we effectively mark liturgical events in the virtual space simply by gathering there at the same time? If so, is this virtual space one in which a sacramental celebration is possible?

❖ ❖ ❖

As a result of living in a society permeated by digital media, it may be that we have come to believe too much in the power of technology to connect us with each other. It may be that we need to adopt less technology in our worship, not more. A determination to adopt and employ every new social media platform as it comes along, to stream every worship and Christian formation event to every conceivable platform—these things are not only out of reach for many congregations, but they are surely the way to madness. We may not even be aware that our new, technology-saturated world is not one that we necessarily asked for. Cal Newport writes that our dependence on social media and smartphones

> crept up on us and happened fast, before we had a chance to step back and ask what *we really wanted* out of the rapid advances of the past decade. We added new technologies to the periphery of our experience for minor reasons, then woke one morning to discover that they had colonized the core of our daily life. We didn't, in other words, sign up for the digital world in which we're currently entrenched; we seem to have stumbled backward into it.[14]

The subtitle to Newport's book *Digital Minimalism* is "Choosing a Focused Life in a Noisy World." Isn't this one of the hopes of the church in a 21st century affluent culture? Isn't it one of the things that we are taught to pray for when we prepare for worship?

---

13. Richard D. McCall, *Do This: Liturgy as Performance* (South Bend, IN: University of Notre Dame Press, 2007), 53.

14. Cal Newport, *Digital Minimalism* (New York: Penguin/Portfolio, 2019), 6–7.

> O Almighty God, who pourest out on all who desire it the spirit of grace and of supplication: Deliver us, when we draw near to thee, from coldness of heart and wanderings of mind, that with steadfast thoughts and kindled affections we may worship thee in spirit and in truth; through Jesus Christ our Lord. Amen.[15]

If video webcasts promote—even in part—a consumerist mindset of liturgy and drive the faithful to distraction, are they really the assets we want them to be?

The free social media platforms like Facebook and YouTube, used as streaming platforms by many churches, are run by businesses that are not interested in delivering us from "wanderings of mind," but rather its opposite. They are fundamentally in the distraction business. They want their users to spend more time on their websites so they have more data about their users and more advertising dollars. To do this, websites like Facebook and YouTube do everything they can to get us to click away and watch something else, even while watching Holy Communion.

Where church music is concerned, technology provides some opportunities, but some barriers as well. The challenges faced by choirs in the early stages of the coronavirus pandemic proved the limits of technology. Rehearsals could be led online, either by way of a virtual meeting or a prerecorded video. But in either case, there was no resulting choral sound, only the experience of rehearsing in isolation. Various methods of producing choral music were employed. One method is to combine separate recordings from individual singers to form a "virtual choir." The editing process can be especially time-consuming. These videos always sort of had an uncanny quality of a group of singers who were not really listening to each other—because that's what was happening. Participants in a virtual choir project need to sing along with some kind of guide recording as a baseline for pitch and tempo, but this process removes any of the traditional abilities that choral singers have to adjust to other voices. There are innumerable microcalculations that go within an in-person choir as singers adjust their breathing, tuning, vowels, tone, color, and relative volume. The kind of communication needed for true simultaneity of ensemble is denied. From the perspective of this singer, the process is generally uninteresting at best and demoralizing at worst. I've heard the same kinds of complaints from preachers about giving a sermon. Without real-time feedback from a room with people in it, the effect isn't the same. This isn't how we were trained to operate. The reality of recording on different equipment and in different acoustical spaces also lends to a kind of disembodied quality to this recording. Choirs who are physically in a shared location don't have these issues.

---

15. *The Book of Common Prayer* (New York: Church Publishing, 1979), 833.

Choral singing, as the art is traditionally understood, is an embodied act. Both the space in which the choir sings and how the individual voices are arranged affect the choral sound. This is to say nothing of congregational singing, which is truly an art that requires real presence and benefits from a slight lack of social distance. The techniques employed during the pandemic, especially its beginning, to record and disseminate liturgy and music were born out of necessity. But these experiences have laid bare the limits of what technology can do well and how far the spatial dynamics of our liturgical life can be stretched.

❖❖❖

Before electric lights and loudspeakers, one of the most pervasive technologies in the Western church was the pipe organ. As the assistant organist at Christ Church Cathedral, Indianapolis, I was privileged to play two very fine mechanical-action organs. The rear gallery organ, built by Taylor and Boody of Staunton, Virginia, was an outright gift to the cathedral and represents an historic form of organ building. Every element of the organ is mechanically operated, including the way the organist pulls out each stop: each stop knob has a direct mechanical connection to the mechanism that allows that rank of pipes to play. This organ also can be operated entirely without electricity; it can be played with the assistance of a bellows pumper. The cathedral's chancel organ, built by Hellmuth Wolff & Associates, is also a mechanical-action organ but with a few added conveniences. The stop action on this organ is not mechanical, but electropneumatic. It also has a combination action, which means that organists can program various combinations of stops and summon them at the touch of a button. This organ does not have bellows that could be operated by human power; it relies entirely on its electric blower. Within these two instruments we see a progression from accepted historic principles of organ building from the way organs operated in the 15th century to the way organs operated in the early 20th century.

As they developed further, organs were made fully electropneumatic: the key action as well as the stop action was updated. Other linkages between the organ console and the pipes have been introduced over time, including direct electric action, fiber optic, and wireless connectivity. Outside of what is traditionally understood as an organ (a musical instrument with pipes), fully electronic simulations of organs can be achieved with loudspeakers. Sampling technology allows for high-fidelity replication of existing organs. The result of all these methods, from the most historic to the most cutting edge, is the same, giving the person seated at the console the ability to have full control of the instrument's resources to make music on the organ. The particulars vary somewhat, but the technology has the same result. We might take organ building as a model for how the traditions of the past can be continually augmented by the technology of the present within liturgical worship. The details have and will continue to vary, but the end goals should be the same: to worship the Lord in the beauty of holiness; to "unite ourselves with others to acknowledge the holiness of God, to hear God's Word, to offer prayer, and to celebrate the sacraments."[16]

❖ ❖ ❖

All of our technologies, even those of the Information Age, can be destroyed and remade, but the God-given information stays the same. "The grass withers, the flower fades," but the enduring Word of God is what defines and guides the Christian life. And the Christian life is a life together, at as close a distance as we can manage. There is a biblical precedent for being face to face with each other (a pandemic notwithstanding) and, ultimately, our God.

> Although I have much to write to you, I would rather not use paper and ink; instead, I hope to come to you and talk with you *face to face*, so that our joy may be complete. (2 John 1:12, emphasis mine)

> For now we see in a mirror, dimly, but then we will see *face to face*. Now I know only in part; then I will know fully, even as I have been fully known. (1 Cor. 13:12, emphasis mine)

No matter how good we think it is at any moment, our technology, when it comes to divine things, is but another dim mirror. But in the flurry of innovation and experimentation that has sprung up since March 2020, more Episcopal churches than ever have explored the possibilities afforded by digital technologies. When we were not able to meet face to face, existing technologies provided options for communication, prayer, and hearing the Word of God.

Technology and liturgy have gone hand in hand since the beginning of liturgical tradition. The impetus provided by the pandemic has and will continue to encourage us to think intentionally and creatively about how we employ various digital technologies. Even before the pandemic, churches were already making more use of the internet and digital tools than we have explored here, but there may also be current technologies still left to be tried. One of the remarkable things about the technology of the pipe organ is that the bulk of its development took place inside the church, and secular society benefited from these advancements. With the digital technologies we now confront, the opposite is true: these technologies have developed within secular society, and now the church is seeking to use them in a beneficial way. It could be that the church itself may want to develop "holy" platforms specifically designed for liturgical use, ones separated from the distraction-driven technologies with

---

16. *The Book of Common Prayer* (New York: Church Publishing, 1979), 857.

which we are already familiar. We should expect new approaches to digital technologies to emerge amid an ever-changing technological landscape in a frenetic Information Age. The future surely holds unimagined possibilities and challenges for the liturgical worship and music of the church.

3

Story of Stories

The Language of Stories in Song

The Rt. Rev. Deon Johnson

The flame of the Paschal candle flickers and darts in a divine dance that grounds the moment in eternity. Shards of sunshine pierce the air and wash the gathered congregation in a sea of light. Everyone is on their feet. Young and old, tall and short, believers and skeptics, standing around the font. For a moment, time stands still. The smell of candles and chrism oil and incense fills the air. The delicate sound of splashing water intertwines with fascinated giggles from a little girl and fills the room with joy. A wave of laughter ripples across the congregation as her dad lifts her, soaking wet from the waters of new birth; she wants to stay in the warm font.

"I baptize you in the name of the Father, and of the Son, and of the Holy Spirit."

A loud and rapturous "amen" fills the space.

"You are sealed by the Holy Spirit and marked as Christ's own forever."

A lone voice sings the opening strains of the familiar tune. One by one, other voices take up the words and join in the song. The symphony of voices fills the room with song. The song transforms and invites. In the song is memory and reconnection. Eternity whispers into the present. Each person makes their way to touch the waters as a reminder of their own sealing and marking. They keep singing. The prayer in song weaves eternity into a single moment, and the melody tugs at the soul, conveying a love that is beyond words, beyond music, beyond comprehension. Joy and awe wash over the room.

I was there to hear your borning cry,

I'll be there when you are old.

I rejoiced the day you were baptized,

To see your life unfold.

I was there when you were but a child,

With a faith to suit you well;
In a blaze of light you wandered off
To find where demons dwell.

When you heard the wonder of the Word
I was there to cheer you on;
You were raised to praise the living Lord,
to whom you now belong.

If you find someone to share your time
and you join your hearts as one,
I'll be there to make your verses rhyme
from dusk 'til rising sun.

I was there to hear your borning cry,
I'll be there when you are old.
I rejoiced the day you were baptized,
To see your life unfold.[1]

The flame of the Paschal candle flickers and darts in a divine dance that grounds the moment in eternity. The mourners gather. Tears rebaptize the cheeks and chins of those in grief and sorrow. Shards of sunlight dance heavenward like angels as incense ascends mingled with prayers and pictures of the past. Through the tears, the grief, the goodbyes, a single flame unites this moment with the moments that had gone before. The familiar rituals begin. The people gather, the faithful and the faithless, to say farewell, to entrust the beloved once more to God's care and keeping. Stories of a life lived unite the congregation in a communion of grief. Sunlight bathes the congregation with a blessing of light as the celebration draws to its end. A single note pierces the silence, and a lone voice wells up with the melody of a familiar hymn. It is a song of the eternal and the infinite, uniting the transitory and the finite. Story, song, and prayer woven together call to the soul in a way that nothing else can. The walls, which had borne silent witness to the many rituals and rites, seem to echo and amplify the lone voice swelling, beckoning others to join in the sacred song. The symphony of earth and heaven join as one in a song of farewell and a song of welcome.

In the middle ages of your life,
Not too old, no longer young,
I'll be there to guide you through the night,
Complete what I've begun.

---

1. John Ylvisaker, "I Was There To Hear Your Borning Cry," verses 1–4 and 7, © 1985. Used by permission.

When the evening gently closes in,
And you shut your weary eyes,
I'll be there as I have always been
With just one more surprise.

I was there to hear your borning cry,
I'll be there when you are old.
I rejoiced the day you were baptized,
To see your life unfold.[2]

Many hymns and other compositions are, at their core, prayers set to music. Our hymns for worship often address God, with the intention of inviting change for ourselves or for God to intervene—to be present. Our music is a way of sharing the stories of our faith and connecting us to the fullness of God found in Jesus Christ. What is unusual about the hymn "I Was There to Hear Your Borning Cry," written by John Ylvisaker, is that instead of addressing God from a human perspective, it finds its beauty in God addressing humanity from a divine perspective. The spirit of the hymn is the love affair of God with each one of us throughout the span of our lives. In its language we are reminded of a God who loved us from the beginning of time and continues to love us throughout the seasons of our life. The text allows us as both listener and singer to hear the message of God's timelessness, the love song that has been sung through eternity. It is the story of a love and longing between God and humanity.

At its heart, music is the distillation of the stories of our encounter with God set to the language of song. In the interplay between the notes and the singer, the words and the melody, we glimpse for a moment in time the divine dance of the triune God. At its very best, liturgical music is the weaving of the story of God together with the story of us in the creation of a new story that preaches, teaches, touches, and transforms. Our songs tell a story of the gathering of God's people in worship. The language of those stories will invite or inhibit others in joining the story of faith. Ultimately, worship is about connecting our story to the story of a God who entered human history. God's first language of love was a song.

Stories matter. Our language for worship matters.

We are shaped by the stories we tell and the stories we are told. Stories tell us who we are and where we come from. Stories locate us in our families and our origins, as part of our micro story, while connecting us to the macro story of humanity and human history. Stories locate us in our past and ground us in the present,

---

2. John Ylvisaker, "I Was There To Hear Your Borning Cry," verses 5–7, © 1985. Used by permission.

all the while navigating us toward an unknown future. The story of humanity is written in the subtle movements of our body, the inhalation of breath, the fleeting sacred touch. Stories not only define who we are, but also shape who we become. We are adrift without story. Stories are the most powerful, transcendent force we can encounter of the divine. To be a part of the story that is greater than ourselves is to be reminded of both the eternal and the transitory. The stories that we tell others and ourselves locate us in time and space, uniting us with the stories of those who have gone before. In the giving and receiving of stories, we find our connection to the past, look for meaning and purpose in the present, and dream of a new-storied future. In the stories of faith, we seek a deeper communion with the divine and more profound connections to each other.

We are a part of God's love affair with the cosmos.

By its nature, language is always metaphorical. Our words are intended to be metaphors for the objects and concepts they seek to explain or expand. Yet words are not the objects or concepts they represent; they can only be a source of reference. Therefore, all language works by displaying both similarity and difference simultaneously. Our language for God points to the nature of God as we have experienced the divine but cannot ever fully express the entirety of God through time. Our use of language to address and describe God is the equivalent of dipping a bucket into the ocean and claiming to contain the entirety of the ocean. While the bucket contains a part of the ocean, it is not capable of expressing the wholeness or the vastness of the seas. The same is true for God. The language and metaphors we use to both address and describe God, by their very nature, point to what God is and what God is not. God is both like and not like a mother hen, a lamb, a monarch, a rock. While metaphorical language will fall short in describing *who* or *how* God is, our language and metaphors will always be influenced and guided by the cultural context in which language has developed. We cannot separate the cultural development of language from the metaphors created by the culture. We also run the risk of alienation or domination by imposing cultural metaphors from one community onto another. Cultural images and metaphors that have meaning in one cultural context may have a completely different meaning in another.

Our sacred scripture is replete with cultural references and images that are specific to a time and place and at the same time universal in their appeal. The translators of the Bible often make cultural interpretations based on the culture in which they seek to convey the love story of God found in the scripture. The specific cultural nuances of more than two thousand years ago can get lost in modern cultural interpretation while the universal metaphorical imagery has the power to transcend cultural specificity. Take, for example, the image of Jesus looking over Jerusalem and longing to gather God's people like a mother hen gathers her chicks (Matt. 23:37). The image Jesus uses has specific cultural connotations of God's divine protection surrounding and caring for the people of Israel through time, and yet the image of a brooding hen has universal appeal that goes beyond the specific culture. Almost every culture can relate to hens caring for their young and recognize the protective nature of hens, which is beyond the specifics of Jesus's lived cultural experience. Our language and the metaphorical choices we make in conveying an understanding of the divine matters.

A word or two about expansive and inclusive language.

God gives the gift of language. God speaks in and through language. God is glorified in our language. God is beyond human classification and language. God transcends time and space, matter and thought, gender and expression. God, then, is revealed to us in scripture through story, poetry, prophecy, law, and many different images. Throughout scripture, the authors continually caution the people, when naming God, not to allow the name to become an idol unto itself. From the burning bush, God speaks a mysterious name: "I am who I am" (Exod. 3:1–14). In the exchange between Moses and "I AM," we hear the familiar and the unfamiliar collide. God reminds Moses that even though the people of Israel may have forgotten the divine name, it is still embedded in their very being and will be familiar to them, even if they have not heard the name in generations. The naming of God in this and other instances becomes an icon imprinted on the people of God. We can never fully comprehend the vastness or the fullness of God. However, by expanding the images of God we experience in worship and in song, in poetry and in prose, we can more ably explore and engage this mystery. At the same time, God is revealed in the cosmos but particularly to humans in ways we can understand through images that connect with our lives and our world.

Language is given so that all creation can respond to God's love present in the cosmos. As the author of Psalm 19 reminds us,

> The heavens are telling the glory of God;
> and the firmament proclaims his handiwork.
> Day to day pours forth speech,
> and night to night declares knowledge.
> There is no speech, nor are there words;
> their voice is not heard;
> yet their voice goes out through all the earth,
> and their words to the end of the world. (Ps. 19:1–4)

Language, while a gift of God, is incomplete, finite, and limited. Language can be used either for the building up or for tearing down, for edification or for eradication. Through language, we forge relationship with God, with each other, and with all of creation. How, then, do we move from language that alienates and excludes into language that uplifts and invites? Intentionality provides an avenue toward language that expands the metaphorical imagery of God and the broadly inclusive naming of humanity.

Expansive language seeks to expand the metaphorical lexicon used in referring to or addressing God. The prevailing image of God in the Western church has been that of God the Father. While this image has historical roots in early Christianity and forms a part of the formularies of the church—namely the creeds and formula prescribed for baptism—it limits the references to God with a gendered bias. We know inherently that God is not just a father, but the continued use of such language is limiting. This also becomes problematic considering the hundreds of images and references to God through scripture. Expansive language, by its very definition, seeks to tell as much truth about God as we can, using the full range of language available to us. It does not displace traditional language for God but uses additional metaphors. Of course, no human language can contain God. Even so, our theologies of creation, incarnation, and resurrection affirm that the material world, including language, is a means to understand God in a more faithful way.[3] Language continues to change and evolve as cultures shift and redefine themselves. Over the last hundred years, Western culture has seen a dramatic shift in language and cultural awareness. Like many Romance languages, English retained for a time the understanding that "man" or "men" could function as a referent for both men and women. While that may have been the understanding of our spiritual ancestors of just a few centuries ago, it becomes problematic in the Western context where men and women are seen as equal and gender expression moves from binary to fluid. As the culture has evolved, the use of language must also evolve.

At its best, inclusive language seeks to draw the circle of language for humanity wide enough that all are included. Our language often has built-in biases that exclude and harm some persons. When exclusive language is used, we fall short of our calling to respect all who are created in the image and likeness of God. By using inclusive language for humanity, we respect the dignity of every human being and the need to self-name, while affirming our faith in the vast diversity of the communion of saints.

---

3. Evangelical Lutheran Church of America, *Principles for Worship* (Minneapolis: Augsburg Fortress, 2002), https://download.elca.org/ELCA%20Resource%20Repository/Principles_for_Worship.pdf.

When in our music God is glorified . . .

The people of God gather. The sun streams through the multicolored glass as beautiful light dances across the wooden floors. An ordinary Sunday in many ways. Babies squirm on the lap-made pews; ushers smile and welcome the community. A voice welcomes the assembly. Words of invitation and hospitality set the tone for worship. The piano takes up a melody that is caught and carried by the oboist and the drummer. The people stand. Worship is beginning. The doings of the week past are a memory. The mystery of the time ahead is unknown. Only this present moment matters. Time seems to stand still. The people of God sing.

> When in our music God is glorified,
>
> and adoration leaves no room for pride,
>
> it is as though the whole creation cried, alleluia!
>
> How often, making music, we have found
>
> a new dimension in the world of sound,
>
> as worship moved us to a more profound, alleluia!
>
> So has the church, in liturgy and song,
>
> in faith and love, through centuries of wrong,
>
> borne witness to the truth in ev'ry tongue, alleluia![4]

The people of God sing. Singing and making music is the breaking and bending of silence. Music is the language of the heart set to the rhythms of our souls. Scripture is woven through with the music of God's people singing. From the silent songs of the morning stars in creation, through Miriam's tambourine song, into the song of praise that Mary the Godbearer proclaims, the people of God sing. The breaking and bending of silence is a part of the worship of God and part of the human condition. Worship would be dull without music.

While rather simple, the hymn "When in our music God is glorified" by Fred Pratt Green expresses the best of inclusive and expansive language and allows the listener to connect to God and each other in songs of praise. Worship by its very nature is about aligning our deep yearning to unite with God, with God's deep yearning to connect with us. How better to express that deep desire than in words and images that expand the circle of praise rather than constrict it to a particular time and place, a defined cultural context that is specific and confined.

Hymns, chants, anthems, cantatas, motets, rounds, and solos all seek to stretch and enlarge the understanding of God through song. Both ancient and modern music seek to increase our vocabulary for worship and to expand our

---

4. "When In Our Music God Is Glorified." Words: Fred Pratt Green © 1972 Hope Publishing Company, Carol Stream, IL 60188. All rights reserved. Used by permission.

capacity for praise. As the people of God, we rehearse the biblical story every time we meet. The histories of our spiritual ancestors spill into the present moment in our music and our songs and are essential for the spiritual growth of the community gathered. Music, then, is not mere filler between the "real" work of liturgy, but rather an integral dance partner in the sacred dance of worship.

Change happens. Our theological understanding evolves and changes over time, and yet the purpose and promise of gathering for worship remains unchanged. In his *Church Dogmatics*, theologian Karl Barth reminds us that singing is not optional for the people of God; singing is always an essential element in the ministry of the church. He writes,

> The Christian church sings. It is not a choral society. Its singing is not a concert. But from inner, material necessity it sings. Singing is the highest form of human expression. . . . What we can and must say quite confidently is that the church which does not sing is not the church. And where . . . it does not really sing but sighs and mumbles spasmodically, shamefacedly and with an ill grace, it can be at best only a troubled community which is not sure of its cause and of whose ministry and witness there can be no great expectation. . . . The praise of God which finds its concrete culmination in the singing of the community is one of the indispensable forms of the ministry of the church.[5]

When we come together for worship, the circle of inclusion expands by the very presence of those gathered for worship. We bring different life experiences that shape how we encounter language for God. We bring our cultural blessings and biases, our lived experience in the world to the altar in the hopes that God might "deliver us from the presumption of coming to this Table for solace only, and not for strength; for pardon only, and not for renewal."[6] We aim to worship in solidarity with a wide variety of people, including people who have faced discrimination because of their gender, rejection because of their race, alienation because of their ability, and dismissal because of gender expression. We long to be hospitable to one another in worship through the words we use. We must strive to be attentive to pastoral needs and to the ways different images of God have sustained, wounded, and liberated those in our communities. We must be mindful and intentional in choosing music that allows a broader sense of invitation and hospitality knowing that we all come to worship seeking the healing of our brokenness. Our hymnals are compilations of many images and metaphors for God—a place from which communities explore, discern, repeat, and internalize these images.

---

5. Karl Barth, *Church Dogmatics*, vol. IV, part 3 (London: T. & T. Clark International, 2004), chapter 16, par. 72, #4.

6. *The Book of Common Prayer* (New York: Church Publishing, 1979), 368.

Music and singing continue to be integral to the worship life of communities of faith across the world and across the Episcopal Church. Music saturates and surrounds us in all aspects of life. Contemporary Western culture coupled with modern technology present a myriad of new possibilities and a host of challenges to the music ministry of the church. With the advent of social media and platforms like TikTok, Pandora, and Spotify, music in a real sense accompanies our whole lives.

Our lives are surrounded and often saturated by music—television, radio, streaming apps, birdsong, video games, Muzak. Yet even with the inundation of music in our lives, there are very few places where we are able to join in singing, in making music together. Music in our popular culture continues to be composed for performance and not for participation. The community of faith gathered for worship remains one of the few places where participatory singing is a priority. This means that the church, when it gathers for worship, should and must be different in some ways from the normative culture. We run the risk of being irrelevant if we move away from communal singing in favor of performative religious concerns. We should be careful, intentional, and hospitable in how we select music to better reflect the expansive nature of God and the inclusive nature of humanity.

As the church, we are granted greater access to a variety of music genres, composers, and presentations. From 4th-century chants to Christian rock, from classical cantatas to Brazilian choruses, such musical diversity is to be welcomed, honored, and celebrated; it reflects the vast treasure trove of diversity present in God's creation. Being mindful of the process of discernment and care in planning and implementing music that is expansive and inclusive is a vital part of the ministry of the church. The people of God sing; what and how and why they sing matters. Leaders of the church, both ordained and lay, should be mindful of the impact of musical selections on worship and whenever possible consider the hospitality of the selections. Here are a few questions for musicians and clergy to consider in planning and preparing music as part of the liturgy for worship:

- What theology is being expressed in congregational or choir singing?
- Is the music selected an expression of current theological understanding?
- Does the music represent the diversity present in the community of faith?
- Do our hymns make use of the full range of biblical imagery for God?
- How can we effectively bring out our musical treasures both old and new in ways that are life-giving and God-affirming?
- Does the whole community feel represented by the language of our congregational songs?

As we gather for worship, we bring different life experiences that shape how we encounter language for God. We aim to worship in solidarity with a wide variety of people, including people who have faced discrimination because of their gender, rejection because of their race, alienation because of their ability, and dismissal because of gender expression. We long to be hospitable to one another in worship through the words we use. We strive to be attentive to pastoral needs, and to the ways different images of God have sustained, wounded, and liberated those in our communities.

Clergy and musicians must be intentional in selecting music for worship. Musical diversity that reflects inclusive ideals and expansive imagery is sadly not the norm for Christian worship. Music in worship has been and continues to be an act of radical hospitality. Deviating from the norms of the church and culture past is possible. The journey toward inclusive and expansive language is not in any form a rejection of the past or of cherished images, but is rather an attempt to walk alongside what has already been, with an eye toward what and who we are as church within this current cultural context. The popular hymn "God of our fathers, whose almighty hand" is a joy for musicians and singers, and even nonsingers. A recent rendering of the hymn recast the opening line into "God of the ages, whose almighty hand." The revision to the timeless hymn does not diminish or distract from the music or the history and certainly maintains God as the primary source and cause of worship. Not all hymns or anthems have or can be recast to correspond with the current thinking or theology of the church. Balancing the often-paternalistic language of 17th-century hymns with music employing updated language is another approach that clergy and musicians might consider in deciding on music selections. We *can* sing a 17th-century hymn alongside a 20th-century setting of an inclusive language text in the same liturgy.

Sing to the Lord a new song.

Sacred scripture is filled with song: the songs of redemption, of deliverance, of hope. Songs are the stories of our faith put to sublime music, and the music has the power to evoke emotion like nothing else. At the heart of the church's worship is a transcendent and eternal God, who surpasses "all human understanding." Our language of worship therefore points to and evokes the mystery of God—God who we cannot fully comprehend or completely imagine and yet who is revealed to us in words and images conveyed across "all tribes and peoples and languages" (Rev. 7:9).

Our language of music matters because it conveys the story of a transcendent God who incarnated in our world and is embodied in God's people. By its nature, the church's liturgical language is transcultural, contextual, countercultural, and cross-cultural. The church's liturgical language is biblical, drawing on the stories and images of scripture. Through expansive, inclusive, and metaphorical language, the church aims to participate in the mysterious abundance of God and to speak to God in language that might delight the one who delightedly created diversity and abundance.

4

You Will See
Rare Beasts and
Have Unique Adventures

Considering Again
the Clergy–Musician Relationship

Jessica Nelson[1]

Introduction

I have always loved W. H. Auden's "He is the Way," an excerpt from "For the Time Being: A Christmas Oratorio," which I encountered for the first time set to two different tunes by Richard Wetzel and David Hurd in *The Hymnal 1982*, each revealing a different peculiar facet of the text. I love this text for all its strangeness, for the way it reveals itself over time, and especially for the way it sounds like the beginning of a fantastic fairy tale. Without fail, every time I program this for liturgical use, someone will approach me following the service with a puzzled expression. They're flustered and insistent, asking, "But what does it mean?" My earnest, entirely serious response is always, "I don't know. Sit with it for a few years, and then let's talk again." "You will see rare beasts and have unique adventures" seems like a particularly apt description of *all* of parish ministry, but especially so for describing the clergy–musician relationship. It's part tongue in cheek and part, well, not. Our rare beasts come in the form of systems fraught with dysfunction, unhealthy patterns of communication, interpersonal conflicts, and a lack of clarity around what it is, exactly, we mean to be doing in the service of parish ministry. When at their best, though, healthy clergy–musician teams'

---

1. What follows is a revision of an essay I wrote about five years into my career as a musician working in parish ministry. I am much older and wiser now.

collaboration can result in a joyful work environment and, even more importantly, beautiful liturgy. I have tried to approach this subject with a little bit of humor, not because it's an issue I don't take seriously, but because I find that being able to poke a little fun at something makes it a bit more approachable. Unique adventures indeed.

"Follow Him through the Land of Unlikeness"

In my career as a church musician, and especially in my current position in cathedral ministry, one of the recurring themes of conversations I have with both lay and ordained colleagues centers around dysfunctional clergy–musician relationships. I'll occasionally get phone calls from a frustrated priest, "How do I *make* my musician do/play/sing fill-in-the-blank," with requests ranging from the entirely reasonable to the, well, not. In the same vein, I perhaps slightly more than occasionally get contacted by musician colleagues who ask, "Why does Rev. Grantchester insist on singing that awful hymn once a month? Doesn't he know that it's trite/unsingable/full of parallel fifths/would be better suited for a monster truck rally?" Most often, though, the majority of these conversations aren't begun by intentionally reaching out, but are rather a conversational byproduct, whispered sideways throughout the course of other interactions: Furious texting to a friend following the postlude, "You're not going to *believe* what Fr. Flavian did today." "If Mrs. Winchester Old doesn't pick up the pace on hymns, I'm going to go sit on the organ bench with a metronome." I can say with a certain amount of confidence that any gathering of musicians typically features at least a handful of these stories, and (in my overactive imagination, at least) any gathering of clergy features at least a few dozen or so of these stories, told with increasing flair and melodrama, perhaps told via interpretive dance or puppet theater.

All of us know this conversation, and most of us have participated in it. Now, I do think that blowing off a little steam every once in a while is not at all out of order, and having a neutral third party or two with whom to commiserate and unpack your day-to-day grumbling, sighs, and eye rolls can be helpful. That goes for any relationship, and I have a few such third parties in my life. But the clergy–musician relationship is unique and is so often fraught with explosive dysfunction and, yes, occasional abuse that entire books are devoted to it. I'm not sure that the church music community needs another hot take on what is often a nuanced, systematic problem, but I do want to offer a few thoughts that I've formed over the years, after working alongside a number of talented clergy and just as many wildly gifted musicians. To begin, it's important to discuss the similarities and differences in our vocations.

Calledness

Clergy often describe their urge to pursue holy orders as a "call," and I believe church musicians have an urge equally as intense and inevitable. In both cases, I think one way to describe the sense of "calledness" is as a sort of Marian imperative—submitting to our call to a vocation and God's will for our lives. We've said yes to the call, leaning into the sacrifice and accepting the risk that it entails and have set out to live into it, devoting ourselves to a life in the service of the church.

Intense Vocational Training

Seminary and conservatory both provide intense, contextually specific training. Both types of education require significant investments of time, energy, and financial resources; require long, lonely hours of study or practice; and are often fraught with disappointment, disillusionment, and feelings of inadequacy. The content of that training is obviously different, though, and prepares us for different roles in the service of the church. If we were all physicians, priests might be the general practitioners in a hospital, expected to wear a variety of hats, have a working knowledge of all systems of the body, and be equipped to treat most common illnesses. These clergy are also expected to be fully formed spiritual leaders upon ordination, ready upon arrival in their first cure with thirty years' of parish ministry experience (but no more than forty years old, please.) Sage and wise but young and energetic.

In most parishes, these expectations are not as often made of musicians—youthfulness is not a highly prioritized attribute, nor is having a well-developed spiritual compass. Musicians certainly *are* sometimes called upon to perform other functions but are not regularly required to have the wide range of skills that clergy do. Musicians are the hospital's specialists, required to have an extensive knowledge of one facet (albeit a large one, with dozens of facets within) of parish ministry. In my own experience, I find that aside from making music, I am most often needed to be a sort of pastoral care triage nurse—monitoring the folks I regularly come into contact with, assessing needs, and suggesting they get further care when indicated.

The Work of Interpretation and Contextualization

A major overlap in the typical parish is the priest and musician doing exegesis—the work of interpretation—together. We take each week's propers and decide how to make those texts resonate with people in the pews through preaching, the hymns we sing, and anthem texts and instrumental music. There are certainly other tasks we share, like creating thoughtful programming, strategic planning, and day-to-day administrivia—writing newsletter articles and proofreading service leaflets.

The Environments in Which We Work

Clergy and musicians put ourselves and our work on display week after week, often encountering unrealistically high expectations (imposed both by the communities we serve and ourselves) and negotiate the fishbowl existence of any church leader. One big difference between clergy and musicians is the matter of authority and the nature of the relationship between employee and employer. In the Episcopal Church, clergy exercise their ministry in specific parishes with localized leadership but are also, by virtue of their ordination, subject to the authority of the bishop and disciplinary canons of the Church. On the other hand, musicians are employees. The nature of the rector's authority over and relationship to the musician is different than that of the bishop to the rector. And there is no codified disciplinary process for laypeople at this point. The phrase used to describe this relationship is working "at the pleasure of the rector," which has always made me squirm a little bit. I understand the meaning of the phrase, but perhaps it would be more accurate to say that musicians work under the rector's leadership or with the rector's guidance. Semantic gymnastics aside, lay professionals simply are not subject to the authority of a bishop in the same sense clergy are. Musicians don't take vows and could, theoretically at least, walk away from a position in parish ministry at any time and pursue employment in another arena without much fuss. Every few years, a little noise is made about developing an order of sorts—something akin to the role of the cantor in Jewish communities, for which musicians would complete a formation process and take vows. While this idea is certainly not without merit, I wonder if this wouldn't be at odds with our understanding of lay ministry, wherein by virtue of only their baptism, laypeople are equipped for service in the church. What message might the ordering of musicians send to laity who are not employed by a parish in a professional capacity—that any sort of *real* ministry requires ordination?

"Seek Him in the Kingdom of Anxiety"

How do we prevent a clergy–musician relationship from going awry? Begin well. Just like with any other relationship, it's helpful to know each other well from the very beginning. Now, I don't mean that you have to memorize each other's entire life stories, and while enjoying each other's company is certainly not a bad thing, it's not necessarily an indication of how successful a working relationship will be. You certainly can have a fantastic, healthy working relationship while keeping your work and personal lives somewhat compartmentalized. I only mean that it is helpful to be intentional about understanding each other and communicating well. Some are dubious of personality typing, and while a little skepticism is always in order, I've found the Myers-Briggs Type Indicator to be helpful and reasonably accurate, and I have more recently become a casual devotee of the Enneagram. They've both been useful tools in understanding how I and others function individually and in relationships. That awareness can stop conflicts in their tracks. There have been countless times when I've been mystified by someone's behavior and realized that whatever I've bristled at is merely a behavioral characteristic that I do not share—perhaps I interpreted someone's directness as curtness when they only meant to be clear and unambiguous. I'm sure I have many personality traits that are equally infuriating and mystifying to those around me. I would, however, caution against using this information as ammunition, such as shouting, "You *always* act this way because you're a 6/ENFP," or for mounting a defense in anticipation of conflicts that may never arise. Least of all should one use a personality type as an excuse for abusive behavior. "It's acceptable for me to yell/intimidate/throw things because I'm a Type R." No, it isn't.

In addition to having a current and accurate job description,[2] it is also helpful to clarify and agree upon processes, particularly those related to liturgical planning, which is a frequently cited cause of friction. Who is responsible for what aspects of the liturgy week to week? What about larger arcs, themes, or seasons? Develop a mutually agreeable plan, write it down, and implement it. Bear in mind that what works for one clergy–musician team may not work for another and that this process may require occasional evaluation, maintenance, and retooling.

There are times in shared ministries when one must operate within the scope of a vision that is not one's own. In my own working relationships with clergy, when my frustration begins to level up in response to, say, requests for hymns I wouldn't necessarily program if left to my own devices, I find it helpful to remind myself that not *all* decisions are mine to make. This may seem a little bit obvious, but with that tiny little admission comes some relief—if I didn't make a choice, then I don't have to defend it. (Though a wise and diplomatic response to parishioner questions or criticism would sound something like, "What an interesting question—we plan liturgies together, and I remember Rev. Rustington being enthusiastic about that hymn," and less like a "Well, *I* certainly didn't pick it," squeezed out through clenched teeth.) While not *all* decisions are mine to make, *some* certainly are, and there are just as many instances when my supervising clergyperson has accommodated my vision for a particular event or initiative. Remembering this usually satisfies my slightly higher-than-average control needs and restores balance in my universe. I also find that when I'm a generous collaborator, that favor is often returned. I'll absolutely program that one piece you like for double kazoo choir and tambourine at the offertory if we can *also* sing David Hurd's "Love Bade Me Welcome" as the communion motet.

Make expectations clear, identify metrics for success, and meet regularly to discuss if and how those expectations and metrics are being met. The most valuable conversations I've had with my supervising clergy have been in the context

---

2. The Association of Anglican Musicians (AAM) has produced valuable resources pertaining to the creation of realistic job descriptions, which are readily available on its website, www.anglicanmusicians.org.

of annual employee reviews. I know that this sounds like a special kind of torture required by some obscure canon, and I'm sure that for many, it is. When deployed appropriately (and not used as an excuse to air grievances or in place of couples' therapy) these conversations have been respectful, generative, and motivating, and have left me feeling empowered and supported. If you are responsible for evaluating a subordinate's work, please learn to do this well. Hold each other accountable. Not just for sticking to agreed-upon liturgical planning processes, but also to deadlines (I'm looking squarely at myself here) and especially for behavior. We don't wait until we're Thelma and Louise–ing over a cliff before we turn the steering wheel. A much better (and safer) course of action would be to occasionally glance in the rearview mirror, maybe stop texting, put the phone down, and pay attention to the road. Inappropriate behavior becomes chronic if left unchecked.

Here's an anecdotal example—a cobbled-together patchwork of stories I've heard over the years, with entirely ridiculous made-up names and any identifying details removed: Sarah Rosedale was the organist and choirmaster at St. Simon's-by-the-CVS, Salinas, a post she had held since the earth cooled, give or take a few weeks. Sarah, having sung in an English cathedral that one time on a college choir tour, ruled the St. Simon's Singers with an iron fist. Over the years, rectors came and went with alarming frequency, and Sarah outlasted them all. In rehearsals, her behavior became increasingly troubling, but the choir chalked it up to having an "artistic" temperament and nervously forgave her for each eruption. One Sunday, she gave a tenor a particularly public and incendiary dressing down for missing again that one spectacular entrance in Edgar Bainton's "And I saw a new heaven." Some weeks later, she threw a hymnal in a fit of pique when nobody (and I mean nobody) had a pencil. "I might as well quit if you won't come prepared for rehearsal," she shouted. Around the parish office, Sarah had developed the unfortunate habit of resigning about once a week, usually in response to some slight, perceived or otherwise, from the rector. One week he forgot she took two lumps of sugar in her tea; the following week, he asked her when they might sing some camp songs. Each time, she would pull out the resignation letter she kept in her desk drawer, place it on the rector's desk, and storm out. Like clockwork, by that evening, the rector would call and beg her to come back. She would breeze in the next morning as though nothing had happened, and the increasingly cowed cleric would depart in fairly short order. This scenario played out numerous times over the years. After a lengthy vacancy, the parish called Fr. Stuttgart. Fr. Stuttgart had a no-nonsense way about him. He'd been made aware that his new organist/choirmaster had a demeanor that required a certain amount of Teflon armor, but the search committee had neglected to tell him about the weekly-ish resignation exercise. The day came: Fr. Stuttgart put a coffee cup on the choir room piano. Sarah exploded, resigned, and went home to await the customary apology phone call. It never came. Her now-permanent departure created waves in the St. Simon's community, but secretly, the parishioners felt something like relief. One wonders if a discreet course correction earlier in Sarah's incumbency would not have resulted in a healthier program and parish.

A big part of mutual accountability is recognizing privilege. Both clergy and musicians have certain amounts of privilege in different contexts and need to be aware of how it's exercised. In the preceding story, Sarah wielded the power in the parish (abused it, actually), but in the regular course of healthy parish ministry, the privilege clergy possess exceeds that of the musician. Abuse of that privilege is at the root of the most explosive conflicts. One example of that abuse may include the cleric regularly scheduling mandatory meetings on short notice without consulting the bivocational musician, who is scheduled to teach a class at the university at that time. Another example would be egregious micromanagement—repeated insistence on certain organ registrations or other interpretive choices with little regard for the musician's training and experience.

Clergy should also be aware that because of the nature of the supervisor-subordinate employee relationship, it is often inadvisable or inappropriate for the musician to tell the cleric how they feel about a particular issue or request, even when pressed. They simply may not feel empowered to advocate for themselves in this arena as they might elsewhere, or the musician may fear retaliation. Taking advantage of this is ill advised. Large parishes may have dedicated human resources officers who can advise both the supervisor and subordinate and help implement best practices, but this is certainly the exception rather than the norm. Borrowing from the corporate world, an essential practice to develop is documentation. It may feel incongruous to do so in the context of church work, but if it's not documented, it didn't happen. If Mrs. Winchester Old's rector told her to pick up the pace on hymns, they should both make a note in writing somewhere that that conversation happened, and Mrs. Winchester Old should also make a note of how she responded to this request. This isn't just a way to develop ammunition for terminating an employee's tenure (or for an employee to have evidence that a termination is unwarranted), but is a valuable way to have concrete, unambiguous evidence to identify trends. Praise should *also* be documented this way.

Here's another tortured work of fiction in the service of illustrating my point: William Wareham had served St. Timothy's-by-the-Texaco, Tulsa, quite capably for about five years and had carefully and strategically established a comprehensive music program. He was finally at the point of being able to enjoy the fruits of his labor now that the scaffolding was in place, and he was proud of the program he had created. It was flourishing and healthy, complementing but never competing with other ministries at St. Timothy's, with a clearly articulated sense of mission and a generous understanding of how the music program fit in with the broader mission of the church.

William's beloved rector retired, and St. Timothy's soon called Mother Catherine. On her first day in the parish office, Mother Catherine stuck her head into William's office, and they exchanged pleasantries and made plans to sit down and look at the next month's lectionary readings together. She turned and started for the rector's study but paused in the doorway and turned back, "You know, they taught us in seminary that the very first thing you do in a new parish is fire the musician." She chuckled as she wandered off. William, perhaps being somewhat prone to anxiety to begin with, felt his face grow hot, and a pit formed in his stomach. *She was joking, right?* Was she, though? Making jokes about firing him? In this economy? Who would be so unkind? Could he trust her? The discomfort gnawed at him, and he grew fearful. Colleagues encouraged him to approach her, but he was reticent. William experienced a crisis of confidence; one offhand comment set off a chain reaction of anxiety throughout the music program. It also made for a rocky beginning to William and Mother Catherine's relationship, sowing suspicion and distrust from the very beginning that they would never quite manage to move beyond. A short while later, William decamped for a parish one town over, and a once-healthy program that immensely benefited St. Timothy's languished. Sure, this is an exaggerated amalgamation of several different reports, but I've heard this same story too many times to count.

Capitalize on strengths rather than seek to change weaknesses. I hear from musician colleagues who bemoan their ordained colleagues' lack of interest in all things musical, absence of musical training, and similar. I would be willing to bet that most clergy would welcome and benefit from respectful and supportive guidance from their staff musicians. I also would be willing to bet that these allegedly nonmusical priests' strengths lie somewhere else, maybe in preaching or pastoral care. These things are also important in the life of the church, and I do hear from time to time that there is a world beyond the choir room (though I do not personally have firsthand knowledge of that myself). From clergy colleagues I hear stories of inflexible musicians who only want to program esoteric literature representative of a certain revered time and place—motets from the brutalist period of the great English composer Sir Thomas Chelmsford, sometime musician of Notre Dame, Paris (Texas. Paris, Texas.). It *is* possible to expand repertoire without losing passion for whatever narrowly focused interest ignites a spark. And if one is able to communicate their enthusiasm for Chelmsford's works rather than using that energy bemoaning a request to sing "That One Hymn That Everybody Hates," the membership of the local chapter of the Sir Thomas Fan Club may double.

Lastly, don't let a past toxic relationship with a priest or musician haunt the current relationship. No two musicians or priests are alike. If the last five musicians have been dismissed because of their hymn tempi, or an organist has hopped from bench to bench because none of their supervising clerics adequately appreciate Herbert Howells, consider that something in the system may be awry.

Until now, this essay has been largely theoretical. In case one is in the market for some very concrete, practical recommendations, here are a few ideas I've picked up from colleagues who have sought to improve upon or repair their relationships, or to simply begin a relationship on a solid foundation:

First, identify shared interests. I've often shared nonchurchy interests with my supervising clergy—cooking, travel, pets, podcasts. Sharing an enthusiasm for something beyond the academic and ecclesial has been beneficial to these relationships. Second, I've also heard of clergy–musician teams who will visit each other's arena of expertise. Perhaps the musician will preach for a Sunday service or the priest will sit in on a choir rehearsal. The goal of this activity isn't as much to gain proficiency in either preaching or singing as it is to experience the *process* that the other requires. Understanding how the other's processes work (or challenging long-held assumptions about how these processes work) can be a beneficial window into their inner workings. This may also help cross-pollinate your ministries and lead to new collaborations. Third, study texts together—not just the Sunday lectionary readings, but anthem and hymn texts as well. Practicing a version of *lectio divina* can reveal facets of texts not yet considered, breathe new life into preaching, and inform interpretive choices in choral music and hymnody.

"Love Him in the World of the Flesh."

Scientific studies indicate that primates, up to and including humans, unconsciously imitate each other's posture, gestures, and expressions. How many times have you found yourself unintentionally adopting someone else's tone or speech patterns or laughing or crying only because someone else was, or realized that your heart rate was increasing in response to another person's raised voice? A staff modeling healthy relationships with clear, consistent, and respectful communication, as well as managing conflict in a healthy and productive way when it does arise, is essential to the well-being of a congregation. Modeling healthy relationships for lay leaders in parishes teaches them how to lead and communicate effectively, better equipping them for service. Conversely, the contagious ripple effects of a strained staff relationship will quickly lead to anxiety in other leaders and groups in the parish.

Healthy relationships among a parish's liturgical leaders support beautiful, well-crafted liturgy, and not just in the sense that it's been thoughtfully planned. I'll elaborate: much like how actors flubbing lines can break the spell of theater, or how one can be driven to distraction by tension between actors, our congregations can intuit discord between liturgical participants and will certainly pick up on telegraphed anxiety. This is hugely disruptive, jerking the worshiper out of a prayerful posture and causing an otherwise well-crafted liturgy to suffer.

Conclusion

It's time to change the narrative and dispense with the myth that clergy and musicians are fundamentally inclined to be antagonistic toward one another. I am deeply grieved that healthy clergy–musician relationships are not more prevalent than they are—or at least that that's the commonly held perception. It's possible that they actually *are* more prevalent, and we just never hear about the healthy ones. (If that's the case, please speak up—we could all benefit from your wisdom.) Yes, there will always be exceptions—extraordinary cases in which the level of dysfunction is worsened by some sort of pathology, or situations in which the relationship is irreparably damaged by gross misconduct.

What might a healthy relationship look like? A third and final round of tortured fiction in the service of making a point: At St. Wilfrid's, Walla Walla, Fr. Walden wandered through the nave and found his organist/choirmaster, Wilma, practicing the Bach "Wedge" fugue. She got to a stopping point and Fr. Walden approached, "Hey, I heard this awesome setting of 'O sacrum convivium' for double kazoo choir and tambourine on NPR. Do you think the choir could sing it next week?" Wilma did love a kazoo choir but could not abide a tambourine. Loathed them. And there was no way the choir could learn all that Latin in one rehearsal. She opened her mouth to respond, "Over my dead body," and hesitated. "Next week might be a little too soon to have it put together, and I buried all the tambourines in the church yard. Could I find something that's similar and get to work on it to use a few weeks from now?" Fr. Walden was perfectly amenable to that and bopped off to continue his day. A few Sundays later, the St. Wilfrid's choir sang a stunning rendition of the William Byrd "Ave verum" arranged for SATB, kazoo choir, and egg shaker. Later that week in a vestry meeting, Fr. Walden praised Wilma's flexibility and ingenuity, and recommended that she be given a bonus, an extra Sunday off, *and* a Mercedes. Meanwhile, across town at St. Mary's, Melita Monroe was prepping for choir rehearsal, making sure that every single folder had a pencil *and* a backup pencil in it. (She had once been a chorister at Sarah Rosedale's church in Salinas.) She was hosting an open rehearsal that night, to let prospective singers and friends visit to see if they might like to join their choir. Fr. Matthew had had seventeen meetings that day, made four hospital visits, and was entirely worn out. But still, he visited the open rehearsal because he knew this was important, not just to Melita, but to the mission of the music program and the larger mission of the parish—and because he'd been trying to explain to the vestry why the pencil line item in the budget was constantly tapped.

So what are we to take away, other than that I'll never have a career writing fiction? Here is what I've both experienced and observed: It's not just about give and take, even though that's the example I used above. Relationships that begin well will typically age well. Establishing trust and expectations early on, maintaining healthy systems, cultivating an ethic of clear, consistent, and respectful communication, and a developing shared clarity of mission will serve both parties and the parish they serve well. Flexibility and graciousness are in order. The world will not come to a screeching halt if you do not get to do your favorite thing every single time, and it may be that you discover something delightful in the process. Occasionally, I will concede unexpectedly, just to keep things interesting. (One of my friends describes this as making "bank deposits." Let the reader understand.) Remember your baptism, and regularly revisit the baptismal covenant as set forth in the Book of Common Prayer, in which we promise again and again to "seek and serve Christ in all persons" and to "respect the dignity of every human being."[3] This includes our colleagues as well. Pray with and for each other, consider other perspectives, and be generous collaborators. If we mean to be about God's work in the world, there is no other way forward.

---

3. *The Book of Common Prayer* (New York: Church Publishing, 1979), 305.

5

Celebrating One Another's Way of Worship

Keith Tan

Not long ago, a clergy friend of mine lamented to me, "The music at our church is too slow! Our worship feels so lethargic, and the congregation doesn't sing. I want us to sing some toe-tapping contemporary praise choruses that you do at your church, but our organist would keel over if she had to play that!" Meanwhile, a parishioner in my church recently pressed me, "The jumpy songs that y'all do are fine once in a while, but let's sing more of those good 'ol hymns, eh?" And again, I was on a phone call with a church organist friend, who admitted, "No, I don't know who's in the contemporary praise band at our church. They do their own thing. The traditional service doesn't have much to do with the contemporary service." And still again, I recently read a gleeful web article, "3 Reasons Contemporary Worship Is Declining," criticizing contemporary worship as a nontheological movement and calling for people to "resist the temptation to 'contemporarize' old songs."[1]

For the twenty-three years that I have led Christ Church's music ministry, I have seen the debate between contemporary and traditional worship styles and the tensions that have arisen. Although the height of the "worship wars" occurred twenty years ago, this heated debate is still not resolved for many churches. Some churches have found to their dismay that what they thought to be settled has reemerged in new disagreements. Other churches are learning that temporary solutions appeasing both tired camps don't work. Finally, more churches are just now entering into the fray.

---

1. Jonathan Aigner, "3 Reasons Contemporary Worship IS Declining, and What We Can Do to Help the Church Move On," Patheos, September 4, 2015. Https://www.patheos.com/blogs/ponder-anew/2015/09/04/3-reasons-contemporary- worship-is-declining-and-5-things-we-can-do-to-help-the-church-move-on/.

What is this persistent disagreement really about? How are we to navigate it? Is it possible for worshippers across the stylistic spectrum not just to tolerate one another but authentically to celebrate our diversity? After all, corporate worship as a central activity in all churches is meant to bring people together. What is at stake is the unity of our congregation and our witness to the world. Therefore, because of the persistence of the traditional versus contemporary worship debate, we need to examine the issues underlying the tensions we face: unclear definitions and understanding of terms, the baggage of contemporary music, the divide between pop and classical music, and secular influences in sacred music. As we look at these issues, we should search for shared perspectives and common goals to build bridges between traditional and contemporary worshippers and celebrate one another's way of worship.

Shared Perspectives and Goals

I've had the privilege of working with pastors and musicians of varying denominations and styles, spanning from high liturgical Episcopal churches singing chants to charismatic, nondenominational contemporary churches using disco lights and fog machines. These worship leaders unanimously agree that they desire a singing, participating congregation fully engaged in worship. Additionally, they share the quest of helping their congregation take their engagement in worship into the rest of the week, transforming how they live. The worship leaders may use different language to describe this. Still, the theology is the same—one of the consequences of corporate worship ought to be the energizing of daily living and mission. Secondly, worship leaders across the stylistic spectrum share the desire for a high level of musical artistry. They agree that quality musicianship and the ability authentically to express oneself well serve to help people better connect with God and lower the distractions caused by poorly performed music. Third, they agree on many roles that music fulfills within the church. Music helps worshippers connect with God. When a choir or band offers an anthem or song on behalf of the congregation to exalt God, music performs a priestly role, serving as a connection from the congregation to God. And when music speaks into the hearts of the congregation, it performs a prophetic role, with the connection flowing from God to the congregation. As it has been said, the congregation's theology is shaped by the songs they sing; therefore, music also has a teaching role. By creating a worshipful atmosphere, music also can provide a soundscape for liturgical action or worship activity in the service. Furthermore, music, in its missional role, attracts audiences into the church. Finally, worship leaders across differing worship styles share a common philosophy regarding the power of Christian music. They recognize that Christian music is powerful because it combines the spiritual power of Scripture with the emotive power of music to reach into hearts and transform lives. When we keep an eye on shared perspectives and goals like these, we will better appreciate both worship styles and navigate the tensions surrounding them. Some of these tensions arise from unclear definitions of terms such as *traditional worship* and *contemporary worship*.

Just What Do We Mean by Traditional and Contemporary Worship?

A couple of years ago, I was invited to a liturgical church to work with their contemporary service musicians. As we began to choose our songs, I soon discovered that what they meant by contemporary music were songs like "Seek Ye First" by Karen Lafferty and "On Eagle's Wings" by Michael Joncas. These are folky, hymn-like songs written in the 1970s and not the contemporary Christian music (CCM) heard on the radio today. Around the same time, a newer church worshiping in a contemporary style invited me to be a guest musician at their worship service. Their pastor insisted that songs written over a decade ago no longer qualify as contemporary and shouldn't be used. Meanwhile, I was chatting with an organist from a traditional church. He revealed that he was perturbed that organist Gerre Hancock's (1934–2012) compositions, while considered contemporary by classical musicians, do not fit that same term by contemporary worship musicians.

Many people mean different things when they use the terms *traditional* and *contemporary* worship. Some think that traditional worship means chants, "thees and thous," and incense, while others envision a choir up front, singing gospel hymns accompanied by an organ–piano duet. For some, contemporary worship means plucking an acoustic guitar while singing "On Eagle's Wings," but others imagine something akin to a rock concert. The lack of definition of what is considered traditional worship and what is contemporary worship is one area that leads to mix-ups and prevents meaningful dialogue between the two. To add to the confusion of terminology, members of contemporary churches often refer to their music as "worship." "How was the worship today?" they might ask. They usually mean, "How was the music at the worship service today?" *Traditional* and *contemporary* are very broad terms. Although they provide a general sense of what we are referring to, we need more explicit descriptions to have meaningful discussions about music.

Using Clearer Terms to Describe Christian Music

I have commonly heard the fallacy that what makes music contemporary is its instrumentation. As a member of a traditional country Baptist church once complained to me, "It's all those drums and guitars that we don't care for! We just want the organ." Yet, he loved the classical soprano singing "Stille Nacht," accompanied by a gently plucking guitar, and praised Handel's *Messiah*, despite its use of timpani. Contemporary music is not just about using guitars and drums. Instead, I believe it is *how* the instruments are used that matters more. If the guitarist changes his eighth-note arpeggiating fingering pattern to a boogie-woogie rock-styled strumming pattern, and the soprano soloist chooses to riff in a bluesy-style, changing her vocal timbre and crooning "all is calm, all is bright," then yes, anyone can recognize that as a contemporary musical style. Another common fallacy about what makes music contemporary is the date of composition. But that isn't a defining factor either. Rick Founds wrote the contemporary hit "Lord, I Lift Your Name on High" in 1989. Yet, in 2020, John Rutter wrote a new carol, "Joseph's Carol," in the vein of "traditional" church music. I do not think there is a straightforward way to define traditional music and contemporary music. Rather, as we engage in conversations among musicians and worship leaders, I believe it is better to describe the music used, using more precise terms that have established meaning in the worlds of music theory and the music industry.

Music theory analyzes and describes the differences between musical styles. Descriptions of form, instrumentation and orchestration, timbre, harmonic rhythms, melody, tonal systems, compositional techniques, ornamentation, and other elements provide a clear and common language between musicians to clarify the archetypes of each musical style. For example, a musician friend asked me what I meant by "blend contemporary and traditional styles." I described, "My church employs a thirty-voice choir in homophonic SATB when singing 'Crown Him with Many Crowns.' They are supported by a rock band consisting of a drum set playing a standard eight-beat rock pattern, a fingered electric bass, and a strumming acoustic guitar in lock-step with the drums, and a piano plays syncopated chords and a synth pad underlaying chord changes. Meanwhile, the organist and a string quartet double the choral parts." This description painted a useful sonic picture for my friend.

Besides music theory, the music industry offers us shared vocabulary too. I was perusing the aisles in a Barnes & Noble music section some time ago and was astounded by the number of genres that the music industry has used to categorize music. Of course, there's classical. Then there's a slew of nonclassical genres like pop, rock, hip-hop, rap, alternative, country, Latin, R&B, dance/electronic, metal, world music, jazz, children, Christian/gospel, and more. I later did a web search on Christian/gospel music. I discovered that it was divided into subgenres such as CCM (Christian contemporary music), praise and worship music, Black gospel, southern gospel, Christian rock, Christian metal, Christian folk, Christian hip-hop/rap, and Christian alternative. Interestingly, sacred music was not in the Christian category; it fell in the classical category. The music industry has given us a large vocabulary to describe musical styles. We don't need to reinvent the wheel. We can simply say, "My father-in-law's church is a traditional Baptist country church that uses predominantly southern gospel music style in their worship." We would get a pretty good idea of what that service sounds like.

Understanding Contemporary Church Music and Music Industry Terms

CCM/gospel is the primary term used in the music industry to label artists like Amy Grant, TobyMac, Chris Tomlin, Aretha Franklin, and CeCe Winans. CCM/gospel has two main streams: "praise and worship" and "Christian entertainment." Praise and worship songs are written for use in worship experiences that occur in worship concerts or in contemporary-styled churches. Meant to be sung by a congregation, they tend to be more repetitive, and their melodies often are less complicated rhythmically. Their vocal ranges tend to be smaller. Their lyrics often are overtly and simply declarative of God's worthiness of praise and worship, or about the relationship between God and humans. Songs that refer to oneself in the first person and God in the second person are mostly in this category. Examples of these songs are "Shout to the Lord" (Zschech), "I Will Rise" (Tomlin), "Way Maker" (Egbu), and many others. Music labels that lean toward this type of CCM are Hillsong Music, Integrity Music, and Bethel Music. These music labels make up the body of work that church musicians use in their contemporary worship services.

The other stream, Christian entertainment, focuses on songs meant to be listened to by the general public rather than be sung by congregations. However, they make for great presentational pieces for a soloist or even a choir, if arranged. They inspire, encourage, teach, and edify. These songs tend to be more sophisticated musically, with wider vocal ranges and more complex melodies and rhythms. These songs are seldom directed to God. Examples of these kinds of songs are "Voice of Truth" (Casting Crowns), "God Only Knows" (for KING & COUNTRY), "I Can Only Imagine" (Mercy Me), "The Great Adventure" (Steven Curtis Chapman), and many others. Some such labels are Sparrow Records, Reunion Records, and Essential Records.

Twenty years ago, praise and worship songs were typically heard only in churches rather than on Christian radio, which played more Christian entertainment–type songs. But today, both streams of CCM are equally pushed. Praise and worship songs have gained popularity in the CCM industry over the last decade. Many Christian entertainment artists and their labels have incorporated praise and worship into their repertoire, blurring the line between worship and entertainment. Outside the mainstream music industry, some liturgical musicians write contemporary music for traditional and liturgical churches. These contemporary liturgical musicians write for the church rather than radio; they find their niche and distribute their songs directly to churches through music publishers like GIA Publications and OCP (Oregon Catholic Press). Examples of these musicians are Marty Haugen, Joseph Martin, and Michael Joncas. Therefore, I suggest that we understand "traditional" church music as stylistically similar to the classical genre in the broader music industry—Bach, Brahms, John Taverner, and John Rutter. Included in this would be the singing of monophonic chants and standard four-part homophonic hymns. The organ is the primary instrument in this style. As for "contemporary" church music, I suggest that this term be understood as music in the CCM and gospel genres, themselves modeled after pop, rock, and R&B genres. Instrumentation commonly employed in this style is the rock band.

But in the end, regardless of whether the Christian music is traditional or contemporary, I believe all Christian music has a shared characteristic—Christian words. Whether you are singing an aria from a sacred cantata, rapping the Nicene Creed to a hip-hop beat, or listening to an instrumental piano version of "Amazing Grace," the meaning that the words (or memory of the words) evoke inspires us to connect with God. That is what truly matters in all kinds of Christian music.

Comparing Elements of Traditional and Contemporary Worship

Earlier, I alluded to other elements besides music that make contemporary worship contemporary. These elements include the following: seeking to "experience the presence of God," "flow," the role of "worship leader," and the use of projectors. Although these seem foreign to the traditional worshipper, each element has a parallel in traditional worship.

The preeminent objective in contemporary worship is to experience the Spirit of God viscerally, that is, to be emotionally moved in the course of worship. Many elements in the service can trigger an overwhelming emotional response. It could be witnessing others visibly adoring Christ, hearing a powerful sermon, entering into a trancelike musical repetition–meditation on a characteristic of God, or loudly proclaiming an attribute of God in song. Such emotional experiences indicate to the contemporary worshipper that the Holy Spirit is present and that the worshipper is experiencing the power and grace of God. This subjective experience is a measure of the success of the worship experience.

However, traditional worshippers also seek the presence of God. They call it "encountering the divine." For them, the sacraments are "visible signs of intangible grace." Although traditional worshippers don't actively seek a visceral emotional experience in worship, they do desire an encounter with God.

Flow is an important concept that many contemporary worship leaders consciously consider. It relates to the order of service, particularly the music. Since the worship part of a worship service for the contemporary worshipper is the music, worship leaders give exceptional attention to flow when planning the worship set, the set of five to six songs sung in the beginning half of the service. They would consider topical themes, song tempo and groove, compatible keys, and, most importantly, how to transition from one song to the next to maximize flow. The idea is that this worship set becomes a seamless emotional journey that takes the worshipper from a parking lot mentality to the holy of holies in order to have an intimate encounter with God. Then, the worshipper is ready to receive the Word of God through scripture and sermon, after which there is an opportunity to pray and offer thanksgiving. Finally, the worshippers are dismissed and sent.

But traditional worship has flow too. Participants call it the service order or liturgy. Because denominational tradition may prescribe the liturgy, many traditional worship leaders don't consciously work to ensure a seamless flow. Most liturgical church service orders follow this arc: Gathering/Entering, Word, Thanksgiving (Eucharist), Sending. In my Episcopal church, opening hymns gather the congregation. After opening prayers of invocation and more singing of praise (the *Gloria*), we move to the hearing of scripture and the sermon (all of which form the Liturgy of the Word). Then, we respond to the Word through prayers and thanksgiving (Eucharist—Liturgy of the Table). Finally, we are commissioned, dismissed, and sent. I appreciate how this arc is very similar to the flow in contemporary services.

Another typical characteristic of contemporary worship is the worship leader, whose role is to encourage and inspire the congregation's participation in singing. In addition to a musical leadership role, the worship leader also has a pastoral role, often leading in scripture readings and prayers. The worship leader is not the choir director, though they work closely together. The choir director faces the choir. The worship leader faces the congregation.

Again, this role of leading congregational singing and offering inspiring solos is not new. In liturgical churches, this job belongs to the cantor. However, sometimes, a cantor who comes to perform her parts can forget or not even realize her role as a congregational leader. I once complimented a cantor after a beautiful liturgical service, "Thank you for your beautiful singing and inspiring leading of congregational singing!" She first nodded and smiled her thanks. A little later, during coffee hour, she sought me and remarked, "I've never thought of what I do as leading congregational singing! I like that!"

Still another common characteristic of contemporary services is the use of projectors. This technology helps to provide lyrics for singing and allows digital art as visual liturgy and movie clips as sermon illustrations. Using projectors to display inspirational visual art is similar to the traditional church's use of liturgical art, such as stained glass windows.

The Baggage of Contemporary Christian Music

Why is there such an antagonistic relationship between contemporary and traditional church music? How did it get started? And why does it persist? Examining the history of CCM reveals the baggage that it carries—baggage that made and still makes it difficult for traditionalists to accept CCM in their worship services.

Modern CCM has its roots in the Jesus Movement in the late 1960s and early '70s and the rise of rock and roll. Rock music was closely associated with drugs, sexual promiscuity, alcohol use, and rebellion. So, when musicians like Larry Norman sang about his faith in rock and roll style in songs like "Why Should the Devil Have All the Good Music?" it horrified many traditionalists.

We see traditionalists reject rock music even earlier. Elvis Presley's gospel music was well received, but his rock and roll was not. As he got involved with drugs and alcohol, many saw further proof of the corrupting influence of rock and roll. No way should rock and roll enter the sanctity of the church. Perhaps if not for its association with a negative lifestyle, Christian rock would have been more readily accepted and adopted, just like any other musical style historically. Today, our culture accepts rock music more than in the past. Fewer people associate it with drug use and crime than in the past. In particular, its more widespread cousin, pop music, has gained much popularity and is possibly a driving reason CCM is generally accepted among most Christians worldwide. The weight of this baggage is a lot less than it once was.

The Commercialization of Worship Music

Another baggage that CCM has acquired is the commercialization of worship. There's always been a financial cost to a church's music ministry, no matter the kind of church. Choir robes and octavos need to be bought; handbells and organs need to be maintained. Businesses exist to serve these needs. But there's a kind of commercialization related to CCM that may lead to unintended, unhealthy consequences in churches that use CCM. The CCM industry is a for-profit industry that is probably worth about $1.13 billion in 2020.[2] Most of the big Christian labels are owned by secular corporations like Sony and Universal Music Group.[3] Music executive producers from the corporations are calling the shots based on profit margins, determining which songs get produced and pushed—and these, in turn, shape the theology of churches all over the world. In an article for the website 9Marks, veteran contemporary worship leader and songwriter Bob Kauflin says, "Worship music is now a product to promote, songs are often chosen

---

2. According to the 2020 Nielsen Report, the genre of Christian/Gospel music sold/streamed was 1.9% of the total volume of all music sold/streamed. Assuming this percentage of music usage across live performances, recordings, and publishing, the Christian/Gospel music genre globally is worth a staggering $1.13 billion in 2020, when correlated with Statista Research (Global music industry revenue 2012-2023 published by Statista Research Department, Jan 8, 2021). https://www.statista.com/statistics/259979/global-music-industry-revenue/

3. Essential Records (Mac Powell, Third Day, Building 429, Mal Maher and others) and Provident Entertainment (Michael W. Smith, Mia Fieldes, Leeland, Steven Curtis Chapman, and others) are owned by Sony. Meanwhile, Capitol Christian Music Group (Chris Tomlin, Amy Grant, TobyMac, Tasha Cobbs-Leonard, Jeremy Camp, Hillsong United, Kari Jobe and many others) is owned by Universal Music Group.

more for their identification with an artist than their theology, and songs that were written more than five years ago can be viewed as irrelevant and not worth singing."[4] Another unintended consequence of the global spread of CCM is that churches everywhere are singing the same contemporary songs. Jonathan Aigner, author for Patheos.com and director of music ministries in a Presbyterian Church (USA) congregation, laments the "Hillsongization" of church music worldwide because it is overriding cultural identities and destroying the unique music offerings of cultures and peoples.[5] Third, the commercialization of worship music and marketing of worship artists prioritize the gaining of fans. To do that, the publishing labels in effect put recording artists on a pedestal by accentuating a culture of performance similar to the secular industry with smoke machines, fancy lighting, photoshoots, and music videos, to create an aura of coolness and desirability. At best, it misses the point of worship, which is to point to God. At its worst, it leads to idolatry of the artists. Fourth, the commercialization of worship, with its professionally produced million-dollar experiences, skews the expectations of the local churches' congregations. These "worship concerts" blur the line between liturgy and entertainment, which can lead to the idea that worship is a product consumed by the attending worshipper rather than an offering given by the worshipper. Unfortunately, congregations then focus on whether their band creates an ideal worship experience instead of whether worship was honest—if its sacraments and theology are true.

As long as Christian worship music is marketed in the music industry, the commercialization of worship will be a source of tension for contemporary church musicians. I feel this tension and actively guard against its pitfalls through constant prayer so that my ministry priorities center on Christ.

The Divide of Pop Music Versus Classical Music

As a classically trained pianist who equally enjoys pop music, I find it perplexing that many stylistic purists strongly prefer one style over another. Yet, the dichotomy between pop and classical music exists. Since CCM and traditional church music are each defined by their pop and classical music styles, considering the relationship between pop music versus classical music genres provides insight into the relationship between CCM and traditional church music. Let us briefly examine the pop–classical relationship from these angles: the musician's perspective, the audience's perspective, technology, a metaphysical perspective, and a stylistic blend between the two. Perhaps even in the differences between pop and classical music, we can find shared values.

---

4. Bob Kauflin, "Pitfalls in Worship Music Today," 9Marks, June 17, 2014. https://www.9marks.org/article/pitfalls-in-worship-music-today/.

5. Jonathan Aigner, "Hillsongization and the Insidious Nature of Commercial Worship Music," Patheos, October 15, 2017, https://www.patheos.com/blogs/ponderanew/2017/10/15/hillsongization-and-the-insidious-nature-of- commercial-worship-music/.

Musician's Perspective

The classical musician typically has had many years of formal training that began at a young age and culminated with a music diploma, perhaps from a music conservatory or college. She is highly skilled in her instrument, sight-reads music well, and is knowledgeable in music theory. She strives for an excellent performance, which for her is defined as one that believably represents a piece as faithfully as possible to the composer's intent, as interpreted by her. For the classical musician, the music score is a treasure to be mined and the foundation upon which to build her performance. There is a significant amount of practice, study, and preparation before the performance. Although pop musicians are also skilled on their instruments, many do not have formal music training. Therefore, music theory and music scores are not usually how pop musicians communicate with one another. Instead, the pop musician improvises in the context of what his bandmates are playing. Classical musicians may tend to look down on pop musicians' lack of formal musical training and make fun of simplistic harmonic progressions or overt use of constant percussion to give rhythmic drive to the music. At the same time, they could be intimidated by pop musicians' sheer creative talent and improvisational skills. Meanwhile, pop musicians may lament the lack of strong drum beats in classical music and ridicule the confines of having to be faithful to a music score and the composer. Paradoxically, they may recognize the beauty of Beethoven and Chopin and could be intimidated by classical musicians' technical prowess, music reading, and training.

I believe that the truth is that musicianship and artistry are not lacking on either side of the aisle. Good musicianship has many aspects, and each side shows off their strengths and is fearful of their weaknesses. Perhaps this mutual intimidation can be transformed into mutual admiration. With humility, we can learn to appreciate the strengths of each side.

Audience's Perspective

Classical music as a genre is not as popular today as the nonclassical genres for the general public. According to the 2020 Nielsen Music Report, the total volume of sales and streams by genre shows that the leading genre worldwide is R&B/hip-hop, at 28.2 percent. Rock is 19.5 percent, and pop is 12.9 percent. Meanwhile, classical nets only 1.0 percent of the total volume of sales and streams in 2020.[6] Ninety-nine percent of the music consumed by the world is nonclassical. In other words, the music vernacular of our culture is more akin to Taylor Swift

---

6. Year-end Report, Nielsen/MRC Data, 2020—Music Business Worldwide, January 9, 2021, https://www.musicbusinessworldwide.com/files/2021/01/MRC_Billboard_YEAR_END_2020_US-Final.pdf.

and Lil Baby rather than Bach and Beethoven. What does this mean for music in churches? It means that church music that sounds like pop music will be more familiar and accessible to the general public.

Technology

One big difference between pop music and classical music is pop music's dependence on technology. Classical music usually does not require any additional electrified amplification. Instead, the instruments themselves are designed to resonate; even classically trained singers are trained to produce vocal resonance. The space in which classical musicians perform is built or chosen for its acoustical resonance. Pop musicians, however, rely heavily on the use of electrified amplification. Not only are the instruments such as keyboards and electric guitars powered, but all the instruments and microphones are channeled through an audio mixer that then feeds powered speakers. This mix is controlled by a "sound guy" (i.e., audio engineer), who is often considered part of the band. Yet, even in this area of stark differences, we can still find similarities. Pop musicians use amplification and audio mixers so that every instrument can be heard and the overall sound is balanced. Without proper mixing and amplification, a drum set overpowers all other instruments and vocalists in the band. Classical musicians also strive to achieve the perfect balance between their instrumentation. Their primary means of doing this is through orchestration. Failure to consider proper orchestration results in poor compositions. My daughter recently performed in an avant-garde classical piece written by a student composer. She was a violinist in a string quartet juxtaposed against a saxophone quartet. As you can imagine, the strings were drowned by the sound of the saxophones.

Metaphysical Perspective

Some have criticized CCM in churches by saying that the sounds of the distorted electric guitar are too jarring and ill fitting for church or that the repetition of pulsating drums has the flavor of tribal animistic incantation. While this criticism seems to come from personal distastes and prejudices, it does suggest a related question: Lyrics aside, do pop and rock music and classical music convey different meanings, with one more fitting for church and another less so? All music conveys meaning because music possesses inherent order and patterns. The ancient philosophers knew that there is a fundamental unity and a meaningful relationship between the physics of sound and the aesthetic beauty of music. Pythagoras discovered a direct mathematical relationship between consonances in music, derived from the harmonic series and mathematical ratios (*logos*). (For example, a string that vibrates precisely one octave higher than another is exactly half the length of the other.) St. Clement of Alexandria attributes this relationship in nature to created order—that there is divine intelligence, Christ the *Logos* himself, who prescribes order, truth, and beauty.[7] Therefore, for St. Clement, the purpose of music is to reveal the divine.

Both pop and classical musicians write music that follows laws of music, employing characteristics like tonal harmony and progressions, counterpoint, meaningful form, and metrical rhythmic patterns. These characteristics suggest that, metaphysically, both pop and classical music reflect the order of the *Logos*. Pop and classical music, sans lyrics, can equally reveal the divine.

Pop and Classical Crossovers

I have long enjoyed the stylistic crossover of pop and classical music. To my delight, pop and classical styles are becoming more and more blended. From Andrew Lloyd Webber's *Requiem* (1985) to Sarah Brightman's duet with Andrea Bocelli on "Time to Say Goodbye" (1996) to current-day YouTube sensation The Piano Guys, we see stylistic crossovers happening. Even orchestras today are trying to shed their serious personae and embracing a more light-hearted and accessible pop character. Recently, the local orchestra where I live, Richmond Symphony Orchestra, presented "The Music of Elton John." The Boston Pops is an excellent example of a crossover orchestra. Under the direction of Keith Lockhart, they record and perform lots of film music, another classical–pop crossover form. Film composers train to write with a wide variety of styles to accompany the broad range of cultural expression and human emotion. They employ fast-driving drum beats and synthesized rhythmic loops to go with an exciting car chase. They use lush, swelling symphonic strings to support an emotional scene and perhaps a minimalistic piano score for a poignant scene. To provide the setting of a cultural location, they would use that culture's instrumentation and tonalities. I believe that church music can learn a lot from film music composers. Perhaps just as film music accompanies and accentuates the drama of the movie, worship music can be employed to accompany and highlight the drama of liturgy.

Crossover pop–classical has also affected Christian music. Sandi Patty's 1986 album *Morning Like This* is a collection of pop-styled songs accompanied by a rock band and supported by a full orchestra and choir. Michael W. Smith's *Christmastime* album (1998) is a beautiful example of pop–classical crossover, employing rock band, full orchestra, full SATB choir, and even the American Boychoir. In 2015, contemporary worship leader and songwriter Paul Baloche and the All Souls Orchestra presented *Symphony of Worship* recorded live from the Royal

---

7. St. Clement, *Exhortation to the Heathen*, trans. William Wilson, from *Ante-Nicene Fathers*, vol. 2, ed. Alexander Roberts, James Donaldson, and A. Cleveland Coxe. (Buffalo, NY: Christian Literature Publishing Co., 1885), chap. 1, rev. and ed. for New Advent by Kevin Knight, http://www.newadvent.org/fathers/020801.htm.

Albert Hall in London. Today, many contemporary Christian songs are arranged for choirs, some to be performed with a rock band and orchestral accompaniment.

Because of the blending of pop and classical styles, the church musician now has a wide array of stylistic options to use. With "contemporary" on one end of the spectrum, and "traditional" on the other, churches can choose to use any blended ratio of styles in their worship services.

Secular Influence on Sacred Music

We have looked at sources of tension that arise from vague terms, from the baggage of contemporary music, and the division between pop and classical music. We've also seen that despite these differences, we can find shared truth and possibilities of blended integration. What about the tension that arises from the fear of secular influences infiltrating the church?

A Historical Perspective

I was chatting with an organist who could not abide the thought of welcoming pop music into the church. "We can't let that secular stuff into the church! The church is holy!" Some look at CCM and feel that the employment of secular music styles is a significant change and are horrified by its inclusion. But if we look at the history of church music, we find that secular music has long influenced the church and her music and, I would say, for the better. One such music influence is Greek modes—the tonal systems on which scales, melodies, and harmonies are based. Plainchants are sung to church modes, which in turn are derived from the Greek modal scales: Ionian, Dorian, Phrygian, Lydian, Mixolydian, and so on. This one secular music influence forms the basic tonal system of all Western music and is arguably the most significant contribution of secular music to the church. Another significant contribution is the Byzantine organ, which came from the Greek and Roman hydraulis, played in the arenas of the Roman Empire during the 2nd century CE.[8] The first Western European pipe organ with "great leaden pipes" was sent from Constantinople to the West by the Byzantine emperor Constantine V in 757 as a gift to Pepin the Short, King of the Franks. Pepin's son Charlemagne requested a similar organ for his chapel in Aachen in 812, establishing its use in Western European church music.[9] Today, the sound of the organ is synonymous with church. A third influence that secular music had on sacred music is the use of instruments. Even during the Middle Ages, sacred music was primarily vocal only. The early church fathers

8. Don Michael Randel, ed., *The New Harvard Dictionary of Music*, 4th ed. (Cambridge, MA: Belknap Press: An Imprint of Harvard University Press, 2003), 578–89.

9. Douglas Bush and Richard Kassel, eds., *The Organ, an Encyclopedia* (New York: Routledge, 2006), 327.

viewed using musical instruments in worship as pagan or Jewish rather than Christian. Even as late as the 13th century, Thomas Aquinas condemned musical instruments such as the harp or lyre when praising God, lest the church should seem to lapse into Judaism.[10] However, by the 14th and 15th centuries, instrumental music became a widespread and regular feature of Western worship. Handel's *Messiah* and Mozart's masses are examples of the vast pieces of sacred music that employ instruments. On the other hand, singing in the Eastern churches remains unaccompanied even to the present day.

Another contribution that secular music made to the church was folk and secular tunes, to which some hymn writers set their Christian poetry. The text "O sacred Head now wounded, With grief and shame weighed down" was a German translation by Paul Gerhardt of a poem attributed to the medieval monk Bernard of Clairvaux (1091–1153). The tune we commonly associate with this text was a secular love song that appeared in 1601, called "My Heart Is Distracted by a Gentle Maid" and published by Hans Leo Hassler, a German Renaissance composer. It was wedded to Gerhardt's sacred lyric in 1644 and was harmonized by J. S. Bach in 1729, who included it in his oratorio the *St. Matthew's Passion*, which gave the tune its present name, "Passion Chorale."[11]

If it were not for secular folk tunes, we would not have "There's a Wideness in God's Mercy" sung to "In Babilone," a Dutch traditional melody; "The Gift of Love" sung to "O Waly Waly," or "I Come with Joy" sung to "Land of Rest," both American folk tunes; "I Heard the Voice of Jesus Say" sung to "Kingsfold," an English folk tune; "What Child Is This" sung to "Greensleeves"; "Morning Has Broken" sung to the traditional Gaelic "Bunessan," and many others.

Over the centuries, church music appropriated elements of secular music and incorporated them into her repertoire, adding to her richness.

A Biblical Perspective

What about the Bible? What clues do we have in the Bible that speak to this issue of musical style? Was there ceremonial worship music? If so, was it influenced by folk music? What theology does scripture have regarding worship and music?

The Bible indicates that God's people used music on many different occasions. In Amos 6:5 and Isaiah 5:12, we see that worship for sacrificial feasts often contained music. Amos 5:23 suggests that songs had already become a regular part of worship services. Popular festivals of all kinds were celebrated with

---

10. *The Summa Theologiae of St. Thomas Aquinas, 2a2ae, 91*, 2nd and rev. ed., trans. Fathers of the English Dominican Province (1920; online edition 2017), https://www.newadvent.org/summa/3091.htm.

11. Robert Cottrill, "Barroom Tunes? Did the Melodies of Our Hymns Originate as Barroom Tunes," Wordwise Bible Studies, January 19, 2021, https://wordwisebiblestudies.com/barroom-tunes-did-the-melodies-of-our-hymns-originate-as-barroom-tunes/.

singing and music, usually accompanied by dancing. Triumphant warriors were welcomed with such celebrations.[12] Music accompanied harvest festivals,[13] coronation festivals, and royal marriages.[14] In the biblical era, we see Jewish culture is intertwined with its religious culture. It is difficult to separate what is sacred and what is secular—all of life orbits around Judaism and temple worship. For this reason, songs that arise from battle celebrations may become part of people's religious worship. Songs that emerge from personal, daily living may become part of the community's sacred music collection. Many of the psalms, the hymnbook for Jewish persons living in biblical times, are personal songs of King David, written for personal edification. The psalms eventually were incorporated into corporate temple worship.

The shofar, a ram's horn, is a musical instrument emblematic of Jewish corporate worship. Leviticus 23:24 and Numbers 29:1 prescribe its use for observing major holidays like Rosh Hashanah. Yet, the ram's horn is likely itself a borrowed instrument from earlier cultures. In "Origins of the Shofar," an article for the educational website My Jewish Learning, Rabbi Dr. Reuven Hammer writes,

> Anthropologists and historians of religion have argued that this symbol was not born *de novo* when Judaism came into being. Long before the inception of the religion of Israel, there existed religions in which the sounding of the horn was part of ritual practice. Judaism, then, did not invent this ritual, but rather reinvented it, divesting it of all former pagan meaning and incorporating it into the framework of monotheism.[15]

Other ancient Jewish music instruments referred to in the Bible are the nevel (twelve-stringed harp),[16] the kinnor (ten-stringed lyre),[17] the *chatzutzera* (silver trumpet), the *tof* (small drum),[18] the *metziltayim* (cymbal),[19] and the *halil* (flute/

---

12. Judges 11:34; 1 Samuel 18:6

13. Judges 9:27; 21:21

14. 1 Kings 1:40; Psalms 45:9

15. Reuven Hammer, "Origins of the Shofar," My Jewish Learning, https://www.myjewishlearning.com/article/the-origins-of- the-shofar/.

16. 1 Samuel 10:5; 2 Samuel 6:5; 1 Kings 10:12; Isaiah 5:12, 14:11; Amos 5:23, 6:5; Psalm 33:2, 57:8, 71:22, 81:2, 92:3, 108:2, 144:9, 150:3; Nehemiah 12:27; 1 Chronicles 13:8, 15:16, 15:20, 15:28, 16:5, 25:1, 25:6; 2 Chronicles 5:12, 9:11, 20:28, 29:25.

17. 1 Samuel 10:5; 2 Samuel 6:5; 1 Kings 10:12; Isaiah 5:12, 14:11; Amos 5:23, 6:5; Psalm 33:2, 57:8, 71:22, 81:2, 92:3, 108:2, 144:9, 150:3; Nehemiah 12:27; 1 Chronicles 13:8, 15:16, 15:20, 15:28, 16:5, 25:1, 25:6; 2 Chronicles 5:12, 9:11, 20:28, 29:25.

18. Genesis 31:27; Exodus 15:20; Judges 11:34; 1 Samuel 10:5, 18:6; 2 Samuel 6:5; Isaiah 5:12, 24:8, 30:32; Jeremiah 31:4; Nahum 2:7; Psalm 68:25, 81:2, 149:3, 150:4; Job 21:12; 1 Chronicles 13:8.

19. 2 Samuel 6:5; Psalm 150:5. Ezra 3:10; Nehemiah 12:17; 1 Chronicles 13:8, 15:16, 15:19, 15:28, 16:5, 16:42, 25:1, 25:6; 2 Chronicles 5:12, 5:13, 29:25.

oboe).[20] These kinds of instruments were all in use in ancient Egypt, as evidenced by Egyptian art.

Theologically, the Bible is consonant with the concept that all of life is sacred—that nothing exists that is not under the reign of God and that all creation declares the power and love of God. Even the "trees clap their hands"[21] and the "rocks cry out"[22] in praise. Since biblically, there is no separation between sacred and secular, perhaps there should be no distinction now between sacred music and secular music, for everything that has breath ought to be "praising the Lord."[23] Isaiah 56:7 declares, "My house shall be called a house of prayer for all peoples." Wouldn't this mean that God welcomes different cultural worship music styles? If God insists on the authentic expression of worship from all peoples of various cultures, wouldn't that include the cultures' Indigenous and vernacular music expressions? If so, how would that be any different from someone who grew up with hip-hop and rap? The moment we acknowledge that God welcomes the worship of all peoples, in all cultures, in all generations, we must conclude that God has no prejudice against any particular musical style of worship. Psalm 150 implies that all things, in their own way, are to worship God. All types of instruments, all voices, cultures, forms, and styles are to, as the psalmist says, "praise the Lord!" Although the Bible tells us to use music to praise and worship God, it does not dictate the musical style used. Instead, we are told not just to sing old songs but "new songs" and to play "skillfully"[24] We are told to "shout for joy"[25] and "make a joyful noise."[26]

Jesus sums it up: we should worship God "in spirit and truth."[27] Matters of artistic style are not mentioned. Instead, what seems essential to Jesus is more about our spirit and God's Spirit moving in us, and about our truth and God's truth revealed to us, in us, and by us to others.

Strengths of Each Style of Music

When we find shared truth and perspectives between contemporary and traditional church music, we build and strengthen the bridge between these ends of the worship stylistic spectrum. But finding similarities is not the only way that helps us celebrate the diversity of worship styles. Another way is knowing and admiring the strengths of each style.

---

20. Isaiah 30:29; 1 Kings 1:40; 1 Samuel 10:5; Jeremiah 48:35.
21. Isaiah 55:12.
22. Luke 19:40.
23. Psalm 150.
24. Psalm 33:3.
25. Psalm 33:1.
26. Psalm 100:1.
27. John 4:23.

Traditional Church Music

The first strength of traditional church music is that it often forms the core of a church's identity. Many churches value their heritage because it implies the fellowship of believers across time. Present-day church members feel connected with the generations of past church members through this shared heritage and identity of their worship tradition. Second, singing hymns, a hallmark of traditional worship, connects us to something larger than ourselves. Not only do we share a connection with believers in the history of our church, but many hymns have endured for generations and crossed denominational differences. We are connecting with an ecumenical Church Militant and the Church Triumphant, unifying with worshippers of God throughout space and time. Third, hymns emphasize poetry and theology. The words are always at the core of hymns, with music playing a supportive role. The poetry is often elegant, picturesque, colorful, and not repetitive. Most importantly, they often clearly point to God. They frequently are loaded with scriptural reference and tend to be theologically sound. Reading the poetry of hymns even without music is immensely edifying and rewarding in itself.

Hymns are musically simplistic. They are rhythmically simple, generally without the use of syncopations. As such, they are easy to sing together in a large congregation. In contrast, contemporary syncopations are impossible for a congregation to synchronize. Hymns have strophic, tuneful, catchy melodies. The repetitive melody and simple rhythm make hymns easy to learn. The vocal ranges in hymns are also within the congregation's range, and again, that makes hymns singable, unlike some contemporary songs. Hymns have the advantage of being tested over time. Decades—and in some cases, centuries—of usage have proved the resiliency of the hymns we still sing today. Another strength of traditional church music is its unique instrumentation of the pipe organ. When we hear the organ, we immediately associate it with the church. To some, evoking a sense of "none other" could be similar to an awareness of the holy.

Strengths of Contemporary Church Music

While traditional church music helps attune us to God's holiness and transcendence, CCM draws us to experience God's immanence. CCM uses the same musical vernacular as 99 percent of today's culture. It is the musical style that is honest and true to most of today's people. If one is to worship in truth, this is the most authentic style for many. Musically, contemporary style is accessible. Because it is familiar, it is appealing to many. Not only does it attract today's culture, but people today may find it easy to sing along since they are used to its beats, its rhythms, its harmonic and structural progressions. This familiarity has powerful evangelistic potential. People unfamiliar with the church may find CCM as the crossover point because it is relatable. Lyrically, CCM uses everyday language that is very accessible and approachable. In contrast, hymn texts are often dated and awkward, and contain unrelatable metaphors that require study, interpretation, and teaching. Contemporary language and metaphors make scriptural truths and the gospel immediately accessible. Another strength of CCM in worship is that we can connect Sunday into Monday. By leveraging Christian radio stations and other social media platforms, contemporary songs sung in church services now can be accessed and played throughout the week on our car radios, in our workplaces, and in homes. The commercialization of worship music may have some redeeming points after all—it can bring worship and church into our daily lives. The greatest strengths that CCM has are its relatability and accessibility. They represent God's nearness.

A Way Forward

CCM is not going away, nor should it. But many don't like the tension that spawns from the arguments that pit contemporary against traditional music among worshippers, congregants, pastors, and musicians. Some try to rid themselves of the tension, saying, "Since musical styles don't matter to God, we don't need to bother with them. Let's not talk about it." But this is burying one's head in the sand. Although God welcomes worship in all musical styles, styles still matter to God because they matter to humans. And they should matter to us because music doesn't occur without form. We need to have the courage to discuss the topic of worship styles. Others try to remove the tension by not being willing to entertain the idea of trying some contemporary elements in their repertoire, categorically closing off options even before due consideration. They give reasons like, "I don't improvise, so we can't do it," or "We just don't do that sort of thing around here." But such an attitude of unwillingness to learn more is a closing of the mind and only builds thicker walls between the two sides. What if we are called to live in and embrace the tension?

Here are three broad areas in which we may experience tensions due to the contemporary–traditional relationship: (1) philosophical–logistical; (2) musical; and (3) relational. In the philosophical–logistical area, we wrestle with questions such as the following: Should our church employ contemporary elements in our service? If so, when and how? Should we do a 50-50 blend? Or a 30-70 blend? Should we start a new service? What would that do to our congregation? Now that we haven't sung hymns for years, should we be concerned that our children don't know hymns? Should we insert hymns back into our services?

In the musical area, we figure out answers to questions such as these: What songs do we sing? What instrumentation should we use? How will the arrangement work if we are trying to revamp a hymn? How do I improvise with a lead sheet? Where should we look for appropriate resources? What audiovisual equipment do we need? Who are the musicians and AV persons that we would need?

The third area in which we may experience tensions is in relationships. Since worship is the central activity of most churches, and religious musical style preferences are personal and subjective, many strong and heated opinions will surface in what feels like a high-stakes argument. Relational tensions also arise when we try to use both styles in church. Musical leaders have to solve questions such as the following: How can we slow our contemporary worship–driving pastor down before our organist quits? How can we help the drummer and the choir get along? What do I do about the friction between the soloists and the choir? How do we get the 9:00 a.m. contemporary service congregation and the 11:00 a.m. traditional service congregation to know and support each other?

Engaging with all these kinds of questions takes courage, wisdom, and much humility. Though a few of these questions may always have true answers regardless of circumstances, most of these questions require a discerning spirit to provide wise, prudential judgments because personalities and situations differ. Further, these are not questions that are one-and-done. These kinds of questions will come up repeatedly because the context is dynamic—people and relationships change, situations change, and cultures change. I suggest that the way forward is to stay open and lean into the contemporary–traditional tension. The ministry that we do is not just about finding the solution to resolve these tensions at a worship-strategy level, but practicing and leading a church culture to embrace a spirit of openness, creativity, patience, humility, and love. When we lean into the worship tensions with this spirit, we will see that the challenges we face are opportunities to grow. We would grow in a greater understanding of ourselves and others. We would grow in grace and love, in knowledge and wisdom, in musicianship, and in our relationships with others and with God. As we grow in these ways, we can then celebrate one another's worship ways.

Some Practical Tips

Some of us facing questions like the kinds mentioned in the previous section may be seeking immediate guidance. Here are some ideas that have worked for me. To help determine what style of music you should use in your church, survey your congregation on what style of music better helps them connect with God. Some poll questions that are helpful are: "What radio station do you listen to?" "With what style of music do you associate church?" "With what style of music do you associate transcendence?" "What style of music is very accessible and relatable to you?" Also, poll non-church-affiliated people whom you'd like to invite to church. (Church language may need a little adapting for non-Christians.) That data may be helpful in evangelistic and hospitality contexts. There are no right or wrong answers to these questions. While the responses that congregation members give are important, the answers that the church's lead musician and pastor give should be weighted more heavily because they are the ones who drive the worship design of the church's services.

What are some ideas to incorporate CCM in a traditional church? If you are a traditional church looking to worship using purely contemporary music, you could start a new contemporary worship service. Creating a new service is a big undertaking and has long-range implications of all sorts. Another idea is to offer a limited number of contemporary worship services, such as once a month or in a weekly summer series. Still another idea is to start a ministry program that shares similar values as CCM such as the value of authenticity, relatability, and cultural relevance. For example, host a meeting at a local café or bar, have an open Q&A about the intersection of faith and real life, and feature a musician to sing some CCM or secular–Christian crossover songs. For worship that blends contemporary with traditional worship styles, musicians could, of course, start by scheduling both contemporary songs and hymns in the same service. But beyond that are other ways of blending the two styles, not just for traditional churches wading into the contemporary world, but also for contemporary churches that desire to restore some traditional elements into their services.

One idea is to create contemporary arrangements of traditional hymns. Try different instrumentation when playing hymns. For example, if a guitarist is to strum "Crown Him with Many Crowns," how would that groove feel? How can other instruments support that? Another idea is to use CCM choruses as liturgical antiphons and congregational responses to the prayers. For example, "Thy Word is a lamp unto my feet, and a light unto my path" by Amy Grant and Michael W. Smith works as an effective recurring congregational sung antiphon inserted within a reading of Psalm 119. Still another idea is to set liturgical texts such as the *Kyrie* and the *Sanctus* to contemporary-styled music. Yet another idea is to overlay or juxtapose a classical, traditional-styled quote or compose a descant (perhaps using Latin text) on a contemporary song. For example, Pachelbel's "Canon in D" works quite well with "Seek Ye First" (Huff/Lafferty). Finally, concerts are an excellent opportunity to introduce your parish to something new. In such a setting, the congregation may not feel like their cherished way of worshiping (their identity) is threatened. If you use a blended repertoire at the concert and spiritually move and inspire the listeners, they may ask, "Why don't we sing this more at church?"

6

A Shift in Tension

Leveraging Music Programs
for Evangelism and Formation

Michael Smith

Choir trainers spend a great deal of time teaching singers to avoid tension; we speak of technique as being free, of open throats, of life and movement in the sound. In reality, there is good tension and bad tension in singing. The very fact that the vocal folds vibrate involves tension and resistance; the abdominal muscles must be tense to support the breath on its way back out of the lungs. Sometimes, in teaching young singers to avoid tension in the wrong places, like the neck or jaw, it's helpful to get them to place tension in some innocuous place in their bodies. I often ask singers to lean into their big toe or perform a plié while singing a difficult passage or a high note. By shifting the tension to another area, their sound is free and their musical efforts are more successful. I would like to explore shifts in tension as a metaphor for leveraging a church's music program for evangelism and formation.

Most of us church musicians were trained first as musicians (often in the Western classical tradition), secondarily as practitioners of church music, and thirdly, if we were lucky, with some degree of theological and pastoral training. It's no wonder, then, that so many of us for so long have approached our work as church musicians with these hierarchies informing our values both in philosophy and in application.

A Culture Shift

Although some do exist, it is difficult to find a church music program that is actively opposed to its participants growing in faith and communicating the good news of God in Jesus Christ to others. Most of us who work in church music do so because we have a vocation, a call to ministry. Much has been written about the value of chorister programs to teach children not only how to sing and read music, but who Jesus is and why they were created. We also know that well-planned and well-executed music ministries can result in evangelism; recruitment grows from excitement, parents and grandparents attend a service and become hooked, previously frozen pew occupants are melted by the sounds of children singing the gospel message. But too often, we experience these as secondary effects of our programming, so we trust that our primary objectives will yield these desirable but secondary effects. Discipleship through osmosis.

The tension point of our default primary objective is music-making. This seems obvious for a church music program that exists to provide music for worship. There is pressure in producing a deliverable: that deliverable is called Sunday morning. We choose repertoire that fits the lectionary and edifies the body, we rehearse and prepare it, and we present it in worship. We teach our singers how to read music and sing with a good technique so that this process becomes more efficient. We teach them how to process in a straight line and with some moderate degree of decorum. We teach them how to be engaged in worship, or at the very least how to be politely bored. Of course, in rehearsals, we engage them about the texts and how they relate to the Christian life.

What would happen, though, if we shifted the tension point of our chorister programs and even our adult choirs to discipleship? Far from neglecting musical development, this approach would continue to yield the same musical results but would organize the music program's experience around discipleship and faith formation touchstones rather than starting with the selection of repertoire or the teaching of the rudiments of music theory and vocal production. For example, I'm currently exploring the development of a children's choir curriculum that is based on the catechism found on page 845 of the Book of Common Prayer. By selecting some of the topics and reordering them to coordinate with the liturgical year, a new framework for selecting repertoire and discussing concepts in the rehearsal is presented. Here is one example of this framework:

Season	Topic	Hymnody
Pre-September Camp or Retreat		
	2 God the Father	372 Praise to the Living God
September-October		
	6 God the Son	448 O Love, how deep, how broad, how high
	9 God the Holy Spirit	511 Holy spirit, ever living
	13 Prayer and Worship	51 We the Lord's people
November		

Season	Topic	Hymnody
	11 The Church	711 The Church of Christ in every age
	14 The Sacraments	304 I come with joy to meet my Lord
Advent and Christmastide		
	1 Human Nature	
	3 The Old Covenant	605 What does the Lord require
	18 The Christian Hope	447 The Christ who died but rose again

At that point, the selected hymnody could be analyzed for the musical rudiments and opportunities for vocal pedagogy it provides. Anthems could be selected that both fill in any pedagogical gaps and suitably complement the musical and theological requirements of worship. The objective of providing excellent music for the worship service is still reached, as is the objective of forming singers as disciples and equipping them for evangelism. The difference is that the latter is no longer a secondary or accidental outcome.

The catechism isn't the only way to organize a music program around faith formation and discipleship, but it is a resource that already exists and that aligns with the beliefs and doctrine of the Episcopal Church. If that's a bit ambitious, what about dividing up the Nicene Creed over the course of the year and exploring different articles and clauses through repertoire and hymnody? If the catechism seems too juvenile for your program's needs, there's always the Athanasian Creed or the Thirty-Nine Articles.

This above is both organizational and pedagogical. Another shift would be cultural: the motivation for belonging to a music program. Think about these distillations of motivators for belonging to a choir:

I'm here because I like the type of music we sing.

I'm here because I like hanging out with these people and learning music together.

I'm here because singing gives me a chance to learn more about God and share what I've learned with others. (And I like the type of music we sing and hanging out with these people and learning music together.)

The opportunity for Christian fellowship is a form of discipleship. So is working together to perfect a piece of music according to a system of training (discipline). Neither of these preclude the overt naming of Christian discipleship as the organizing principle of a music program. By doing this, it's clear to students, parents, and adult participants what they're getting themselves into. I have found that the more I talk about faith in my recruiting efforts, the more successful I am in drawing singers who stick around for the long term.

This shift in tension does not require changing your parish's musical style or aesthetic, and it certainly does not require dumbing down your music ministry or your rehearsals. The former would be foolish, the latter unthinkable when children are involved. Organizing a program around faith formation and discipleship actually makes repertoire selection all the more crucial. It demands pieces of choral music and hymns that can stand up to the weight of the theological ideas being discussed. It requires music that singers have to wrestle with and strive for. The idea of excellence and objective beauty is part and parcel of discipleship. To watch a singer wrestle with an anthem, grasp onto it firmly, and exclaim, "I will not let you go until you bless me!"—this is formation.

The shift does require two things that are nonnegotiable: flexibility and creativity. This is not the place to provide instruction on how to achieve those two things; there are myriad materials for doing so.

If you are a member of the clergy reading this chapter, I need to make what might seem like an obvious point at this juncture: your musician must be on board with this shift if it is to be successful. Trying to drive this change without the buy-in of the musician won't end well for anybody. We all know the myth of the organist and the rector engaged in perpetual struggle since the beginning of time. While that stereotype is a little dated (although it definitely exists), most of my colleagues have a firm grasp of their role as pastoral musicians and take the faith formation of their choirs and congregations seriously. Some of us might need a little time and assistance in expanding our mindset to include all the possibilities of using music for faith formation and evangelism. Think about offering your musician funds and opportunities for continuing education outside of and apart from musical skill development. How would your music ministry be supercharged if the musician did a unit of clinical pastoral education or attended a summer conference on evangelism?

When the musician takes direct ownership of the spiritual development of the participants and congregation and then allows that goal to guide decisions from choice of music to structure of rehearsal, the program is well on its way toward the shift in tension from a musical starting point to one of discipleship.

Evangelism: Tension, Vibration, and Resonance

When a pair of vocal folds is silent, there is no tension on their surrounding musculature, no resistance of wind built up behind them, and, consequently, no vibration. Even when the tension, resistance, and vibration sequences are initiated, sometimes the sound doesn't get very far. We usually blame this on too much carpet or the dreaded pew cushions and kneelers. There's something to that: vibrating sound waves, sent out into the universe, encounter surfaces that either dampen, reflect, or amplify them before they reach our ears and are translated by our neurons into recognizable patterns of sound. This is how evangelism does (or too often, doesn't) work. In church, we are good at talking about the gospel inside our church walls. It's not unusual to hear the good news proclaimed from the lectern, pulpit, or choir stalls. It's unremarkable to begin a vestry meeting or a parish dinner with prayer. We might even be so bold as to discuss our own personal faith and our journey toward discipleship with other Christians in a small group. Often, this results in the Holy Spirit calling us to share more broadly this thing that has changed our lives. And then we get out into the world, and our song seems to get muffled by the upholstery. What are the resonant surfaces we need for our message to be amplified and reflected?

When I began my tenure at my current church four years ago, I was tasked with rebuilding a chorister program that had seen decline. My first day on the job was a few weeks before an already-scheduled vacation Bible school. I asked to lead the music for VBS, including a free lunch and two hours of music enrichment after the morning's programming for any participants who wished to stay. I thought I would get a dozen interested children. Well over thirty of fifty total campers signed up. After a quick trip to Costco and wrangling of volunteers to serve lunch, we jumped in with both feet and had a blast. Because I led the usual fare of VBS singing in the morning, the children knew who I was. When we got into the choir room after lunch, I was able to use that familiarity to get them moving and making a good sound. Over the course of the week, they learned a few hymns, one anthem, toured the church and learned about the different areas, and had a great deal of fun. I made sure to show an interest in each camper and hang around at pick-up and drop-off times to meet their parents or guardians and engage them in discussion. At the end of the week, I gave the pitch: come and be a part of our new chorister program. If this is the point where you expect me to tell you that all thirty signed up immediately, you will be disappointed. Only a handful came on board as choristers. But that handful saw the value of what we were doing, were excited about it, and wanted to come back and commit to the program; furthermore, none of them were previously parishioners.

You may recall the metaphor with which we began: the mechanism of the vocal folds, lungs, and lips all uniting to produce sound that is heard. Let's check into that metaphor with this story:

Resistance of breath behind the vocal folds: A team of parishioners and I spent time in prayer in the days leading up to the camp. We prayed for the Holy Spirit to prepare the children to experience Jesus's love, and we prayed that some would be moved to become choristers.

Good muscular tension surrounding the vocal folds: The conditions were set. I let the children and their parents become familiar with me. I gained their trust by singing silly songs in VBS. I served a lot of dino nuggets.

The vibration of the vocal folds: They learned hymns. They learned about prayer. They learned that we could work together to accomplish something excellent that none of us could do individually.

And yet, this still did not become an evangelistic endeavor. It was only after a year and a half of this initial crop of choristers that we began to see real growth. A few choristers brought friends. A few brought younger siblings who had aged in. News of the chorister program attracted other children from inside and outside the church. The resonance came not from preparation or execution, but from giving the Spirit time, space, and trust to act according to God's purpose. The resonance that we need for our musical endeavors to become evangelism is found in faith. If I prepare my singers to learn about the gospel, practice talking out loud about their faith, and send their sound out into all lands, I must have faith that it will fall on good soil. The preparation part is easy enough; it's the practice that we often skimp on. Take the old "How do you get to Carnegie Hall" joke and replace "Carnegie Hall" with "an evangelistic culture that grows your parish deeper in the knowledge and love of Jesus Christ." The answer is still the same: practice, practice, practice.

Recruitment into a music program is a form of evangelism. Savvy social media campaigns and slickly designed brochures are certainly useful, but the most effective way to recruit is often overlooked because it takes a lot of time and energy. By the way, it's the same reason the most useful technique in evangelism is often overlooked. This crucial step that yields long-term commitment and growth is relationship building. By taking the time to let someone know that you are interested in their life and want them to be involved with your program not because of what it will do for them, but because of the value you can see that they will bring to it—this is the tilling of fertile soil. Another oft-neglected facet of evangelism in a music program is peer-to-peer recruitment. I often ask my adult choir members to develop a choir elevator speech. One prompt that I often use is this: After a long day of work or school, what makes you want to come to church and spend an hour or two working on challenging music? For choristers, I often ask them to think of their friend group. I then ask them to narrow down the group to only those who they think would really be interested in the kind of work we do. I stress that it's really all right if they can only think of one or two names. They are then tasked with inviting that friend to a low-stakes, no-obligation rehearsal. With no shame, I admit that I have employed cash signing bonuses as a reward to current choristers who bring a recruit who sticks around for at least two months.

Practical Applications in the Choir Rehearsal

The most important, effective, and easy way to focus on discipleship in a rehearsal is by using prayer. Having a routine of prayer, talking and teaching about prayer, and occasionally modeling spontaneous prayer are all facets of developing prayerful singers. Choose a prayer that you will use to begin and end each rehearsal, and stick to it. Your choir eventually will memorize the prayer and can say it with you, or you can ask a different singer to lead the prayer.

We begin each rehearsal with the following collect:

> Direct us, O Lord, in all our doings with thy most gracious favor, and further us with thy continual help; that in all our works begun, continued, and ended in thee, we may glorify thy holy Name, and finally, by thy mercy, obtain everlasting life; through Jesus Christ our Lord. Amen. (Book of Common Prayer, page 832)

At the end of the rehearsal, we all say together the Royal School of Church Music's "Chorister's Prayer":

> Bless O Lord, us thy servants, who minister in thy temple. Grant that what we sing with our lips, we may believe in our hearts, and what we believe in our hearts, we may show forth in our lives; through Jesus Christ our Lord, Amen.

It's important not to relegate prayer only to the beginning and ending of rehearsals; this approach can lead to viewing prayer as a perfunctory task. Our attention spans need breaks; what if at regular intervals in the rehearsal, some sort of guided prayer with a physical component was practiced? I take it quite seriously that my singers (of all ages) need to be taught to pray. Any of the techniques that would be used in a good Christian formation text or scheme can be used to accomplish this.

I have my singers keep journals in their music boxes and give them prompts for prayer journaling:
Write down:

> *The name of someone you're concerned about*
> *A situation in the world that troubles you*
> *Something that happened today that made you smile*

I then ask them to spend some time simply talking to God silently about those things. As with any educational endeavor, I include a great deal of modeling, prompts, and repetition. One of my favorite moments in ministry occurred when a parent told me about her child jumping in the car after rehearsal and saying, "I think I know how to pray now!" Of course, hymn and anthem texts often function as prayers, and so do various parts of the liturgy. After the violence in the US Capitol on January 6, 2021, we met for a Zoom rehearsal and I simply said, "Sometimes, when awful and scary things happen, we don't know what to pray. You can memorize simple short prayers and use them because God hears those too and knows what you're trying to say even if you can't say it." We had just been rehearsing a portion of the evensong service. I told them "O God, make speed to save us; O Lord, make haste to help us" is a fine prayer to use when they are confused, afraid, or anxious. We even talked about how the alliteration (speed/save, haste/help) makes it easier to memorize. If your program sings evensong regularly, the *Magnificat* is a prayer that will stick to their hearts and help them to understand God's role in the confusing world of revolution and greed that confronts them day by day.

Another technique I use in the rehearsal is a Book of Common Prayer scavenger hunt. The first time, I have them spend a few minutes looking at the table of contents. I might begin with some simple questions: How do I find out what feasts are in March? How can I pray at noon?

Once they are more familiar with the Book of Common Prayer, the questions can get trickier: What are the suggested canticles for Advent? What's the date of Easter in 2034? The beauty of this is that they become familiar with the book as both a devotional tool and a resource.

There is no greater teacher in the choir rehearsal than the hymnal. In addition to the anatomy of individual hymns and the hymnal as a whole, I try to emphasize that each hymn is a treasure trove to be explored; on each return there is a new gem to find. If this is taught with passion and conviction, children will be glad to go exploring on their own. This is also true with the psalter; in teaching singers to sing psalms, we are forming them to be Christians who pray the daily office and encounter a psalm with the warm greeting of an old friend. Of course, it goes without saying that some of the wild imagery in the psalms can be a springboard for great discussions in rehearsal. Much of this discussion has focused on children's choirs. It's worth mentioning that for most adults, religious literacy cannot be assumed. I often walk my adult singers through the reasons I chose a particular hymn or anthem; when they understand there is a matrix of decision-making (lectionary, liturgical season, language style, musical style, placement in the service), they are more likely to engage with the texts on a theological and devotional level.

Conclusion

Formation, discipleship, and evangelism as organizing principles are just the starting place. Through intentionality in planning, an excellent musical diet, the liturgical year, the poetic imagination of hymns, and living out our mission through a sacrifice of praise, we are uniquely poised as church musicians to offer a program that forms intelligent, committed disciples of Jesus.

I began this chapter by using the process of tension as a metaphor and discussing how a shift in tension from one organizing philosophy to another might enable desirable outcomes on multiple fronts.

Tuning an instrument is an act of changing the relative tension. The act of forming Christians into disciples is also an act of transforming tension. To be "in tune" means that multiple instruments are vibrating at the same frequency. If one violin is flat compared with the concertmaster, that player must increase the tension on the string until the vibrations are aligned. When we increase the good sort of tension in our music programs by leaning into faith, discipleship, and evangelization, we are aligning our work as musicians with the work of God in Jesus Christ through the Holy Spirit, and we are equipping future disciples to be the church in the world.

7

Reckoning with the Anglican Inheritance

Stories from the Episcopal Chaplaincy at Harvard

The Rev. Rita Teschner Powell

What Is the Anglican Inheritance with Which We Must Reckon?

Let me open with a statement of personal location: I am a white, fourth-generation Massachusetts woman and a priest in the Episcopal Church. I do not consider myself an Anglophile, but I love Sherlock Holmes and J. R. R. Tolkien, my parents loved the Beatles, and I drink tea from Fortnum & Mason. The cultural footprint of England is a part of my aesthetic and cultural pattern. I did not grow up with church, but I did grow up with King's College Lessons and Carols broadcast live on the radio on Christmas Eve. My uncle sang in the choir at All Saints, Worcester, Massachusetts. As an adult, I learned that my grandmother had been confirmed in a tiny Episcopal church in northern Vermont and that my mother and father's best friend was a sometime parishioner at St. Mary the Virgin in New York City and his uncle a High Church priest at the church in Newport, Rhode Island. My ethnic background and context were Anglican informed without my even being a member of the church.

The Episcopal Church today, like many American institutions, is in the midst of a process of reckoning with our history. We wish to celebrate the charisms that are our authentic inheritance, yet we must face the reality that our inheritance includes the very building blocks for the structural racism, misogyny, and gross economic inequity that continue to plague our nation to this day. How do we know which things can be received as treasured family heirlooms and which are Trojan horses, carrying on patterns we wish to change in the name of the gospel?

In the realm of the aesthetic experience of music and liturgy, this issue is acute. We wish for our music and liturgy to show us the way to a beloved community, to open our hearts and spirits to a rich and diverse world. And, too, we wish only to hear what we have known, holding fast to memory and mood without the ability to think critically about what we actually value. What, then, of our Anglican inheritance is of deep value? How might we reimagine that inheritance now in light of what we know now about values to which we wish to cleave?

In *Stand Your Ground: Black Bodies and the Justice of God*, the Rev. Dr. Kelly Brown Douglas has illuminated in searing terms the ways in which Anglo-Saxon exceptionalism is a driving force in the creation of a nation built on inequity and oppression. She traces this from Germany through England and across the Atlantic to the founding of this country. This myth saturates the imaginary political and religious convictions that are the building blocks of our churches, and it has traceable consequences for how we treat people of color to this day. When we unthinkingly wish to celebrate our Anglican roots, we risk continuing to perpetuate the mythology of white supremacy.

According to CNN, the Anglican Communion—arguably a large part of what it means to be Anglican—represents approximately 85 million people in 165 countries. Only 26 million of those are baptized in the Church of England (with a mere 854,000 attending services in 2019)[1] and a tiny 1.8 million in the Episcopal Church in America.[2] Is it a mistake, then, to identify Anglicanism with the myth of Anglo-Saxon exceptionalism and, in particular, white English heritage? The Anglican Communion itself is a complicated inheritance, because its origins are tainted by the energy and consequence of the colonial movement. The reason the Church of England is alive in those 160 countries is the presence of the legacy of colonization of those countries, which included religious teaching, conversion, and compliance as part of the project of domination. Since the end of colonization, trusting people's autonomy to inherit and reshape religion in their contexts, we need not dismiss the majority of the Communion as a product and perpetuation of white supremacy culture. However, the strength of this colonial legacy cannot entirely be ignored either. But this is a subject for a different essay. For the purpose of this chapter, I'd like to focus on the elements most common to what we experience as Anglican in our American church today, primarily the legacy of liturgy and music.

I have been part of a group in the church, the American Sarum Movement, for the last ten years as a way to explore these questions. As described on the American Sarum website, this movement is an

---

1. Church of England Research and Statistics, "Statistics for Mission, 2019" (London: The Church of England, 2020), https://www.churchofengland.org/sites/default/files/2020-10/2019StatisticsForMission.pdf.

2. "Table of Statistics of the Episcopal Church," The 2020 Parochial Report, The Episcopal Church, September 2020, https://extranet.generalconvention.org/staff/files/download/28748.

on-going liturgical and musical laboratory examining Anglican liturgy and music which has been bequeathed to us from the medieval liturgies of Salisbury Cathedral. In an age when it is increasingly difficult to define what it means to be Anglican, [their] conferences examine the origins of our liturgical and musical Anglican heritage. Discussions and re-creations of early liturgical practices provide liturgical and musical insights that are intrinsically Anglican and completely relevant to the liturgies of the 21st century. . . . Do we espouse the recovery of glorious Sarum rituals for our liturgies today? No. What we do is mine the depths of Sarum liturgy to find ways in which the spirit of Sarum liturgy can inform our contemporary worship.[3]

American Sarum provides a collaborative and conversational place to sift through and explore those pieces of the Anglican liturgical and musical inheritance that may still nourish and inform us. In this work, I believe it is possible to ask different questions of what we have received without losing the knowledge and concern for the patterns these are part of replicating. But here is where I think we might wish to be most careful; to read our heirlooms may mean submitting to a logic and sensibility that has something to teach us, even if it is foreign to us. If we only read our past with the lens of the evils of today, we may lose our ability to learn wisdom from our ancestors.

A short example may illustrate: in Sarum and other Cathedral processions for major feasts, it was customary to have local or regional officials or nobles in the procession. The ordering of processions was a visual map of rank, with the bishop or dean asserting the power spot at the end of the line. (As Matt. 20:16 reads, "the last will be first.") In this way, the sacred ritual served to enshrine and reify the class and power order of the secular community in a way we might today find abhorrent, noting all those whose powerlessness was rendered visible and sanctified by their absence in the procession. But it would be a mistake to assume all vested processing is or was nothing more than this enshrinement and parading of power. To excise grand processing from our liturgies in the name of leveling the power dynamics is to lose the ideas of enacting sacred, ritual pilgrimage as a central activity in our liturgies. It is to lose the power of performance and movement through our spaces, and it is to lose the sense of obligation and duty to treat each space in our church, as well as spaces in our community, as animate places that need our attention, our devotion. Processions as a practice allow the church to enact the need for movement as part of what we offer to God, part of how we keep alive the tension between a static place of worship and a God who is with us when we move.

---

3. See "American Sarum," American Sarum, accessed February 16, 2022, www.americansarum. org.

And yet I certainly wish to keep alive the knife-edge of discomfort that forces us to acknowledge and worry about the unexamined consequences of the ways our Church and liturgical patterns shape our social and political patterns. At the Episcopal Chaplaincy at Harvard, we began to ask this question with some urgency and energy: How can we make a home in an inherited structure? How can we reimagine our way forward, acknowledging the wickedness and oppression that have come from these structures and yet learning deeply from the spiritual insights of our ancestors in this tradition?

The Sacred Tent: Dwelling in the Wilderness

Three tall wooden triangles rise from a pentagonal platform tucked in a corner under a pine tree in the backyard of 2 Garden Street in Cambridge, Massachusetts. It seems as much an object of art as a dwelling. When its triangles are lit in the nighttime darkness, it feels like a Berlin loft party space. When the sun is blazing on it in the morning, blue jays and bunnies are at home in it. It is solid with its beams of oak and pine, held in place against wind and storm by thin steel cables pegged to the ground that recall the fact that it is a tent. Hooks on the triangles are ready to attach fabric, which can make the space change again and again. It can be taken down and reassembled in a day.

In 2020, the Episcopal Chaplaincy at Harvard designed and built a Sacred Tent. Through a process of community and collaboration, architect Benjamin Bromberg-Gaber and architectural historian and consultant Dr. Matthew Gin (both recent Harvard School of Design grads) worked with the chaplain and students to imagine a dwelling in which to reimagine our relationship to the structures (architectural, liturgical, and conceptual) of the church. Ben is a student of midrash as well as architecture, so we started with texts:

וְעָשׂוּ לִי מִקְדָּשׁ וְשָׁכַנְתִּי בְּתוֹכָם:
And let them make me a sanctuary; that I may dwell among them.
Then have them make a sanctuary for me, and I will dwell among them.
(Exod. 25:8, Sefaria, KJV, NIV)

הדבר נהיה ושכן בתוכינו
And the Word was made flesh, and dwelt among us.
The Word became flesh and made his dwelling among us.
(John 1:14, HHH, KJV, NIV)

The very relationship between God and humans is a sanctuary in its most elemental form. Sanctuary is a place where God dwells among and with us. To honor the specificity of that encounter, that meeting, that dwelling, we are inclined to create demarcated areas. This is for the purpose of seeing, pointing, witnessing, and acknowledging something distinctive and sacred. But what kind of *space* should serve to create such a place? Thus begins the unending stream of varieties of sacred architecture. Many kinds of spaces can be created or designated as sites of divine encounter. In the story of Jesus, a theme from the Exodus is rearticulated: the place where God encounters us is *among us*. We are sacred places; we are ephemeral dwellings of the creative word, the Holy Spirit. If, in our earnest creation of demarcated sanctuaries, we forget that the essential sanctuary is created flesh itself, we can be confused about who God is and how to dwell with God. Churches, therefore, always must be careful about their buildings, lest we transfer our sense of the sacred onto built and inherited structures and forget the basic, fleeting, fleshly quality of sanctuary.

So how, then, could we imagine a created space that called us to renewed attention to this holy space? An ephemeral structure that is porous to the created world can be a beginning—a structure that will not be mistaken for the solid enduring presence, but that can point us both inward (the sacred body each of us carries, the sacred body of the gathered ones) and outward (the world itself as the dwelling of God.)

We wanted something that both recalled the shapes and feel of our traditional spaces and yet was freed from the tyranny of those spaces. We wanted a way to try to be the church that wasn't entirely, irrevocably bound to the systems of oppression the church has helped to legitimate. We wanted a way to take seriously church outdoors, church of the wilderness, church who knows that the God of creation is greater than us, greater than our hearts, and whose creation can be our teacher—our way back to the one who made all things. We wanted a place of hospitality, where we could gather and be and share a cup of tea and a story or two. We wanted a place to play with music and theater and dance. And when the coronavirus pandemic hit and our traditional buildings literally became condemned as harmful to us, we needed what we had been imagining in new ways. So we arrived at a design to meet all these desires.

The tent, first and foremost, felt like an exercise in the discipline of ephemeral as an antidote to the reification of our church buildings and patterns. Claiming the world we live in as a time and place of wilderness, a dwelling for people on the move speaks to the need to inhabit the place of unknowing, of temporariness, of instability and change. It is in this context that we may dare to imagine being led into something new. And yet, of course, we wish to retain something of the traditional shapes—not absolutely all must be lost. So the tent is made up of triangles that recall the Trinity and the perduring shape of arches in our sacred architecture. Equally important is to disrupt the traditional shapes—so the floor platform is an irregular pentagon, with no single orientation, no simple allegorical reduction. It asks, Why not *this* shape? The tent disrupts the border of inside and outside; it is made up of five doors with no walls or ceilings. It is all thresholds— so the boundaries of what is inside versus outside are called into question, both the opposition of natural world to constructed space and the question of which people have been kept out or let in.

The tent is designed to be able to be a place of hospitality, inspired by the tradition of Japanese tea houses. The tent is grounded by a platform on which to sit, on the wood or in chairs, and the triangles hope to create a sense of protected interiority, even as they integrate into the air and life around it. The tent is also a play space—the colored lights in the triangles and the rounded feel of the shape call to mind the circus, the traveling theater. Absurdist liturgical theater coming this spring. Finally, what began as a requirement to be a COVID-friendly church space also allowed us to imagine the church as significantly more informed by and porous to the natural world. Squirrels have run through prayers, and blue jays have chimed in from the tops of the triangles, with leaves drifting in and the breezes dancing with the fair linen and vestments.

The tent creates a location from which to imagine a kind of minimalist-essential sacred space, and yet questions are asked by it, and it allow its people to ask questions with it. What is sacred—what activities? Can a space hold more than one layer? Can it be liturgical and hold other uses too? Does its liturgical use consecrate those other activities too? Perhaps. Hospitality, art and play, and contemplation of the natural world are all possible from this same space. Are those activities rendered more obviously holy by sharing the same footprint and portal as the divine office?

Sarum Liturgy in the Tent: The Consecration

The afternoon of Sunday, October 4, 2020, was sunny and crisp in Cambridge. Because of COVID, we could not assemble in a large group or invite as many as I had hoped. We had to remain small in number—liturgical actors only—spaced and outside. And so we gathered: a photographer, a sound person, a lector, two cantors, the dean of the cathedral (the bishop had taken ill that day) as deacon, the architect and lector, the thurifer, with myself as the presider. We formed a small circle on the Cambridge Common. This idea was based on the medieval practice of *collatio*, in which a text is heard, and reflection occurs apart from the liturgy itself as a preparation for the liturgy. The thurifer and the deacon were vested in cassock and surplice and hoods. The presider wore a chasuble and cope of white and gold for the solemn occasion. The vestments took on a new meaning: out there on Cambridge Common, they had to do the work of communicating the church itself. The vestments were the only thing that spoke that we were the church. We had worried that we might feel out of place, but in fact, our gathering with music and reading and homily and vestment costume easily took its place as one activity among many in the Common. We felt acutely our surroundings, and as the sermon spoke of the wilderness as a state—a way of perceiving landscape—we could feel that we were not in our church home, that we were outside, that we needed a different kind of dwelling.[4] The text from

---

4. The full text of the short homily follows this essay.

Exodus reinforced this desire, and the homily gave us a moment to consider what kind of dwelling we needed and what kind of dwelling we were to consecrate. Separating the sermon, and indeed the instructive or active and reflective component of corporate worship from the flow of the liturgy is an element of the Sarum liturgical pattern I wish to embrace wholeheartedly. Located here, before the liturgy, meant the readings and sermon served the purpose of preparing the assembled to perceive and experience the liturgy. We could then hear the subsequent texts with the ideas of the sermon in mind but as a result of our own engagement with the texts.

We then processed to the garden, across the street, waiting at a traffic light, in full processional order. Moving from a space outside the church or its property made the feeling of procession as journey palpable. We paused at the gate, censed the threshold, and chanted a verse and response. Being outside in unfamiliar liturgical spaces made it easy to observe and attend to places as conceptual essentials. In other words, while we might not have observed every single door as we were processing in the church, being familiar with its pattern here gave us a heightened awareness of something like the humble backyard gate as a threshold space. And it created another layer of beginning. Now, we entered the garden.

The main body of the liturgy had been adapted by the inimitable Dr. John Harper from a liturgy for the dedication of a church in the Bishop Leofric Missal, a medieval sacramentary originating in Exeter, now residing in the Bodleian Library at Oxford. This liturgy imagined the church as a body, and the consecration read like a rite of baptism. The lines between the body of the tent and the body of the people assembled were intentionally blurred. Everything done to the tent was done also to the garden and to the people. It recalled the Sarum liturgy for the asperging of the salt and water, in which those elements, generally considered inanimate, were accounted for as creatures. So the thurifer censed the tent and its portals, then the garden and the people. The presider then asperged the body and portals of the tent with water and likewise the garden and the people. Then came anointing with chrism. The open and impermanent nature of the tent made it easy to feel it as a body, which in turn made it clear that our own bodies are themselves ephemeral architecture. COVID rules about speaking and space made it easy to perform another Sarum principle, in which the words of the liturgy were carried through the chanting of the singers, so that the thurifer and presider's words and voice were less the site of action than their actions. The bodily performance of cleansing and anointing replaced the more cerebral premise of communicating meaning through the indirect medium of words as the only site of action.

The altar, like the gate, was reduced to a minimal essential and called to mind the story we read of Jacob and the pillar at Bethel. A tower of cinderblocks was topped with a piece of slate that bore the main significance of the blessing. The rock, the stone—a creature—was washed and anointed like all the others. It was set up to face east, and as the sun began to drop behind us, the meaning of that direction was felt concretely. The east! The place from which the light arrives. The very Orient, to which we ought to be oriented if we wish to turn to the light, was no abstract metaphor, but a tangible reality of the created world.

The eucharistic elements—again, due to COVID—were received only by the priest. Combined with the orientation east and the demarcated space of the platform, it was clear that the Eucharist is first and foremost an offering made to God. Our consumption of the offering is of a second order of meaning to the offering itself. Of course, consuming the body and blood literally incorporates us into this risen body. But *not* receiving made it clear that the benefits of the Incarnation far surpass our small ritual, which is an enactment of the Incarnation, yes, but is most importantly a humble response to it. Our desire to see and respond to the Incarnation by offering to it is the place where we are enlarged—made bigger. The offering—the love it creates—is more important than the consummation in receiving. Our receiving is not limited to what we receive from church, and this point is made apparent in the noncommunicating mass.

The liturgy ended with a procession back out of the garden. Here again, the spaces spoke clearly. The concept of journey—from wilderness back to the garden, and then from the garden again back to the wilderness—was easy to grasp. This journeying was a wandering, a way of being oriented even as we are lost, a way of realizing God's presence precisely because we have lost our familiar patterns and had to become reacquainted with older, deeper ones. Suddenly, the possibilities of reimagining the historic patterns of Sarum liturgy in a new context itself took on a new sense—as a doubling, as a discovery, of precisely this pattern of wandering in trust, of losing what is familiar to find what is both more fleeting and more enduring.

Sarum Principles Revealed: Learning from the Anglican Inheritance

Having made a case in general for the careful sifting of the liturgical and musical inheritance of the Anglican tradition, specifically in the retrieval of ceremonial and pattern of the Sarum use, let me now enumerate some principles that the experience of this liturgical form, in the surprising context of tent and wilderness, have revealed. I believe these areas to be potentially useful in correcting our dominant liturgical ideology and occasioning a renewal and reform that is in continuity with the tradition and yet, as reimagined now, something new.

Return to Facing East

East-facing celebration of the Eucharist has become equated with a reification of male clerical power. It has been objected that the distance between altar and congregation is alienating and diminishes the power of the people. But practicing east-facing Eucharist outside brought home two very different essential qualities of the practice: First, that being oriented east means taking account of the natural world as central to worship. East is not about men or women or clergy or church—it's about the earth. The symbolic nature of the east, as the place from which light comes, is recovered when the service is outside. It also helps reframe the supposed supremacy of the "Western" culture we inhabit, by insisting we look away from the west and toward something else, toward a light that, even when we cannot see, we know will come. Worship facing east orients us to a reality of geography and symbol that reminds us that God is bigger than the church.

East-facing celebration also achieves a very important recalibration of what is happening in the Eucharist and what the role of the priest is. When the priest faces the congregation, it is nearly impossible to avoid the very serious error of conflating priest with teacher—with Jesus—and to imagine that the heart of the sacrament is an interaction between priest and people, in which the priest stands in authority to make something happen to give it to the waiting community. This is all wrong. This is precisely the distortion of clerical power and capacity that must be avoided. Rather, Sarum teaches us that we might understand the Eucharist to be an offering we make to God, all facing the same direction, all offering together, even if the priest has a particular role of voice, body, and gesture. But when we remove the priest–people interaction, we cannot imagine the priest is giving us something they made for us. Reclaiming the Eucharist as an offering goes a long way to counter the pervasive culture of consumption that we find in church today, in which I go to church to get something that someone else made.

Performing these Eucharists in the time of the pandemic, as a university chaplain forbidden to gather students, also shed light on the role of sacrament and community. If we think of it as an offering, our consumption of it becomes less essential, and we see that our giving to God is the best response we can make to God's salvific action in the world for us. But in this way, we see that God's action for us is not primarily accomplished in or by the church. This liberates liturgy from community, properly calling us to build community that is porous and proximate, rather than congregational and insular. The liturgy should not be seen as the glue that makes a finite community led by a priest, but rather as a mode of response that calls us to seek the love of God and the presence of God in the world around us.

The celebration of the Eucharist without consumption also allows us to reevaluate the liturgical role of the people. If they are not primarily there to receive a "product" made by the priest, what are they there to do? Their role could be understood as to be part of the body making the offering. This changes our role from receivers who are getting something into devotees who are giving our bodies, our time, our hearts and minds and spirits to the worship of the triune God.

Illuminated Embodiment

Other familiar charisms of the Anglican or Sarum liturgical inheritance include music and chant as the auditory mode of the words in the liturgy, a large amount of attention to gesture, incense and purifications, and processions as liturgical acts in themselves. In each of these categories, what can be recovered or reimagined is an awareness that our bodies know and speak differently than the simple cognitive brain functions we tend to rely on in white Episcopal culture. Shifting our location of engagement away from the simple brain cognition into the intelligence of the body allows us to understand ritual differently and upend the hierarchies imposed by that limited brain cognition. The more embodied our practice, the more we see the sentience and vitality of the nonhuman world of our rituals and find ourselves opened into a different relationship with words and language, architectural elements, and objects.

The experience of Sarum worship has radically changed my view of how words work in liturgies. In Episcopal worship today, a large emphasis is placed on words as the primary site of action. In this way, when someone says they wish to "make a liturgy" about creation care or lament about racism, they go to words. Which texts will illuminate the points they wish to get across? Which prayers will say what we want the church to say? When we wish to eradicate misogyny in our liturgy, we look to words: pronouns, names for God, names of women. When a congregation wants to feel more involved, we give them more words in bold to speak. We imagine the words in liturgies to be delivery systems for content, to be given and received with conscious, straightforward reception. I've come to think this reduces language to a thin surface—words as vehicles for the content behind them to be used as tools to accomplish ends. But as people committed to a story whereby the fullness of divine life can be understood as a word, we must push ourselves to a larger and more expansive sense of what words are and how they operate on us.

The practice of the chanted offices and Eucharists in the Sarum pattern uses words and scriptures in a different way than we do. They do not place the primary emphasis on linear transmission of text or ideas from the one singing to the one listening. Rather, the offices are composed of an ecosystem of texts put into play with one another and ordered by themes of meaning rather than simple didactics. Almost all the words in a Sarum liturgy are sung. Word is expanded by sound, and the sound is part of the transmission and reception. Already, the word is given a more full life. Sung words communicate by both tone and melody and content of the words. The listener is able to receive and respond to this from a place beneath (above? beyond?) the cognitive and thus is less likely to reduce the content and meaning of the words to an idea already imagined to be known. Singing the words, which are arranged in complex layers of nondidactic "fabric," allows the words to hold mystery as part of their essence.

The experience of Sarum liturgy outdoors has also changed my sense of where the action of the liturgy resides. If it has changed my orientation, if it has shown me that words must be treated as creatures, not tools, it has also shown me that the primary vocabulary of ritual is gesture. Once I begin to see that all the spaces, all the objects, all the people, all the words are alive, are kinds of bodies, I realize that only in my body can I commune with all of these types of beings. The movements and gestures of my body perform this reverence and awareness, and this is part of the offering and part of the practice. My body speaks to all the other bodies from within its own language of movement, shape, and symbolic gesture. This is highlighted, too, by the insistence on music, and the resistance to the discursive flow of language. All assembled become sacred ministers whose bodies can speak, gesture, and perform. The music allows the assembly to be held in a fabric of sound, which in turn allows the discursive mind to rest and the body-mind to rise.

If part of the ritual, then, is the laying aside of our usual dominant mental patterns, and training to move with and from a different place in ourselves, we must also ask about the sermon. In the Sarum use, there was no sermon in the liturgy, and this, too, is part of what must be reclaimed. In the practice of *collatio*, as we explored in the consecration liturgy, the assembly can gather in a separate space and begin with a time of teaching and conversation with text. But once the liturgy begins, to interrupt the sacred dance with talking breaks the spell, disrupts the very practice, and prevents all—liturgical ministers and congregational ministers—from finding this embodied sense. Moreover, it recalls the question of teaching power and authority and reinscribes the sense of the priest as a person of power and authority, rather than as an actor playing a part (with utmost seriousness) in the liturgy. Moving from a place of illuminated embodiment shows a way forward in ritual that does not reinscribe clerical power or human supremacy, but puts all the varieties of bodies—architectural, object, human, animal, textual—in a layered dance, a communion.

Conclusion

The problem of living into our inheritance as Anglicans is complex. In this chapter, I have explored one strand of the tradition, the Sarum liturgical pattern, in one reimagined context—the Sacred Tent in the Garden of the Episcopal Chaplaincy at Harvard. This is by no means exhaustive or even conclusive. It is meant to have been an exercise in asking our ancestors what there is to learn. I feel confident there *is* much to learn. It is also an important task to continue to work through and to ask where and what parts of our patterns must be left behind. Different parts and pieces of the legacy can be similarly mined and reinterpreted. Fundamentally, though, to stand in relation to the tradition and believe it may have wisdom to teach us, is an act of faith that we must practice.

What might that mean, concretely, for our churches today? It means doing some homework, and it means being brave. The homework is to find ways to study, explore, recover what the liturgical patterns of our Church have been and to treat historical liturgy as though it might have knowledge of ritual and gesture that we have forgotten. The bravery required is to be willing to try on ways of church that contradict patterns on which we have come to rely. We have become accustomed to asking certain questions of our liturgy that preclude others: if we only ask what the words mean, if we only ask if we are immediately intelligible to a brand-new person, if we want our liturgy to do work of social justice that it cannot do, we will not be able to explore how space and object and bodies are alive and speaking. From our Anglican inheritance we may at least take the invitation to restore attention to the ways in which we engage the divine in sacred space and ritual practice, and not imagine we already know what we need to find.

A Sermon Preached by the Rev. Rita Teschner Powell for the Dedication of the Sacred Tent, October 4, 2020

We are in a time of wilderness.
We had forgotten what that feels like.
We had mistakenly taken the word *wilderness* to mean
a luscious scenic backdrop for our restoration.
The wilderness is not an inanimate backdrop
nor is it simply geography.

The unknown, untamed wild is a present, living truth, only superficially suppressed. In the biblical stories we remember our ancestors' experience in the time of their Exodus from slavery. The people wanted to be set free, but liberation is brought forth through a process of undoing. The time of wilderness is a time of loss, loss, loss. Family, friends, health, stability, comfort, home. The familiar ways and buildings that framed and anchored our lives are behind us. Our patterns were oppression, but they were ours and we lived in them, and to lose them is also loss.

The liberation that beckoned, was promised, is gone from view. We the people are not free, and we are tired, and sad, and disoriented. This is not a story of an endurance sport, with a known finish line to which we steadily advance. Our bodies are in motion, and there is distance to cover, and endurance is needed, but there is no end in sight. We do not know where we are going. We do not know where we are. This is a time of alienation, of becoming strangers to the world we thought we knew. This is the time of our undoing.

How shall we make a home in such a time?

What kind of dwelling do we need to survive the ceaseless movement, the inhospitable terrain?

From our ancestors in Exodus we see that the tent is the dwelling for the time of wilderness. There are tents to live in: providing shelter. A tent makes a home less solid than the ones we left behind—a home that is porous to the world outside, so that we may belong to that world rather than be cut off from it. There is the tent of tabernacle: a ritual space held in the midst of our living, our cooking, and our sleeping. There is the tent of meeting: where one meets God as a very intense friend.

Our story today reminds us that our God meets us in tents. The God of the wilderness asked us to build an ephemeral sanctuary, a tabernacle, that God might dwell among us. And again, our God came to us, to dwell among us, in a tent, the body of a man. In John's great Gospel prologue, "The Word became flesh . . . pitched his tent to dwell among us." We can tell it like this: Mary, visited by the angel, understood that a time of wilderness was all around her. Freedom was on the horizon, but to dwell in that vast place of undoing with us, the divine One would need a home. And so she gave her body for shelter and tabernacle and meeting place, that God might have a way to be with us here.

And what is here but a place that is this time? To dwell, with God, in this present time will be the undoing of the patterns that bind us. This is what Mary sings in her *Magnificat*: Cast down the mighty from their thrones, for God does not dwell in thrones, but in the bodies of women and men, fleeting tabernacles pitched in the wilds of time.

And if God is precisely in this wild time, then with what kind of time must we be oriented by to see and know this God? The pattern of time we have grown accustomed to is the very time of our oppression.

Then as much as we need a structure suited to the wilderness, we need a pattern of time for such a dwelling. We need a time that is not measured by markets, but by creation itself, and by the divine life that is creation's source. We will need liturgical time to live into our tents in the wilderness. Liturgical time is held by the daily pattern of morning and evening of this created world, and liturgical time is held by the divine life "which is eternal" even now, "in the midst of things passing away." In the liturgy we remember that we are a people with a home that is in God through all eternity. And this memory reminds us that we are aliens here in this time that is passing away. Liturgical time is the time of alienation, of being lost, the time of the wilderness, of passing away, and liturgical time is a time of belonging, of finding a way of being at home in this very moment. Liturgical time is an ephemeral dwelling in time itself.

And now, in this liturgy, on this day, we will awaken our tent as a body in which God is at home. We will wash and anoint it as a newborn, a new incarnation, a new dwelling. The altar faces east, and even as the sun will set behind us, we will set our sight to the place of dawn and orient our course to the rising of the Light that is not overcome.

8

Approaches to Decolonizing Our Church Music

C. Ellis Reyes Montes

[Jesus] said, "'You shall love the Lord your God with all your heart, and with all your soul, and with all your mind.' This is the greatest and first commandment. And a second is like it: 'You shall love your neighbor as yourself.' On these two commandments hang all the law and the prophets."

Matthew 22:37–40

"Unidos, tomándonos las manos iremos por el mundo cantando al amor. La gloria de Jesús al fin resplandecerá y el mundo llenará de amor y de paz."

Benjamin Villanueva[1]

"When we love, we are committed to our church, our community, and the world. . . . When we love, we are committed to listening to others. When we listen, we are able to understand what people need. We are not trying to give people what we think they need, but through love we are able to help them genuinely."

Sandra T. Montes[2]

---

1. "Together, holding hands, we shall go into the world singing of love. The glory of Jesus will finally shine, and the world will be filled with love and peace" (trans. Ellis Montes). *Wonder, Love, and Praise*: A Supplement to the Hymnal 1982 (New York: Church Publishing, 1997), #796.

2. Sandra T. Montes, Becoming REAL: And Thriving in Ministry (New York: Church Publishing, 2020), 104.

It is exhausting to approach the issue of colonization within the Episcopal Church; it has been a foundational part of the institution since its establishment. As a gay, Indigenous Latino, I am constantly faced with the colonizing practices that continue to prevail throughout this Church, able to confront only so much of it. In this chapter, I will explore the different ways that colonization continues to work within the Episcopal Church, considering issues of liturgy, culture, and our published resources. Throughout, I will offer some practices that can help decolonize these aspects within our lives of faith and within our worship communities.

What Does Colonization Look Like?

Colonization is a complex topic, manifesting itself in different ways in different regions and times around the world. For the sake of this chapter, I will focus on Western colonization, since that is what has influenced much of the current cultural situation within the Episcopal Church. When thinking about Western colonization, the images that come to mind are the ones that I learned in grade school, where, in the 16th and 17th centuries, the Europeans were depicted as exploring new lands in their great ships to bond with the natives and settle in the land that the Europeans claimed was their own. Since then, I have learned about the atrocities committed by the Europeans against my Indigenous ancestors, particularly in their desire to pillage the New World of its natural resources and human lives.

While this is probably the most literal example of Western colonization, it brings a common pitfall with it: thinking of Western colonization as having occurred centuries ago distances our current cultural climate from the realities that colonization has created. Even while people around Anglophone North America have begun to pronounce land acknowledgments at the beginning of meetings, seminars, and liturgies, they continue to neglect the pressing issues that colonization poses today. I am currently writing from Montreal, Canada, which was built on land stolen from the Haudenosaunee and Anishinabeg nations. I am grateful to have been able to interact with the First Nations communities here, meeting people with ancestry from this land and from other North American nations, namely Mohawk and Cree. However, when I think about the land where I grew up, southeastern Texas, my land acknowledgment includes the Karankawa, a tribe that has very little representation in southeast Texan communities today. I often read that they were repeatedly pushed aside by the Spaniards since the 16th century and then by the white Texans since the 19th century to the point that the Karankawa almost seem to be extinct. As a result, I think of the colonization of the First People in southeast Texas as having taken place over a century ago and that the current social climate in the Greater Houston area is influenced by other factors.

However, colonization still happens today. Called by different names, such as gentrification, highway expansion, urban development, commercialization, and consumerism, it often affects groups of people other than the older European versus Indigenous American example. Currently, while colonization continues to affect Indigenous communities, it also affects every community of color, poor people, people with disabilities, and people with different sexualities and gender expressions. It is the warehouse refitted with massive office spaces for tech companies, raising the prices of the dilapidated properties all around, leading to mass evictions. It is the oil pipelines being built, threatening communities already struggling for clean, running water and electricity. It is the declining of artwork, articles, and content from underrepresented communities because they are not composed within a certain style nor written in an artificially formal register.

Colonization also manifests itself within the Episcopal Church. It usually involves those in power telling underrepresented communities which prayers or songs or instruments are permissible in our liturgies, citing an authority, generally a text authored by a white man, as the source. This also involves giving preference—including in allocating financial resources—to Anglophone or European sources for prayers and music, including translations of Anglophone or European resources over resources originally developed in other languages or by other communities.

In the following sections, I will highlight some issues of colonization that we face within the Episcopal Church while suggesting some steps we can take toward fixing these problems.

Decolonizing Our Liturgy

Decolonizing our liturgy requires that we approach liturgy with an open mind. While the prevailing assumption throughout the Episcopal Church is that by using the Book of Common Prayer, every single worship community will worship the same way, this is not the case at all. As a lifelong Episcopalian, I have worshipped with a variety of communities, both as a visitor and as a member. With each visit, I experienced a different approach to liturgy.

One experience that illustrates this liturgical diversity happened during my time as the music director at Grace Episcopal Church in Houston, Texas.

In planning service music for an upcoming season in the liturgical calendar, I discussed with the vicar the use of an upbeat setting of the *Sanctus* (#255 by Grayson Warren Brown in *Lift Every Voice and Sing II*), an idea that intrigued me because I had grown up singing upbeat settings of the *Sanctus* in my home church, Iglesia Episcopal San Mateo. We decided to use it for the next several weeks. The choir learned the setting easily, even though it was strikingly different than the settings we had done in the previous months. During the Sundays of use with this setting, more and more of the congregation made an attempt to sing along, though I noticed that no one was clapping along with the music. The lack of spontaneous clapping surprised me because it was a practice I had experienced regularly within my home parish.

It was this experience that made me realize that different worship communities will treat different prayers in the liturgy with different attitudes. While some say that this indicates the degree of reverence around a prayer or liturgical practice, I must disagree. In *comunidades latinas*, we often show our reverence by how much of ourselves we put into our prayers and music. For example, when we sing a sacred song, we sing it with our full voices, we may try to clap along, and we may feel moved to dance as well. In the liturgy I grew up with, this was how most of our liturgical music was performed. We clapped and danced with the choruses of angels forever singing the hymn. We sang and danced in acknowledgment of the glory of the Holy Trinity. We exclaimed (not just proclaimed) the mysteries of faith. This was the reverence I grew up with, and I wanted to feel that reverence in my new community.

What I learned from this difference in interpretation of liturgy is that different communities have different ideas of reverence during worship. During my time as music director at Grace, I tried to incorporate more of the liturgical practices I had grown up with; sometimes they worked while other times they did not. Every week, I would reflect on the general reception of these ideas with the vicar and talk through how to reconcile any differences that arose because of them. In the case of the *Sanctus*, we ended up deciding to use Brown's setting during the green seasons, when the general approach to music was livelier, continuing to explore different styles of music for this liturgical prayer. I appreciated the opportunity to try out new things, especially when they were drawn from my personal experiences, and the opportunity to reflect on how to bring these ideas into a new situation.

This series of conversations between the vicar, the congregation, the choir, and me were what helped us all explore new understandings of our common liturgy. We were all blessed with our leaders being open to conversation. However, when these conversations are not happening and our leaders are not open to exploring these issues, we encounter one of the characteristics of colonization: imposing one idea upon others. As our churches continue to face demographic shifts in the surrounding communities, we will encounter people we know nothing about. They will come from countries we have never heard of, and they will speak in ways we may not yet understand. When we are presented with these situations, we must be willing to engage newcomers in conversation rather than imposing our comfortable liturgical practices on them. Maybe a prospective congregant feels at home with the liturgy as it is. Maybe they have other spiritual needs that our communities do not yet offer. We will not know without having conversations and building relationships. We must treat the stranger as Jesus did: welcoming, conversing with, and loving them.

Decolonizing Our Instrumentation

What is the most essential instrument to sacred music?

Of course, this is a loaded question, and I am certain that your current worship community's musical makeup came to mind. Perhaps this included the ubiquitous organ and choir, or maybe just voices. Does a guitar come to mind? Does that cause you to cringe?

Instrumentation has become a divisive issue throughout the Episcopal Church, although it is an important discussion to be had. Throughout the United States, the organ and choir continue to be *the* definition of sacred music generation after generation, and there is great literature for this medium spanning centuries. However, there is also quite a lot of bad literature for this medium. In that same vein, many great songs have been written for guitar and voice, or percussion and choir, or unaccompanied singing. At the most fundamental level, the music director must discern the purpose behind choosing one instrumentation over another.

One of the blessings, of which many worship communities do not take advantage, is that we do not have an admonition against using certain instruments over others. In the past five centuries of documented sacred music in the West, there have been many different musical ensembles encouraging the faithful to worship and glorify God. Although the organ is documented as one of the first instruments to be allowed to be played in churches during Mass,[3] there were several other instruments used in different functions not too long afterward, such as heraldic brass for the elevation of the host or even cornetti and sackbuts to support the choir. In addition to what was happening within the church walls, there are many instances of dance bands accompanying sacred functions outside, giving the faithful different ways of listening to the music they could have heard sung during indoor liturgies. The Western sacred musical tradition has continued to incorporate this variety straight through today.

As a result of the lessened constraints on our music, different communities of faith have developed different instrumentations for liturgical use. Throughout much of Latin America, this includes the use of guitars as the main accompaniment, alongside hand percussion and wind instruments. In Black churches across the United States, ensembles incorporate piano, bass, drums, and a variety of other percussion, from clapping to tambourines. Several sacred music ensembles have experimented with different kinds of instruments as well, from electronic soundscapes to a traditional Chinese ensemble. Each one of these instruments can support our sacred music in different, often overlapping ways.

---

3. There are some documented uses of the organ alternating verses with a choir as early as 1400. See Victor Coelho and Keith Polk, *Instrumentalists and Renaissance Culture, 1420–1600: Players of Function and Fantasy* (Cambridge: Cambridge University Press, 2016), 37.

When considering instrumentation, the first step should be to evaluate what you have access to within your worship community. Ask what instruments people play. Ask what kinds of songs people know how to sing. Once you know your musical forces, you can start to think about how to incorporate the instruments into your music. If this is the first time that you are considering including instruments unfamiliar to you, keep in mind that this also will require some new ways of thinking. While the most convenient way to incorporate different instruments is through an existing composition or arrangement that specifies that particular combination of instruments, this is not always an option, let alone a good one.

For example, say your resources include a staff organist and a member of the choir who plays the guitar. Perhaps the first thing that comes to mind is "the keyboard and guitar should not sound together."[4] While it is true that the style of music an organist might find familiar may be remarkably different than the style of music a guitarist is used to, this should not prohibit the two from playing together. For example, consider having the instrumentalists play together in "Seek ye first" (*The Hymnal 1982*, hymn 711). First, make sure that both instrumentalists are reading from the same arrangement. (If you are unfamiliar with the notation, have both instruments play together in a rehearsal, and then tweak the arrangement from there.) Next, come up with the right registration and amplification so that the two can be heard without one overpowering the other. This will require some working out, but the result will involve a new interpretation of a hymn.

At Grace, I have experimented with different instrumentations for different hymns and songs with varying degrees of success. One enjoyable result was in our interpretation of the hymn "O heavenly Word, eternal Light" (*The Hymnal 1982*, hymn 64). We had one musician play the tambourine while our keyboardist played on the organ with a reed stop, and I played recorder in between verses of the hymn. All of this was inspired from 17th-century performance practice, since the hymn's tune, "O Heiland, reiss," had been published in a collection in 1666. While this may not have been the original intention or considered a correct interpretation of the hymn when it was first published as a sacred song or even at its incorporation into *The Hymnal 1982*, this was an experiment drawn from my experience as a performer and from the musical resources available to me in my worship community.

In my home church, San Mateo, we have interpreted several 19th-century hymns in a variety of different styles with our ensemble of keyboard, guitar, bass, drums, and voices. While for hymns of joy, such as "Joyful, joyful, we adore Thee" and "Alleluia! Sing to Jesus," we would usually set the music to more of a rock

4. This is a direction specified in several hymns from *The Hymnal 1982*, such as hymn 488, although this often occurs when there is a chord chart written above a keyboard accompaniment. Oftentimes, the chords differ from the harmonies in the keyboard accompaniment (such as in measure 4 of hymn 488, where the keyboard has an E-flat major chord, whereas the guitar chord is marked G minor), hence leading to potential dissonances between a guitar and organ (or other keyboard) playing together.

style, for other hymns, such as "Thou didst leave thy throne," we would play them closer to how an ensemble of just piano and choir would interpret it, having chords change on almost every beat.

When it comes to instrumentation, it is important to approach the situation with an open mind. Ask what the different possibilities with an ensemble are. Ask what resources are available to you. Research the music typical of the musical resources available. Arrange music in ways that work best. Try different things out in rehearsal.

Decolonizing Our Language

Decolonizing our language in the Episcopal Church is a significant topic, especially with the ongoing conversation about potential revisions to the Book of Common Prayer and the creation of new liturgical materials. Although there are several issues surrounding colonized language in the Episcopal Church, I want to focus on one issue that pertains directly to liturgy and music. Colonized language involves emphasizing the status quo, especially in the face of changing understandings around issues affecting speakers of the language.

Word choice is an ongoing issue, particularly when discussing revisions to liturgical resources, because language is constantly evolving. Linguistic change is often at the core of the arguments both for and against revision, the former stating that our understanding around different topics evolves over time and that language adapts to these new understandings, and the latter stating that language changes too much and that using the same language as it was originally published is reason enough to continue using it. As a gay, Indigenous Latino, I, too, have been learning to use different terms throughout my life in my native languages. For example, when I was young, I identified as Hispanic because that was the prevalent term used to describe people with heritage like mine. However, after high school, I started to notice a shift in preference for the term *Latino*, which was often paired with *Hispanic*, such as "Latino/Hispanic Ministries." Nowadays, I just use the word *Latino* because that is what my peers within *comunidades latinas* use to speak about our identity. I use "Latino" and "Latinx" in different contexts in my writing. This is because I, myself, am a cisgendered male; my pronoun in Spanish is él, and my adjectives end in -*o*. However, when I refer to the general community, especially when not using the Spanish term *comunidad* (which is feminine because of its grammatical properties and not because of the identity of an individual) I use "Latinx" to acknowledge the current understanding around gender expression in Spanish in the United States and Latin America. While this is the term that I use today, it may become obsolete in the future if Latinx trans+ people develop different terminology and encourage its use.

In a similar manner, I have changed how I use indefinite pronouns in my writing in English. I was a stickler for the traditional pairing of "one/his." However, as I learned more about how gendered language affects our perceptions of others in our society, I tried using "one/one's" to avoid the issue of gender in language altogether. Nowadays, I use "one/their" to be gender inclusive while also using a preexisting pronoun.

All the changes mentioned so far have come from conversations and interactions with different communities affected by my use of language. There are other terms in our liturgical and musical writings that may become problematic. If a term is raised as problematic, the most important thing to do is to listen. If the problem brought up is unknown to you, ask for more information about the issue. Then, ask for suggestions on how to improve your use of language.

As we develop more prayers to include in our liturgical resources, I urge liturgists to reconsider using the word *dialects* as in "in their languages and dialects." This is because the word *dialect* has been used to denigrate the status of Indigenous languages, particularly in Latin America, where Spanish speakers tell speakers of Indigenous languages that their languages are merely dialects, either to prove that Indigenous languages are incapable of perceived refined speech, or (even worse) to say that Indigenous languages are ultimately bastardizations of Spanish. When describing the diversity of languages of the world, the word *language* is enough to describe that variety.

As we consider the difficulties around gender and language, the question of meter in hymnody comes to the fore. There are several ways we can go about dealing with problematic language in metered verse. First, in longer hymns in which a single verse may be considered problematic, just omit the problematic verse. Many of the hymns in *The Hymnal 1982* are much longer than the texts included within. One of my favorite hymns, "Come, O thou Traveler unknown" (hymn 638/639) appears with only four verses, even though the text originally includes fourteen. Of course, it would be impractical to include all the verses in the hymnal, but it does show that some hymns contained in the volume are not exact reproductions. I am certain that even in churches that rely solely on *The Hymnal 1982*, they omit certain verses in some hymns, especially for those that are longer than four verses.

If a metered verse has one problematic term, this can become more complicated. I encourage people to try rewriting the specific phrase in question or try to compose an additional verse to the hymn, as has been done several times throughout *The Hymnal 1982*. If the composer or songwriter is still alive, contact them to see if they could rewrite a part of the verse. Remember, a metrical verse does not automatically make it divinely inspired, and the texts that we consider traditional today may be altered versions of even older texts. Just as our language and our prayers can evolve, so can our lyrics.

Decolonizing Our Resources

When considering the resources at our disposal, we must evaluate every contribution contained within. In essence, each published resource is a snapshot of the priorities of the editorial body and the contexts in which they worked, and while we can continue to work toward the stated intention of each, we unfortunately cannot change what is already published. While several attempts have been made to diversify the resources available to Episcopalians, each has had its successes and its problems. In the following section, I will point out some issues that are contained in some of our denominational resources and then discuss an exemplar of a decolonized hymnal from outside the Episcopal Church I have encountered recently in my personal studies. While the resources I will discuss are (or in the case of *El Himnario*, were) published by Church Publishing (except for the last one), each one has been developed by a different body of compilers and editors, as explained in the footnotes.

One of the most unfortunate situations from among our resources for diversifying our music in the Episcopal Church is the cessation of the publication of *El Himnario*.[5] While a thorough evaluation of this resource, from its inception in 1979 to its unfortunate demise in the 2000s, would benefit future attempts to compile music from our *comunidades latinas* all over the Episcopal Church, a brief discussion of *El Himnario* explains how a resource made to serve a specific community can still engage in colonization.

First, here are some of *El Himnario*'s accomplishments. In the preface and introduction, the committee members explain their desire to create a resource that compiles hymns and songs from different styles and eras of sacred music. They also explain that they wish to present the music with simple accompaniments and Latin American rhythms and harmonies. I am grateful to own a copy of this resource and draw from it from time to time for liturgical music, especially in some Psalm settings. I credit the mostly Latinx committee for including songs that are significant to *comunidades latinas* where a connection may not be obvious. For example, the song "Tú dejaste tu trono" (hymn 80) was originally written in English, and it appears in several Protestant hymnals. However, it is absent from *The Hymnal 1982*, most likely because it is not widely known in the Episcopal Church. However, in Spanish-speaking communities, this is a well-known hymn. It was not until I prepared to bring it to the Anglophone congregation at Grace that I discovered it was originally written in English.

This musical cultural crossover happens many times in *música latina* and in other cultures. *Lift Every Voice and Sing II*[6] includes several songs that are highly regarded by Black communities, written by white composers and not typically sung

---

5. Published in 1998, this resource was developed by the ecumenical Comité Ecuménico del Himnario Español, which included several members from the Episcopal Church. According to a report from the Standing Commission on Church Music to the 72nd General Convention, some members of the Standing Commission served as liaisons to the Comité.

6. Published in 1993, this resource was compiled by the Episcopal Commission for Black Ministries in collaboration with the Standing Commission on Church Music.

in white communities. Recognizing who the composers were might not be the most pertinent information for understanding where a song fits into a cultural context. These sorts of facts are often only discerned by members of these communities, and that is why they should always make up the leadership responsible for compiling musical and liturgical resources.

Perhaps the main issue in the negative reception of *El Himnario* is in the amount of Anglophone and European music that is contained throughout. Many hymns are translations of popular Anglican or Episcopalian hymns and not known among *comunidades latinas*. Moreover, these hymns are usually presented in their four-part or even six-part organ scores without any chord notation, a terrible oversight on the part of the editors. Rather than giving people the resources necessary to learn new music in a Latinx context, the hymns stand out as colonizing impositions of Anglican or Episcopalian music. I hope that future attempts at creating a resource for *comunidades latinas* will take these and other issues into consideration, for our communities need and want good resources.

Aside from the resources compiled for communities of color, other musical resources present different issues. The Leader's Guide of *Wonder, Love, and Praise*[7] includes several egregious descriptions about the multicultural music that is printed within, presenting musical styles as appropriate to a genre when, in fact, that may not be the case.

Now, does this mean that nobody is allowed to cross cultural boundaries to create new music? Certainly not! What needs to happen is a respectful relationship between the community and the outsider wishing to participate and contribute.

At the same time, I wonder how many Latinx composers were turned away in the compilation process of this volume so that the compositions of Anglocentric composers might be used as representations of *música latina*. Since one of the stated goals of *Wonder, Love, and Praise* is to honor and affirm "the participation of all in the Body of Christ the Church, while recognizing our diverse nature as children of God,"[8] I can only wonder how many other spaces in the volume were taken up by white representatives of underrepresented communities rather than actual members of these communities.

Within our resources, we also come across the issue of linguistic diversity. When it comes to respecting that diversity and encouraging relationships to be built across linguistic boundaries, it is essential to keep in mind the presentation and the treatment of foreign languages. I still hear native English-speaking celebrants murmuring through prayers and even sermons in Spanish, not knowing how to pronounce the words or even how to emphasize the prosody in the language. This is not to say that one must speak with an impeccable accent and without stopping to think through a long word or confusing grammar point,

7. Published in 1997, this resource was compiled by members of The Standing Commission on Church Music, and Vice-Chair Rev. John Hooker wrote the *Leader's Guide*, published in the same year.

8. Hooker, *Wonder, Love, and Praise*, preface.

but it does mean that one needs to be familiar with more than just the pronunciation of individual letters to be understood to any degree in a foreign language. I applaud those who have made the effort to learn how to speak and write in Spanish, continuing their education through their relationships with native Spanish speakers and engagement with native materials. In fact, when someone speaks Spanish with an English speaker's accent but with the timing and intonation typical of Spanish speakers, it is more comprehendible than one who might be able to pronounce every word correctly but monotonously or, worse, with English prosodic patterns.

The first step to approaching a foreign language, especially in music, is knowing which language is being spoken. Unfortunately, this information is absent from several songs in *My Heart Sings Out*, as is the case with too many hymnals and songbooks.[9] While this book is not identified as a supplement to *The Hymnal 1982* or called a hymnal, it is a publication by Church Publishing and appropriate to this discussion of language.

The song "Amen, siyakudumisa/*Amen, we praise your name*" (hymn 34 in *My Heart Sings Out*) is a prime example of the issue of language appropriation. While this song, as far as I know, is from South Africa (according to the citation associated with the song), the compiler does not indicate the language. Instead, the words in the unnamed language are printed above the English translation. As a result, the presentation of the text encourages singers to make pronunciation choices and to view the song as one that is detached from its culture.

To say that a song is "South African" without any other indication of the language or culture surrounding it would be just like labeling any Western song as "European." South Africa has many different languages spoken aside from English and Afrikaans, including those from different language families, and each has a different pronunciation of the Latin alphabet. I was able to discover that the song is in Xhosa and found information on how to pronounce the language. In researching the other song labeled as "South African," I found that it is in Zulu. In the book, two songs are from the same country, but their lack of language citation provides no clues to singers of their interpretations.[10]

Going further with this issue, though, the book does not provide information on pronunciation. While I am usually not a fan of such guides based on American English pronunciation (or any other accent for that matter), they at least provide some information to begin with. Even if a pronunciation guide were given in the International Phonetic Alphabet with the appropriate additional symbols

---

9. Published in 2005, this resource was compiled and edited by Fiona Vidal-White. This resource was not funded by the Episcopal Church nor created by the Standing Commission on Church Music/ Standing Commission on Liturgy and Music.

10. There are several other songs in *My Heart Sings Out* in other languages that do not specify the language or country of origin. Some of these credit the composer, but the publication information does not explain anything else about the background of the composer.

indicating accentuation, syllable length, and even intonation, guidance from a native speaker of that language would still be helpful.

While I appreciate that *My Heart Sings Out* attempts to broaden the scope of music within the Episcopal Church, it perpetuates colonization of our church music. The volume's introduction states that the songs contained are fulfilling the need for "good church music for children," causing a reader to assume that the music contained is just children's music. Now, Vidal-White does not state this in the introduction or anywhere else in the book, but it does remind me that people have labeled *música latina* as infantile or unrefined. This prejudice on my musical heritage often leads to the treatment of these musical genres as somehow "less than" those that represent other cultural traditions.

Perhaps future hymnals and supplements will provide additional information about the contexts of the material included. What is the cultural significance to each song? How can these songs build community? What should leaders and singers know about the musical style, performance preferences, or appropriate pronunciation? Perhaps answers to these questions could build on the ever so important relational aspect to learning new music from other cultures.

Now, what would be an example of a decolonized hymnal? I have found a variety among my collection of hymnals and songbooks, but perhaps the best example with respect to the issues I have brought up in this section comes from my nearly ten-year-long study of Mandarin Chinese. My Chinese studies also have compelled me to buy hymnals and songbooks in Chinese from different denominations, and perhaps the most pleasant surprise acquisition is a copy of *Seng-si 2009*,[11] a hymnal of the Presbyterian Church in Taiwan. As I learned more and more music from it, I became intrigued by the makeup of the hymns, and I delved deeper into their sources. What I found was a model of a decolonized hymnal.

Perhaps the most important feature is that the editorial team of *Seng-si 2009* consists mostly of people of Taiwanese descent, including some who are of Aboriginal, non-Han descent. This leadership has helped to prioritize the mission to incorporate more Taiwanese and Chinese hymns into the hymnal and lessen the dependence on Western European hymns.[12] This mission has manifested itself in the form of compiling hymns written since the 19th-century

---

11. 聖詩 2009. In this section, I am using I-to Loh's romanization, which he uses in his article about this hymnal.

12. Although I am just beginning to learn more about Christianity in China and Taiwan, it is evident that Western European colonization played a major role in establishing churches there, and much of Christianity there still has many Western European and North American influences, especially on the music. For more information pertaining to the decolonizing effort of *Seng-si 2009*, read I-to Loh, "The Significance of Seng-Si 2009. The New Hymnal of the Presbyterian Church in Taiwan," trans. David Alexander, *Global Church Music* (blog), May 3, 2011, https://globalchurchmusic. org/en/article-the-significance-of-seng-si-2009-the-new-hymnal-of-t.html.

in a non-Western style, including finding hymns from the underrepresented Aboriginal people, and commissioning new works for this publication. While many of the contributions by Taiwanese Aboriginals have lyrics in other languages, some are written in Chinese characters.[13] However, each hymn contains a citation pointing to the country or ethnicity of origin for every tune and text, and the Taiwanese contributions include information about which people group the composers come from, including what language is used when not in Chinese.

In addition to addressing the issues I have raised above, *Seng-si 2009* is forward-looking in its use of gender-neutral language. For lyrics and prayers describing God, the Chinese lyrics avoid using a gendered pronoun, instead using an ungendered pronoun. This approach turns away from many Protestant Chinese prayers, including the Chinese translation of the Book of Common Prayer, that exclusively use male pronouns for God. While the linguistic issues around gender and God are different from those happening in English, Spanish, and other European languages, it is still remarkable that *Seng-si 2009* makes the effort to use gender-neutral language.

As I have pointed out, several examples of colonization can be found within our musical resources in the Episcopal Church. While each resource serves as a snapshot of the priorities for different editorial bodies over the past several decades, we can still move forward from there. Unfortunately, we have not had a major publication of new music in the past several years, but I hope that the future publications will learn from past ones while also looking at the hymnals and songbooks at the forefront of decolonization and reconciliation for inspiration and best practices.

How to Incorporate New Music from Unfamiliar Communities into Liturgy

Amid the conversations and arguments over the colonizing practice of cultural appropriation, it might feel safest to avoid engaging with other cultures entirely. If there is no cross-cultural interaction, then there can be no appropriation. While this logic might be one way to dodge the issue, it goes against our mission as church musicians to help our communities glorify God. If we keep a distance from those within, or in proximity to, our worship communities who are seeking God, we are ignoring them and their needs. Engaging with different cultures is difficult to do, especially if it is unfamiliar. Even as a person of

---

13. While the official language of Taiwan is Mandarin, much of the text and many of the hymns in *Seng-si 2009* are written in other Chinese languages, particularly Taiwanese Hokkien. Because of this variety, for the sake of simplicity in this section, I will say a text is either "written in Chinese characters" or "is in Chinese" interchangeably. I do not mean Mandarin (or any other Chinese language) when I write the word "Chinese."

color who grew up in one of the most diverse counties in the United States,[14] I face the same challenge of engaging with people from different backgrounds. However, I do have some practices that I have developed in my experience with learning new music from other cultures, and I encourage you to try some of these as you incorporate music from unfamiliar cultures into liturgy.

1. Form a Respectful Relationship

Before doing anything else, develop a relationship with the community whose music you wish to learn and share. You may have recently learned a new song in a different language, encountered a new family in your worship community, or even learned about a demographic shift happening around your area. Engage with people from that community, and get to know them. Speak to newcomers, and ask them about what they hope to experience in your worship community, especially around music. Maybe they know some songs already in your repertoire. Maybe they have some suggestions or ideas that pertain to the upcoming liturgical season. None of this information can be known without a genuine conversation and the initiation of a respectful relationship.

In my previous parish, I met Nelson Flores, who was active in the community and often served as an acolyte. I also learned that Nelson was from the Philippines. He told me about his familial traditions and offered to share some music with me.

2. Select Music to Learn

In the excitement of learning a different community's traditions it can be tempting to incorporate all of it into the liturgy. This can lead to too much unfamiliar text or too many unfamiliar rhythms or harmonies, creating the potential for burnout even before getting to engage with the music. Instead, focus on one or two songs to start. First, ask for recommendations of songs from the people within the community whose music you would like to learn. If the songs are in languages uncommon to your worshipping community, ask about the text and a good translation. This can be a great first step for an ensemble to learn unfamiliar music, focusing first on building a comfort level with rhythms and harmonies that may be new.

After finding out more about the music you want to learn, determine where and how to incorporate the song into an upcoming liturgy. If the song is

---

14. In 2010, Fort Bend County was named one of the most diverse counties in the US (Corrie Maclaggan, "What Ethnic Diversity Looks Like: Fort Bend," *New York Times*, November 23, 2013, https://www.nytimes.com/2013/11/24/us/what-ethnic-diversity-looks-like-fort-bend.html.), and in 2021, the county continues to be the most diverse in Texas (Solange DeLisle, "Census Bureau Data Shows Fort Bend County Is 'the Most Diverse County in Texas'," *Houston Daily*, August 27, 2021, https://houstondaily.com/stories/606861667-census-bureau-data-shows-fort-bend-county-is-the-most-diverse-county-in-texas.).

devotional, it might work well as a communion anthem or music during prayer. If it is a song of praise, it might suit the space for the *Gloria* or song of praise.

Nelson recommended I learn a song by Filipino musician Raymund Remo, "Ang tanging alay ko,"[15] which translates to "The only thing I can give." Unfortunately, there was not an existing singable translation of the song, but Nelson did send me the lyrics with a phrase-by-phrase translation so I could study it. As the title implies, it is a song about devotion most suitable for an offertory, so I planned to use it as an offertory anthem in an upcoming liturgy.

3. Learn the Music by Yourself

This step is crucial when considering incorporating music from an unfamiliar culture into the liturgy. As a church musician, it is essential to understand the music fully before rehearsing it with other musicians, especially if you are the only person with direct contact with the community whose music you are learning.

When learning, it is important to learn it beyond what might be notated or what you can mimic from a recording. Involve in the process the members of the community whose music you are trying to learn. If they are musicians, have them teach you the music, or at least have them record the music for you, perhaps in a simplified form if there is usually ornamentation involved. If they are not musicians, check in with them as you learn the music. Play or sing it for them to see if it sounds right.

Moreover, make sure to learn the version that they know. Many songs, especially those that are popular with multiple communities, exist in several different forms. For example, the song "Montaña," which has been quite popular throughout the Episcopal Church, has variations throughout Latin America. In the opening phrase, I have encountered two versions of the lyrics: "*Si tuvieras fe, como un grano de mostaza . . .*" and "*Si tuvieras fe, como un granito de mostaza . . .*"

With these two versions comes a slight variation in the melody, a difference that becomes more obvious every time it is repeated. If I were to teach you the song, I would use the first version because that is the way I learned it. While we Western classically trained musicians might feel a noble obligation to find the original, authoritative version that was documented in the earliest source when learning new music, this is not often appreciated by the communities whose music you are trying to learn. In fact, this is a colonial mindset that has been used extensively among the compilers of the musical resources I have discussed above. Honor those teaching you by learning the song as they know it. As an outsider, to tell a community they have been singing a song incorrectly is a grave sign of disrespect.

---

15. There are a number of recordings of "Ang tanging alay ko" available on social media and YouTube.

If the song is in an unfamiliar language, consult with the members of the community about the pronunciation. Have them record themselves speaking the words slowly. Repeat the words to them so they can correct your pronunciation, paying special attention to the accentuation (which can affect how you approach singing the song). After learning the spoken pronunciation, learn the words with the melody, and sing the song to the members of the community. Again, have them check your pronunciation throughout the song. Perhaps the unfamiliar language will present some differences when sung rather than spoken. For example, in sung French, often the unspoken syllables are sung. In sung Spanish, we often combine several vowels into one note, especially if they are unstressed vowels.

When I began learning "Ang tanging alay ko," I wrote out the chords and the melody so I could sing the song while playing it on the piano. Nelson sent me a recording of him pronouncing the words, and I met with him to make sure I understood the pronunciation. One of the things I noticed in Tagalog orthography is that some vowels have a glottal stop in between them, and others are pronounced longer than I had anticipated (since I often approach Latin letters with a Spanish pronunciation). After working out the pronunciation and reviewing my notes, I began to sing the words along with the recording before starting to play the song on my own. I received Nelson's approval before continuing onto the next step.

4. Teach the Song to Your Ensemble

Once you become comfortable with the new music, you can begin to rehearse it with your ensemble. Make sure to set aside enough time to go over new rhythms or harmonies with the instrumentalists and the pronunciation with the vocalists if it is in an unfamiliar language. Also, ask members of the community whose music you are trying to learn to attend your rehearsal, if possible. They can give you feedback about how the music sounds, especially if it sounds like it is going in the right direction or falling astray.

Pay attention to the pitfalls that you encountered while learning, and address them if they arise. Although many of us have trained for years and acquired many skills, we might apply them inappropriately to unfamiliar music. This is not to say that a musician should not feel free to play musically, but it is important to ensure that the basic structure of the music is present before personalizing it. No matter how long you spend learning the music for the first time, it probably will still feel unfamiliar, but it can be a first step to learning more music in this genre, building on what you establish.

I was fortunate enough to have Nelson attend our first rehearsal when learning the song. He went over the pronunciation with our choir and provided pointers about the tempo and rhythm of the music. I felt supported by having someone familiar with the music in the same space and who was able to answer any additional questions that may come up with in the rehearsal. Nelson's presence helped us know when we were comfortable enough with the music to move onto something else during rehearsal without any lingering doubt about how it would end up going on the upcoming Sunday.

5. Glorify God

When it comes to incorporating new music into our liturgies, we must remember the ultimate purpose of our liturgical music: to glorify God. When we learn music form different cultures, we praise God for the diversity that surrounds us, and we glorify God in partaking in the beauty that music is to so many communities. On the day you will sing the new music, remember to thank God for the gift of this new music, and pray for the music to be another example of God's love in the world.

I was grateful to Nelson after we sang the new song in our liturgy. Our ensemble enjoyed learning the music with its beautiful harmonies and text. The congregation also appreciated the new music, since it was a different way to express gratitude to God for all that God has done in our community.

Conclusion

Decolonizing our church music is a complicated process that takes a continuing effort on our part as musicians. We must reflect on our own practices and engage with other communities in our efforts to decolonize. While this is not something that happens instantaneously, there are several practices we can use to find the love of God in our neighbors. By building respectful relationships and continuing to learn about the factors that influence our communities, we can make our way toward reconciliation.

II

CONVERSATIONS IN VOCATION

9

Claim the High Calling

Jessica Nelson

At the onset of the coronavirus pandemic, musicians were advised that, due to the emission of aerosolized virus particles, singing in groups was a particularly risky activity. News stories broke early on about choir rehearsals being super-spreader events during which many contracted the virus from one asymptomatic participant. Any sort of group music-making ground to a halt. Restrictions on making music in schools and religious organizations have since become common and are complicated, following an ever-shifting formula that takes into consideration group size, room size, and local transmission rates, posing endless questions: How many times in an hour is there a complete exchange of air in the room? Is your mask sufficient? Is mine? I've learned way more than I could have ever imagined about spit, airflow, and virology. They did not teach us this in school. Many parishes suspended singing altogether. As of this writing, restrictions in some areas are beginning to be lifted and more singing is permissible, but it is still impeded by mask usage, time limits on the duration of hymns, physical distancing requirements, and other safety measures. I don't want to leave room for misunderstanding: these restrictions are necessary in the interest of community health. But the whole situation has been heartbreaking and, frankly, has thrown me into a vocational tailspin. What am I, *who* am I, if I cannot perform the most basic functions of this call to make music in community in the service of the church's worship? Sure, I can make plenty of music on my own and certainly have, but to what end?

It sounds like I'm trying to relay a much less funny version of that old Abbott and Costello routine,[1] but bear with me: A conductor friend once explained to his choir that there is always a *what* and a *how* in music—that the music that reaches our ears is the *what* and everything on the page is just *how*. Our *what* has been gathering in community to make music to offer to the glory of God and in

---

1. Jokes lose something when they must be explained, but just in case this one is unfamiliar: Bud Abbott and Lou Costello were a vaudeville comedy duo active in the 1950s known for their sketch, "Who's on First?" In it, confusion results from a team of baseball players with names like "Who," "What," and "I Don't Know."

the service of the church's worship. We know that *how* we do this has changed. Is *what* we do changing as well? If so, into what? Because I'm an external processor, I sought out a handful of colleagues with whom I could have frank conversations in an effort to regain some of my lost clarity. I presented each with the same basic set of prompts to shape our conversations, beginning with considering Alec Wyton's understanding of church leaders as pastor-teacher-performer, in that order.[2] Wyton was a native Englishman who served churches all over the United States, taught at Union Theological Seminary, and played a significant role in the creation of *The Hymnal 1982*.[3] Each conversation went down its own little rabbit trails, unsurprisingly. I intentionally chose these colleagues for their range of perspective and experience as well as their thoughtfulness and ability to consider critically the questions at hand. I was also particularly interested in conversations with church musicians in different phases of their careers: some are closer to retirement, some have been established a while, and one is just dipping his toes in. These five prompts were generated partially out of my own recent pandemic-induced vocational crisis and partially because I realized our professional landscape was rapidly changing even before the pandemic, which merited reflection on its own.[4] I also wanted to capture a snapshot of this strange, liminal time in the interest of historical self-consciousness and documentation. What follows is the content of those conversations, with some personal reflection woven in.

Conversation with Dr. Marty Wheeler Burnett

Marty is in her first year as the associate professor of church music and director of chapel music at Virginia Theological Seminary, succeeding the Rev. Dr. William Bradley Roberts upon his retirement. Immediately prior to this appointment, she was the canon precentor of Trinity Cathedral in Omaha, Nebraska, and has spent the majority of her life working in some capacity in the service of the church. I start out by asking her to comment on Alec Wyton's formula. She says, "Interestingly enough, we were just talking about that quotation in class yesterday, so it's all fresh on my mind. I think that that's still absolutely true, and even more so now, in the pandemic and moving out of [it]. . . . As I told my students, that's

---

2. Alec Wyton, "The Function of Music in Corporate Worship," *The Journal of Church Music* (December 1987): 9

3. Craig R. Whitney, "Alec Wyton, 85, Organist Who Updated Church Music, Is Dead," *New York Times*, March 23, 2007, https://www.nytimes.com/2007/03/23/arts/music/23wyton.html.

4. Here is a summary of the questions and prompts, which were loosely followed. (1) Do you think Alec Wyton's description of the church musician as "pastor-teacher-performer" is still accurate? (2) Do you believe you're called to this work? Do you think this is God's will for your life? (3) How did you come to understand yourself as a church musician? (4) Has the coronavirus pandemic given you any vocational anxiety or clarity? (5) Do you think the vocation of the church musician is changing, pandemic notwithstanding?

certainly proved true for me in my work in the parish." I'm glad to know that she's teaching this to seminarians. "As I've told my students," she begins, "things that were once considered revolutionary we now take for granted, and this is one of those things. When Alec said that, it was controversial. . . . Church music programs . . . were geared toward performance. And certainly within my lifetime, we've seen that shift within the Episcopal Church to something that more closely resembles Alec's model." She continues, "I think [seminarians] are always a little surprised by this. . . . I think they really think of [church musicians] as performers and don't really understand the pastoral and teaching aspects of the ministry," prior to their arrival at seminary. "They haven't really thought about the fact that the choir spends more time together than any other small group in the parish— that they're immersed in worship and the life of the church. Hopefully it opens their eyes."

Marty has had the benefit of excellent training but notes that musicians in her generation rarely, if ever, received any sort of formal instruction in the pastoral care arena, nor did they learn to teach beyond how *their* teachers learned to teach. That is, they received plenty of training in how to teach in an academic context but never in other environments. "We received training about how to teach our instrument," having been required to take courses in organ pedagogy, "but nobody in school ever taught us how to teach music to a volunteer choir. . . . It was all focused on performance." Marty affirms, "The ministries of pastor and teacher are things that most of us learn along the way from other sources—whether it's conferences or seminars or books, but mostly from practical experience—learning how to do those things and do them well. I'm not sure how much time is spent [in academic church music programs] in training for pastoral skills and teaching skills, but certainly here in the seminary, we see that as a model for all ministry, that first and foremost is the ministry of pastor." She continues, "As a church musician, the choir really often functions like a small congregation within a larger parish, and the director of music is the pastor to that small congregation, so it's very natural that people will come to the musician with pastoral concerns. . . . You never know when it's going to happen," she says. "You have to be open and ready for it."

In addition to her service to the academy, Marty has had long tenures in parish ministry. I wonder if she's felt called to this work. "Do you think this has been your calling—or *a* calling?" I ask. "I do see it as a call," she acknowledges, remembering, "from a very early age, I felt called to be a church musician. I remember going to church when I was five, six years old and seeing a Christmas pageant . . . with choir . . . there was wonderful music and a small orchestra, and I thought, *I want to do that*." She continues, "Music was how I connected to God; it was what was meaningful to me in worship . . . and I felt drawn to it." She began piano studies in fourth grade and very soon started playing for events in the United Methodist congregation of her childhood. "I loved that, and we were lucky to have a church where choir was open to young people," she remembers with appreciation.

"In high school, I was really focused on doing work in church music and making that my life's path," remembering that multiple guidance counselors tried to talk her out of it. She had good grades and SAT scores—why not pursue a career in something more lucrative? Even then, she had a clear sense of call, which further crystallized in college at Rice University in Houston, Texas. "When I went to college, two things happened," she reflects. "My teacher was the organist and choirmaster at the Episcopal cathedral, so he'd constantly rope us into doing things," like filling out choirs or turning pages at the organ. The second thing was realizing that she valued the quality, quantity, and range of music she was hearing there and felt a tug. "Coming to the Episcopal church felt like coming home—it wasn't so much turning my back on my past, but finding the connection to where I felt at home." Following studies at Rice, Marty had a number of parish ministry jobs in a few different denominations. Looking back, she realizes, "The ironic thing about all of this is that even though I felt called . . . I didn't have a full-time job in church music until I was in my fifties," holding jobs alongside her work in parish ministry. "I've done everything from working in a music therapy setting to teaching piano and organ students to teaching in a school. You name it, I've done it." Marty also remembers that, having discerned and articulated to others a call to parish ministry, many well-meaning colleagues, both lay and ordained, interpreted this as a call to ordained ministry and repeatedly suggested she pursue orders and attend seminary. She is clear, though—her call was not—*is* not—to priestly ministry: "The things that I feel the most called to do in the church don't require ordination. They're baptismal ministries."

It occurs to me that Marty's work at VTS so far has been entirely under coronavirus conditions—she hasn't known work at VTS in their absence. We commiserate about that, in particular about how prerecorded liturgies feel strangely disembodied and sterile. She tells me about the first in-person service she played at VTS, having only participated in remotely recorded or livestreamed services. "I remember being nervous about it because I'd never done an in-person service in this chapel," even though she'd been there for a year at that point. She remembers being concerned about how all the mechanics of the service would come together—especially the timing of the processions, given that the organ's position in the chapel only allows the organist to see the proceedings through a small mirror as they're playing. But something interesting happened. "As the service went on," she begins, "what I became aware of was all the different senses that came into play. I could smell the incense as the procession got closer—I could hear the jangle of the chains as things were being censed. I could feel the vibrations of peoples' footsteps as they were moving through the space. I became so aware of the sensory experience—the embodied experience of worship." She wonders if this might be due in part to having done collaborative piano work for so long. "When you're really in the zone, when you're in sync with other people . . . it's almost like you don't have to see them—you can feel their presence. Although I couldn't see the presider, I knew exactly where he was." "That's what we missed" while not being able to gather in person, she lamented, "that integration of the senses and that embodiment in worship. It's intangible, but it's central to what we do, and it can't be captured."

I ask her how she imagines the musician's work in parish ministry might evolve moving forward. I'm particularly interested in her thoughts on this, since she's in regular contact with those being trained for parish ministry, though mostly for ordained ministry. "I think it *will* change—that's the one thing we can count on," she asserts, going on to say, "Things that were once revolutionary are now commonplace, and things that are now commonplace will change." She also acknowledges that many musicians are experiencing cutbacks in hours and salary and will likely continue to do so—but this was true even prior to the pandemic. "I think we're going to see fewer and fewer full-time church music positions, so the challenge—if we're working with people in part-time positions—is how we can provide the education and training they need in terms of pastoral skills, teaching skills, performance skills," since these skills aren't being taught widely in university or conservatory programs. "It's a changing terrain. I do have issues with the prophets of doom and gloom who say that the Episcopal Church is dying—I don't believe that; I believe that if you have qualified, motivated, and well-trained people as leaders, you can do remarkable things and see the church grow." Does the church still need us to do this work? She thinks so: "If you are really committed to the work and have the skills you need, people are hungry for what we have to offer. With creative planning, you can create liturgies and music programs that draw people in." She sees this creativity at work in the seminary, and explains, "In working with seminarians today, there is much more emphasis on being out in the community and finding ways to move ministry beyond the walls of the church building." Is this an idea that needs musicians' attention as well? Perhaps. Marty does anticipate seeing a widening gap between large and small congregations moving into the future, saying, "I think we're going to see a divide of sorts—I think there will continue to be large Episcopal churches with large music programs, but I think we're going to see a lot of smaller churches using different and innovative models." I've been marinating on this lately as well, particularly as I consider how a cathedral lives into the unique role it plays in its diocese. How do larger parishes who may have the benefit of more financial resources and greater visibility support smaller parishes without annexing them? And what can these larger parishes learn from the ways that smaller parishes are adapting?

Conversation with Ellen Johnston

Among her roles in the service of the church—including educational initiatives, running conferences, and providing consulting services to parishes and dioceses—Ellen Johnston has served parishes as their principal musician, most recently Church of the Holy Comforter, Richmond, Virginia. Ellen is also a lifelong church musician—more or less—having started as a teenager in Camden, Arkansas. We sit down to chat, and she wonders right away if the most overlooked aspect of our vocational model is the church musician as teacher. She says, "I think by virtue of what we have to do, particularly in small and medium churches where we don't have staff singers, the teaching part may come first. . . . On a scale of 1 to 5, I'd put pastor as 1 and teacher as 1.5," with performing being a not-at-all urgent priority. I wonder if she meant teaching musicianship or teaching in the sense of Christian formation, so she clarifies, "Part of what we do falls under formation, but yes to both. There's teaching of basic musicianship skills, . . . [teaching] the congregation new hymns, . . . [and also teaching] about worship and liturgy—why we do what we do when we do it." I press her a little bit and ask her what she thought teaching reading music, fundamentals of singing, and other concrete skills had to do with the mission of the church. She believes that teaching basic musicianship to volunteer choir members is a way to equip them, to lessen their anxiety about making music in a public space so that they feel successful. Teaching them "what a phrase is, or how to listen for an interval to get from note to note, and about dynamics and why and how you make that happen," she says, will make them less anxious about making offerings of music in the church's public worship.

But this isn't just in the interest of making polished offerings in worship. "I think there's a pastoral aspect to that," she continues, using the example of a parish she once served: Upon arrival, the rector remarked that the choir was noticeably anxious and wondered if there might be a way she could address that, since this anxiety was apparent and distracting during worship services. Ellen's assessment was that their anxiety was due to not feeling successful; poor repertoire choices requiring skills they did not possess had caused them to feel inadequate, and the liturgy was suffering as a result.[5] We agree that there's certainly a pastoral element to repertoire selection—that being able to lead worship from a less anxious place benefits the whole parish: "Anxiety is contagious. If the people leading are anxious, then [worshipers] become anxious." I've seen this play out any number of times as well.

I ask Ellen if she believed being a church musician was her calling, to which she wryly responds, "God, I hope so. I've been doing it long enough. . . . I'd always

---

5. Ellen contends that every choir needs three types of literature in their folders at any given time: one piece that they "can sing with thirty minutes of rehearsal, one that requires a moderate amount of work, and one that really challenges them."

been a 'church' person," she remembers, "but it didn't 'take' until I got to the Episcopal Church."[6] Her work in Episcopal churches began at age sixteen, when her friend Victoria asked her to come sing in the church choir she was conducting at the time. Ellen fell in love with the Episcopal Church, cottoning to it quickly after having grown up in another tradition. When Victoria moved on to another parish, Ellen inherited her position, making $40 a month. It was 1967. She says, "I caught the bug then, even with four people in the choir." I ask if she remembered what about that experience was so magnetic. Maybe it was inevitable that this would happen? Ellen wonders if perhaps this inevitability had started even earlier, reaching back to when, as seventh graders, she and Victoria would go to the younger Sunday school classes to lead hymns on the piano, partially in an effort to cut Sunday school class. "We'd go and play 'This Is My Father's World' and 'I Would Be True' and 'Dare to Be Brave' . . . so maybe *that's* how I got started." Something about this feels familiar to me. I speculate out loud about how many musicians shared that experience of being pressed into service simply by virtue of having had a few piano lessons and being, well, *there*, only identifying a call much later.

I ask her who she thought she would've been without this call—what would her life have been like? What would it look like now? "Well, I would've loved to have been a professional tennis player," she says, laughing, "but I don't know what I would've done if I hadn't done this. It's shaped my life." Ellen, like many of us, has done a number of what you might call secular jobs either alongside or between her parish ministry gigs—things that would pay for the groceries as she continued serving churches. I wonder at what point she began to realize herself as a *church* musician who worked in the service of the church and not just a musician who *happened* to work in churches. Was this something she realized as it was happening, or is it only identified in hindsight? How was she formed? "I think singing in the [Centenary College] choir, "alongside a staff singer position at nearby St. Mark's Cathedral in Shreveport, Louisiana, "had a lot to do with forming me as a church musician, because I was there *every* single Sunday." She continues that singing in these two choirs formed her in the sense that she was introduced to repertoire and grew as a musician but mainly because it left time for little else. I ask if she could remember if there was a point in her work in parish ministry she could pinpoint as the beginning of a vocational identity. She reflects back to St. Peter's-by-the-Lake in Brandon, Mississippi, a church that was being planted in the early 1980s, when she happened to be living nearby. "The rector heard that I played the piano. . . . He and the senior warden asked me to come interview for the job." Was that the beginning? Life later took her north to Tupelo, Mississippi.

---

6. Ellen has not, strictly speaking, always been an avid churchgoer. She relates to me a funny childhood story about skipping church with a friend to go to the Camden Hotel downtown to eat French fries on Sunday mornings and unfortunately being spotted by her grandmother. "They came in at 'mawmaw' time—11:00 o'clock—for Sunday lunch, and there I was."

Ellen continued, saying that All Saints', a parish she served for twelve years (and one of the positions I succeeded her in) helped her further distill her identity as a church musician. She pauses for a moment when I ask her what it was about All Saints' that helped her clarify that. "I'm not really sure," she admits. "[Maybe] starting from zero," like she had at St. Peter's—"Starting from nothing." She had moved to Tupelo following her marriage to Shannon Johnston, the then-recently installed rector of All Saints', who is also a capable musician in his own right. "There were four people in the choir, singing unison hymns out of the hymnal," until Shannon encouraged them, telling them that at their best, Episcopal churches have vibrant music programs. "The next day, fourteen people showed up for choir rehearsal." I sense a theme emerging. I wonder if starting programs has been her own version of church planting. I ask Ellen, "Is this your mission?" "Maybe," she says. "I hadn't really thought of it that way, but maybe that *was* my thing: getting a program off the ground." She certainly seems to have done that over and over again.

"I had no idea what to do," she says, recalling the earliest days of the coronavirus pandemic. I wonder if it has been as profoundly disorienting for her as it has been for me. Holy Comforter is a congregation that loves to sing, she says, but "in the first days, I was in my living room sitting at my piano, just playing stuff" for services held over video conferencing platforms. Like many of us, she began to experiment with recording technology, "Frankly, there was a part of it I had a ball doing. I don't particularly want to ever do it again, but it sparked some creativity in me. I was the only one in the church, so I could record an accompaniment, then call in someone who played the flute" to record another track to cobble together, recording a few weeks ahead of time so that their services could have more substantial music. She remembers feeling like a one-person band. "There was a little bit of 'Well, this is kind of fun,'" she recollects, "a way of doing things that I couldn't have done [before COVID]." I agree with her that there was certainly a novelty in all the recording options suddenly made available and in having time to explore them since there were no in-person rehearsals to prepare for. It *was* novel at first but quickly became tedious and more than a little soul-crushing. At any rate, she embraced the technology quickly, leveraging it in the interest of helping her parish make as much music together as possible. "Frankly, now that all that's over, but we're indoors and masked, we're making less music at this point," due to restrictions on singing indoors. "This is just the season we're in now."

I ask if she thought the profession as we know it would be recognizable in fifty years. She wonders what it might mean for making music in the church if people aren't joining groups and organizations as they did in previous generations. This is a phenomenon identified only fairly recently—a shift that people who pay attention to data and trends have noted and starting stewing on. Ellen says, "I don't know what's going to happen. I think this year and a half, or however many years [we still have ahead of us] of COVID has changed the church, and I'm not sure what it's going to be changed into yet—I don't think anybody knows. I don't think we can continue to do the same thing over and over." I ask what she meant. Was it that we would have to become more versatile? "I think we're going to have to be flexible, be better pastors, and we're going to have to advocate for ourselves in a way that we haven't had to do before." She continues, "I think we need to know our value and understand that we still *do* have value." I've also felt that deeply lately—that part of my responsibility is to leave the profession in a better place than I found it, by advocating for lay employees, especially in regard to salary, benefits, and church-wide policy.

Ellen contends that part of making parishes recognize the musician's value is to advocate for music and music programs in churches by finding new ways to cross-program initiatives to integrate it into all facets of the church's life, resisting the urge to isolate ourselves in the choir room or at the organ console. She's resolute, saying that we must push "for what we value and love, keeping it in front of the congregation, vestry, and clergy. Because I'm not sure if we don't, that these programs will [flourish.]" She then offers what may be an unpopular opinion in some circles: if they must choose only one, "clergy need to think about hiring a full-time musician instead of an extra priest, but we have to show why that's important to the life and mission of the church. . . . [Making music] *is* Christian formation, and I think that we as church musicians need to be more proactive about advocating to our parish leadership that it is. Some know it already . . . but I'm not sure that all clergy understand that . . . and they're not going to absorb it by osmosis. It's part of our role as teacher, as well to teach the clergy, because we're educated so much differently than most clergy are."

Conversation with Kyle Ritter

I often joke that Kyle and I are personality twins, since we're both Myers-Briggs ISTJs and Enneagram Sixes. We also share a similarly dry, occasionally irreverent sense of humor. Maybe this was why I was so surprised that our paths are so different. Kyle has spent the better part of the last two decades as canon for music at The Cathedral of All Souls in Asheville, North Carolina. As we begin our conversation, I'm immediately reminded of what struck me about him when I first met him: he is so keenly interested in other people's lives. He has a superhuman memory, can remember details of things that I told him years ago, and always asks about my family by name. "I love being in touch with people," he says. "I love hearing people's stories—[that's] really an extraordinary thing—you learn so much about people, and your relationship with them deepens. So much of the work of church music doesn't really have to do with music. It has to do with relationships and with people." Kyle is emphatic about this. I wonder if he might be a better person to be collecting these vocation stories. He really does deeply love people.

Kyle tells me about his Indiana upbringing. He grew up in a United Methodist congregation that benefitted from an extensive music program, but what he remembers most about that time were the relationships formed between members of these groups. "I had it modeled for me from the beginning that music in the church was a ministry that involved people. I saw how it really affected people and how these groups prayed for each other. . . . There was a lot of care in how people treated each other." This is a theme that he's carried with him throughout his career and into this position at All Souls. "The pastoral side of [parish music ministry] actually thrills me," he claims. "It's the most important thing for me—being in relationship with the people who are in the choirs *and* in the pews."

I wonder if Kyle can remember when he first felt a call to this work. He says, "I've wanted to be a church musician since I was three years old—that's when my mother said I turned to her in church and said, 'I'm gonna do what [that] lady's doing over there at the organ.'" That early interest resulted in piano lessons at five and organ lessons at ten, then undergraduate and graduate degrees from Indiana University, where he encountered Marilyn Keiser and Robert Rayfield. He cites their influence as incredibly formational, still speaking of both with a sense of awe and incredulity, as though he can't believe his luck to have known them. Robert Rayfield died in 1999, but Marilyn Keiser has been an ongoing presence in Kyle's life. "She's still in my life; she's still at my elbow, moving me forward," he says. Would that we all had such devoted teachers. I wonder if, in the course of his organ performance studies, he'd ever considered another path, maybe performing or academia. Still no—he knew this was it, though he does enjoy playing occasional recitals. "It's where I saw myself, and it's where I've been," remembering that his favorite thing since early in his musical development has been playing hymns. He's not wrong—playing hymns *is* actually the best part of this work. There's something thrilling, sometimes almost overwhelming, about accompanying a room full of people singing. For me, the most electrifying part is the split second before people open their mouths to sing—when they're sucking in a belly full of air. It's like a lightning strike.

I think Kyle is a little charmed in that he's known for so long and had such a clear understanding of what he wanted to be and do, and I suggest that to him, though perhaps in different words. "It's been Holy Spirit-led; there have been too many experiences I've had in this vocation. . . . It can't be any other way," he says confidently. He pauses a beat for effect, then says, "Lord knows we're not in it for the money." We laughed. "It really has to be something that you feel like your heart is called to. Things have unfolded as though it was the way it was supposed to happen." This is a point at which our experiences diverge. As a person with higher-than-average control needs, I've always been resistant to acknowledging the work of the Holy Spirit in my life—or naming it that, at least. I'd much rather believe that everything is the result of hard work and self-determination, but I know that this is not the case.

I feel like I know his answer already, but I ask Kyle anyway to tell me about his experience navigating music ministry during the coronavirus pandemic. He admits that though signs point to improvement and though he is resolved to be a joyful and stable presence in his ministry, there have been nights where he has lain awake at all hours wondering what might happen, hearing an internal monologue that might as well be my own: *Am I going to be able to stay the course? Is the church going to stay the course? Will the church be recognizable to us in the future?* I had an inkling of something before the pandemic that has crystallized during it: the church is no longer strictly a Sunday morning endeavor. Are physical and temporal proximity even necessary anymore? I think the church at large has been pondering this for quite some time, but musicians have been assuming that it won't have an effect on our work. Is that still a safe assumption? "We have to be outside the doors because it's not a given anymore that people are going to come *to* church. I think now that a very active member will come once a month," he notes, "except for the choir—they seem to be the people who are really invested in it." This rings true—by its very nature, what we do requires gathering frequently, regularly, and in the same space. But can we assume that the midweek rehearsal and Sunday obligation will continue to be the norm? He continues, "It's not a given anymore that people will walk in the door and know the Lord's Prayer or know what we're about; they're going to come to a community because it feeds them, not because they were raised in it. So how do we keep the best parts of our tradition alive . . . while also imagining new possibilities?"

Looking past the pandemic, even past his own retirement, which is still a bit down the road, I ask Kyle if he can imagine this profession being any different than it is now. "[I'm grateful for] the education I received thirty years ago, but I've had to think bigger. . . . I'm having to be more open," he says. "Our role is not to be a museum, our role is to be about vital and honest liturgy." He cites shifting trends in choral music and congregational song as evidence that church musicians are more flexible than we may think: "Look at *The Hymnal 1982.* Look how visionary that was and how it incorporated new material," citing the wildly progressive (for the time) range of genres that were represented. "We have to pray into the future and be open to the future, or there isn't going to be a vocation," he insists. "I don't think the Holy Spirit is ever going to give up on the church—that as long as people are worshiping God—and music is a key element of that—the profession is going to exist. I have every confidence that our work as corporate music-makers will thrive, but what that looks like, I don't know, really. The church is going to have to go through a renaissance, and maybe it's the next generation that just says to the church 'This is important to us.'" (Church, consider yourselves told.)

"I have felt great joy in this work. It's all I've ever wanted to do. It's been a life-giving thing and *still* brings me great joy," even in a difficult season. "It's innately in my being; inspiring people's worship doesn't get any better." "When it works," he begins, and I finish the thought before he can, "it's totally magical." He says, "It happens in people's funerals, it happens on Sunday mornings, it happens when we gather at choir retreats—these magical moments that you can't imagine your life without."

Conversation with Robert McCormick

Robert McCormick is a fellow native of the Deep South, any discernible accent he once may have had tempered by living away from Georgia for some time now. I'd forgotten this fact about him until we sat down to talk and he pointed the iPad camera at the thoroughly unimpressed cocker spaniel next to him on the sofa. Robert encouraged him, "Beau, say hi to Miss Jessica." (I will always talk to a dog.) "Miss [*first name*]" is a distinctly Southern appellation that has nothing to do with age or marital status and is what my youngest choristers usually call me, so I find this terribly sweet and endearing. Robert is the organist and choirmaster at St. Mark's, Locust Street in Philadelphia, an historically Anglo-Catholic parish planted just steps away from the Curtis Institute of Music.

I ask Robert to remind me about his educational background, in the interest of documentation. He holds an undergraduate degree in organ from Westminster Choir College and confesses that, due to not having an advanced degree, he has at times felt lowly among other professional musicians. I'm terribly surprised by this—not that he doesn't have an advanced degree, but that he's ever felt insecure about that. Robert is a tremendously gifted musician. "My story is kind of unusual. . . . I essentially got a really lucky break . . . because in my senior year [at Westminster Choir College] the position at St. Mary the Virgin in New York was open." It wound up being his first position after graduation. This was a parish that had recently experienced some turbulence following abrupt staff changes. He began his tenure figuring out parish ministry as he went and continuing to study organ and improvisation with McNeil Robinson, a celebrated teacher who had also served churches in the New York area. As a twenty-two-year-old newly minted graduate, he remembers thinking, "If this job doesn't work out, I'm young, it's not going to ruin my career, I'll just go back to school. . . . I made it my business to read a lot of professional material on all sorts of things—church music, performance practice, choral music—to try to educate myself alongside learning on the job."

I'm aware the parish Robert serves now is accustomed to very fine music offered with a great deal of artistic merit and technical excellence, and he's clear about what excellence and beauty have to do with the prayer of the church. "The goal is to glorify God and to enable the prayers of God's people," he declares. I've encountered a school of thought in some corners of the church that pursuing excellence in the execution in the public worship of the church is somehow incongruous with the church's mission. I don't share this opinion at all. What musicians produce within the context of a liturgy is the result of time spent in community devoting energy to a common goal with the intention of magnifying the praises of the assembly. If anything, excellence (and the pursuit thereof) makes all the more apparent the work of the Holy Spirit in our midst. But Robert is also aware of how deeply fallible musicians are, which is a comfort to me. He references one of the Thirty-Nine Articles—the one that says, in effect, that a priest's "unworthiness" doesn't affect the efficacy of the sacraments. "The challenge is living with being human," he says, "having egos and insecurities, doubts and anxieties that stand in the way. We as musicians . . . just by being faithful and doing our job . . . move [the listener] to deeper prayer." I hope to remember this conversation the next time I stumble through some Bach chorale prelude on a Sunday morning without the benefit of a good night's sleep or a second cup of coffee.

We chat more about his work at St. Mark's, and I ask what functions he saw himself fulfilling in the course of his ministry. "I guess it depends on what I'm doing at any given time," he begins. "I'm not a pastor in a sacramental sense, of course, but I do see myself in a pastoral role" to those participating in the music ministry at St. Mark's, in addition to having a responsibility to the entire parish. He muses on caring for the parish as a whole, saying, "I think about how the act of music-making in a parish *has* to be pastoral, [and] the choices I make for the parish are different than they would be in another parish," bringing up an important element—that all music-making in the church is deeply contextual. I note that all the parishes Robert has served are representative of worship in an Anglo-Catholic tradition. He confirms this and is careful to articulate that "these parishes have many similarities, but there are still distinct differences" and pastoral considerations that inform his ministry. He also sees himself as a teacher, particularly to the children participating in his chorister programs. "I sometimes think that if I knew then what I know now, I would've gotten a double degree in music education," he says, maybe just a little wistfully.

I ask him the big question: Does he think this is God's will for his life? He's certain. "I've felt that way for a long time; I knew as a child that this is what I wanted to do. I had a very clear sense of vocation." Robert tells me a sweetly funny story about when, as a young child, he began to show interest and promise in music. His practical investment banker grandfather expressed concern to his mother that Robert wouldn't be able to make a living. His mother mentioned this to him, and Robert confidently replied, "Mom, don't you think that if God wants me to do this, he'll make sure I'll be well taken care of?" I think that maybe his understanding of how all this works has evolved a bit, but I wonder, Has he ever doubted this calling? "In a certain sense, I never seriously doubt the vocation, but sometimes I wonder what it would be like to have a job I could leave at 5:00 p.m., because I've never known what that feels like." Robert insists that he doesn't have any other marketable skills. "I have a hard time imagining myself doing anything else, really."

Robert grew up in a large United Methodist congregation in Macon, Georgia, and cites participating in music programs there as being central to his formation as a church musician. These are happy memories for him. "It's where I learned to love Jesus," he says. His first mentor, Camille Bishop, was the musician there, who also gave him his first piano and organ lessons. Robert remembers thinking, "I want to be like her; I want to do what she does." He says, "I couldn't have asked for a better model." He's clearly still very fond of her. He does, however, recall that in college, after he began to worship in the Anglican tradition, he wondered if he wouldn't have been better off having grown up as a chorister in an Episcopal church or attending the St. Thomas Choir School. I've often had these thoughts, as well—what if I had grown up in a larger city? What if I'd taken organ more seriously in college? But now, having the benefit of an adult perspective, Robert realizes that he wouldn't change anything about this time.

We look into the future a little bit: What will the profession look like moving forward? Robert does mention concern about numerical decline, particularly following the coronavirus pandemic. He wonders if, in the future, musicians will be able to earn a living, or even a portion of their living, from a church position. "There's a risk for a young person who is entering the profession," he thinks, but believes that what we do is needed now more than ever. We commiserate further about the pandemic, both being people who are prone to anxiety if we can't control a certain percentage of the variables in our lives. He says, "Like many, I suffer from the illusion that I control a lot more than is actually true, because each of us actually controls very little." He's had to learn to be flexible and gracious with himself lately. "Each day I try to remind myself that I can only be faithful in what I've been given that day. I can only do the best I can."

Conversation with Dr. Margaret Harper

Dr. Margaret Harper—Meg—was raised in the Philippines from the age of six until she left for Wheaton College, the daughter of evangelical seminary professors called to work in the mission field. Her first exposure to church music in the Episcopal tradition was at Lake Delaware Boys' Camp in upstate New York, which sounds like a magical place, with a daily sung High Mass at 6:30 a.m., along with weekly evensongs. Meg reports that wrangling a boychoir every morning was not for the faint of heart. I can't imagine, but it does occur to me that this might be excellent training for parish ministry. She's now the associate director of music and organist at St. Michael and All Angels Episcopal Church in Dallas, Texas.

Meg is deeply invested in teaching opportunities at St. Michael's, where she's developed a series of modular classes geared toward the adult nonmusician, with the goal of raising the level of music literacy in the parish. She gets enthusiastic in a mad scientist sort of way when I ask her to reflect on what role music literacy plays in the life of the average churchgoer. "It has *everything* to do with it," she insists. Her reasoning is that it's based in evolutionary science. I am momentarily confused. Evolution? "We like to be able to understand the world," she says, continuing, "because it makes evolutionary sense. . . . You have to think about people as being a product of what allows them to thrive." This is not an aspect I'd ever considered, but her enthusiasm is compelling. She also understands that musical education promotes biblical literacy, since so many of the texts we sing are direct quotations from scripture. This does resonate—I don't think of myself as a person who has a particularly high degree of biblical literacy, but what I *do* know is mostly a byproduct of choral singing. Aside from preaching, in her estimation, "music is the most communicative piece" of the liturgy. "Sundays are packed with meaning. [We're sent] out in the world to do things, to live in the world and therefore anything we can do to deepen people's [worship] experience . . . enhances the mission of the church." In addition to this missional element, she seems to be articulating a pastoral one too, so I ask her how *hearing* music in the liturgy might have an effect on the average person. Meg still has her mad scientist hat on and offers a theory: both music and human thought patterns exist in time and happen in a linear fashion. The music that we hear and the thoughts we form are by nature sequential—one leads to the next. This lends itself to mindful, contemplative engagement, Meg reasons. "You are stopping [your] life to do this one thing: to sit and listen . . . and part of the beauty of what allows it to be so communicative and have so much teaching power is that it happens in time, so you have to engage with it in time." She's deeply invested in her role as an educator, emphasizing, "Building a congregational culture where engaging with music on a deep level is just what we do."

Meg doesn't know that she's experienced a sense of call in the same way many others describe—there was no moment when she thought, *Aha! This is it!* In fact, she actively avoided it, admitting, "I explicitly did not want to be a church musician." She grew up in a family that valued music and was exposed to plenty of it from an early age but can't recall hearing any remarkable music in a liturgical context as a child in the Philippine mission field. She came back to the United States for college and, being a clarinetist, briefly considered a path that would lead to an orchestral career. "In the mill of the university, when teachers get a great student, they want to mold them into themselves. Part of this is just how we are as humans. I do this too," Meg says, "when I see a fantastic chorister who's really geeky, and I think, 'Ooh, she could be an organist!'" Meg remembered that at Eastman, a high level of contact with exceptional teachers made her think that perhaps teaching should be her goal. "This is what happens when you get to university—the person you're modeling yourself after is a university professor." She continues, "It's easy for a lot of people to envision themselves doing that. So I had this plan for when I was done at Eastman. . . . I applied for *all* the university jobs that were open," thinking in the back of her mind that she'd apply for church jobs too, just as a backup plan. "I'm going to work in a church for maybe four years, get some experience, and be more marketable . . . and *then* I'm going to switch over," she remembers thinking. "Church work was supposed to be just a temporary thing." I articulate something to Meg that I'd only realized in that moment and about which I feel more than slightly ashamed: as a younger musician, I remember feeling that working for the church was a consolation prize. To be clear, none of my teachers ever said this or implied it. In fact, what they modeled to me was quite the opposite. My earliest piano teachers, all highly trained and competent, had church gigs on the weekends. I simply suffered from a lack of exposure. I accompanied services through most of my teenage years at a very small church plant and only occasionally wound up at the Episcopal church across town. There *was* good music happening there, but I was determined in my apathy. If you're trained in the traditional sense—private study, conservatory or university, then more conservatory or university—the goal *is* to do what your teachers have done, following that arc until you, too, are teaching in a conservatory or a university with a calendar full of recital engagements.

Meg took her first job following graduate school at St. John's, Portsmouth, New Hampshire, and was surprised to discover that it was so rewarding. "It's actually incredibly fulfilling work, and I just didn't see that coming," she remembers. She leaned into her work and thrived. Even then, there were surprises. She tells me about the first time a choir member came to her with a pastoral care issue. "It had not occurred to me that this would be a part of my job," she acknowledges. "To provide some kind of spiritual support and presence for them . . . at the time I felt like I was wasting my work hours; I felt like I should be doing something 'real' with my time, but then it happened more and more, and I came to appreciate that role . . . but I felt unworthy of being trusted in that way." "My sole merit," she remembers thinking, "was that I was in the job." I think perhaps she was underestimating herself. Portsmouth is a bedroom community to Boston, home to wealthy financiers and executive types but also with a number of people living at or below the poverty line. This is where Meg established the St. John's Choir School, which recruited from the most at-risk neighborhoods. She remembers that this was particularly eye-opening for that congregation, because it put them in touch with a population that they might not have encountered elsewhere.

"I think the pastoral nature of a church musician's role is a little bit deeper and more meaningful" as a result of the coronavirus pandemic, Meg muses. We talk about our shared resistance to vulnerability and lack of control but acknowledge that we are grateful for the ways the professional community has become a little smaller, a little more connected and dependent on one another as we've all had to reconfigure our work. She wonders if a positive byproduct of the pandemic is this sharing of knowledge and resources. "I think in music we can get a bit territorial," she admits, thinking about the ways musicians are prone to compare ourselves to one another, "but I think it's so important to recognize that we build culture together and that when *your* program that's similar to mine succeeds, it changes culture."

Conversation with Dr. Stephan Griffin

Dr. Stephan Griffin has had a remarkable performing career for someone so young. At the time of this writing, he's in his early thirties, has an impressive academic résumé that includes degrees from the University of Texas ("with Gerre and Judy," he says, warmly) and Boston University, and has an enviable list of performing credits and reviews. He's currently leading a large music program at All Saints Parish in Brookline, Massachusetts, an affluent town in the Boston metropolitan sprawl. "It's a one-man show, for the first time in fifty years," he says a little dryly, making me wonder if he, too, is feeling a little over-tapped and overextended these days. He praises the clergy he's worked with, reflecting on what has contributed to the success of those relationships. "Getting that relationship off on the right foot from day one has been the best piece of advice I got before being launched into church music," he says, remembering being told, "When you take that interview, *know* who you're going to be working for." This piece of advice has served him well.

I ask him what, if anything, he would add to the pastor-teacher-performer roles.

"The first thing that I always add to it is just a giant comma," he begins, adding that he would finish that statement with, "at the discretion of your rector. . . . I think it was fine to make a blanket statement [at the time Wyton made it] that we should be [pastors], but I think that every job is going to be different in terms of how pastoral we get and what the expectations of the job are, and being sure that we don't cross lines that we aren't trained [to cross], or that [our supervising clergy] don't want us to cross." This is an important reminder. He's aware that he hasn't had much in the way of formal training in the pastoral care arena but knows that in his context, it begins with at least "reading a rehearsal room and seeing . . . where everyone is" spiritually and emotionally, acknowledging that "it's a little bit different when I have staff singers and section leaders who may not be members of the church but [who are] looking for a church community. . . . I think I ride that line between boss and pastoral counsel" with them, he says.

"I've spent a lot of time in the teaching arena" throughout the course of parish ministry, Stephan offers; it sounds like he has lots of energy around this role. "In terms of teaching, Boston is overly academic most of the time; a lot of the volunteers come in asking questions," indicating a general propensity for nerding out over minutiae and trivia. "I understand Byrd was Catholic, but his relationship with the monarchy . . ." he begins, trailing off in a gentle and loving impression of an enthusiastic chorister. Of performing, he says that he will sometimes flippantly say, "at the top of the show," in a preservice rehearsal, but at the same time, he makes a concerted effort to impress upon his singers that what they are doing is *not* a performance, though it certainly shares some of the same qualities. "I really make sure that the understanding is that we aren't here to put on a show, and I try to keep [the word] *performance* . . . out of the rehearsal room, while maintaining performance-quality work." I appreciate this subtle distinction he makes and make a note to remember it for my own use.

I ask Stephan if he sees the role of the musician in parish ministry shifting over the next generation or so. He's thoughtful for a moment, then says, "I think it's evolving—parish staffs in general are evolving." He also acknowledges that the role of church in society is shifting as well. "For me, most of my experience is in the northeast, so it's a different church culture. . . . Not a lot of people go to church," he says. This is markedly less true here in the Bible Belt, where it's not uncommon for a total stranger to ask you where you attend church. "That said," he continues, "I think staff positions are constantly evolving to become combined, because you've got to steer this big ship with fewer and fewer people," citing in particular reduced budgets and volunteer fatigue. This often results in the church musician, likely bivocational and cobbling together a full-time salary by working a number of part-time jobs, a few more hours in exchange for, say, clerical work or some other administrative function. He gives an example, saying, "I'm thinking of all the people who have become musician *and* tech verger," since technology has come to play such a large part in many of our weekly services. I wonder how a multitasking musician keeps all the plates spinning while honoring a call to serve primarily through making music. How do you acknowledge your own limitations and capacity, while maintaining collegial relationships with your supervising clergy? Stephan acknowledges this dynamic, saying, "They can't do it alone, we can't do it alone, and we've got to find some balance and very clear expectation of what's reasonable and equitable."

By this point, I've participated in enough of these conversations to have noticed the surprisingly wide variety of responses to my next question: Do you feel called to this work? He laughs. "When I read that question," he says, still laughing, "I thought, *I just need to walk away for a second*," perhaps a little dazed by that idea. "So, my honest answer is yes," inflecting upwards as though it's more of a question than a statement. "I feel called to serve — in what capacity I serve, I think for me personally, remains open. . . . I am open to the movement of the Holy Spirit. Do I feel called to be where I am at this point in time? Absolutely, yes. Will I be called here in ten years? I have no idea. . . . I remember having the moment," sometime in college or graduate school, he remembers, "of, 'I will go if you send me.' I'm flexible with where God moves me," Stephan says, recognizing that he'll likely always be called to serve the church in *some* way. "[I'm] not going to get out of being a musician," he realizes, conceding that he may, further down the road, be called to serve the church in a different capacity. He's piqued my interest in something, and I say that I want to back up a little bit, telling him he's free not to answer the question that follows, since I recognize the topic seems to give him a little heartburn. "You say that where God is calling you now might change in a few years. Are you considering a call to ordained ministry?" He's laughing again. Hard. "I don't know that I hear a call to ordained ministry. It's been brought up in the past, and I'm not actively listening for it. . . . I won't rule it out if it comes . . . but please don't let it come. I feel called to be a church musician . . . but at the same time, I don't know that [I'll feel the same] in twenty years." Stephan grew up Methodist, "low-church, in the Black church," as the son of a minister, he tells me. "When the Holy Ghost hits," he says, "I think it's hard to fight off. You can try, but it will trouble your spirit until you go where God is sending you."

He doesn't know that there was a single moment that led to realizing that he was on the path to parish ministry. "I think it started out as [being] the kid in church who could play the organ . . . and you have adults trying to help shape you and pour into you as much wisdom as possible . . . having people constantly say things like, 'Well, there's anointing on your life—*you* don't quite see it yet.'" Stephan was thinking he'd rather be playing football. He later realized, as a student singing in the Marsh Chapel choir at Boston University, that he felt fulfilled by this work. "It was being in worship with other people, making music, and seeing the impact" that it has on people's lives, he recalls. "So that was the *first* lightbulb." His studies later took him to graduate school to study sacred music, where he saw the Hancocks model career paths that seemed appealing to him. He remembers taking his first church job out of a sense of duty—that it just seemed like the right thing to do—but realizing that once he was in it, he found himself "in the deep end, completely unprepared" for the pastoral aspects of this ministry. He was surprised what his singers would bring into rehearsal—big feelings, emotions, prayer requests. I remember feeling the same way in one of my early church appointments—a little overwhelmed by other people's needs. He recalls that the most valuable thing at that time was having a supportive rector sit him down and give solid, practical advice on how to navigate the spiritual care of a group of people. After a few years, he realized that this *was* what he was called to do, witnessing the "impact that music ministry [had] on the community, on me, and individual choir members," giving the example of a chorister with debilitating social anxiety blossoming as a result of participation in a youth choir. Stephan recalls thinking, *Oh, this is why we do this.* "Okay, fine, I get it. I'm going," he acquiesced to the universe. "This is what I'll do."

"I've learned new skills," Stephan says, reflecting on the pandemic. This was followed by a pause. "Do I think there is redemption? Yes." This was followed by an even bigger pause. "And a needed and somewhat painful wakeup call for a lot of congregations to assess their values . . . and what will and can sustain them," continuing by saying that what the congregation he currently serves has missed most during this wilderness time was being formed by corporate worship. "We missed being fed during worship. All these other [outreach] activities are nice . . . but we really miss *this* . . . I think for us to realize . . . how people spend money, how they use their platform to preach the gospel . . . has been an awakening. People are at home with options to go elsewhere at the click of a button. I'm a firm believer that the 'Word of God will not return void,'" he says, quoting Isaiah, "but [the church had] better sit down and do some discerning," Stephan says. "It can't be about chasing numbers. . . . I think the pandemic has given us time and space to reevaluate those things," he says thoughtfully, and "see what can, should, and will survive."

Conversation with Janet Yieh

Janet and I get together via Zoom on an afternoon that is sunny in both Jackson and New York City. Janet is the associate organist and director of the St. Paul's Chapel Choir at Trinity Church, Wall Street. She grew up in what might be described as a "churchy" family on the campus of Virginia Theological Seminary, where her father is a New Testament Professor and where Ray Glover[7] was a childhood neighbor. Somehow it seems inevitable that this would be her calling, growing up in such an orbit of influence.

We begin our conversation talking about vocation, and she reflects on meeting up recently with high school friends in Brooklyn, with whom a similar conversation occurred. She remembers that one friend insisted that a job is just a job, what you do from 9:00 to 5:00 every day, and that your *real* life is what happens outside of that. She's not so sure, and neither am I—when we leave the church for the day, are we not still attentive to the parish? I ask if she feels like the same person at home and work. She pauses, then responds, "I think I always have a part of my brain ruminating on what hymns would be best for the next Sunday. I can't help it." I'm relieved to learn that she, too, has hymnals strewn on her dining room table. Any boundary between work and home seems porous at best right now, especially after a year of working at home. I wonder out loud if folks who work at Starbucks carry their work around with them, if they're the same person at work and at home. "You'd be really bad at spelling names *all* the time," she says, with a little humorous irony, then continues more thoughtfully, "but I'm *not* just clocking in and clocking out; that's part of what I love."

Janet tells me about her work at Trinity and St. Paul's Chapel, where she conducts a volunteer adult choir, among myriad other duties. "Perhaps 90 percent of being the director of a parish-based choir is pastoral . . . the other 10 percent is emails," she jokes. I can confirm this. "But at its heart, it's about creating community." She goes on, elaborating, "I think a lot of what I see as a church musician's

---

7. Ray was, among other things, a cofounder of the Association of Anglican Musicians, professor of church music at Virginia Theological Seminary, and the general editor of *The Hymnal 1982*.

. . . calling comes back to this idea of community and relationships. As much as I love playing the organ in a dark room, I found myself loving the aspects of music-making with other people . . . working with choirs and congregations, teaching kids and choristers. That's something that I find so fulfilling." She shares a tender story about one of her adult choristers at St. Paul's, who joined the choir following a particularly tragic and life-altering event. Although the family weren't particularly regular churchgoers, this chorister felt so loved and supported by the church community in her time of need that lending her voice to the choir seemed like a way she could repay that favor. "To me, that's a big part of what we do," Janet says, providing the space and opportunity "for whatever reason God brings people to want to come and sing on a Thursday night."

Janet is a Juilliard and Yale graduate and is mindful of the role mentors have played in her life in addition to her formal study. "I do think what formed me as a church musician really has a lot to do with the people who were my mentors early on, the people who encouraged me to follow this road," counting Ray Glover among that number. She reflects on his influence—particularly the ways in which he created opportunities for her. "Looking back, I was seven years old, and he would always have me come and play the piano for preludes" for the seminary community's daily offices. She also recalls discovering his habit of early morning practice, saying, "We would go [to the chapel] at 7:00 a.m., and he would be practicing—someone who had [done this] for his entire life. There was something clearly important and serious about what he was doing and what he was preparing to do for everyone else."

When thinking about these mentors, Janet articulated a trend of which I'd only been vaguely aware and had certainly not yet considered the implications it may have for me: in our parents' generation, it was not uncommon for a recent college graduate to take a position and stay with that same company for their whole career, moving up through the ranks until reaching upper management. In our own field, it has not been uncommon for a musician to graduate from school, take a position in a parish, and stay in it for decades. That may be the only parish that musician ever serves. These are the musicians who are now reaching retirement age and are being succeeded by those who seem much less prone to so long a tenure. The anticipated employment arc now seems to be something like this: finish training—which may or may not include university or conservatory study, take a job, then move into increasingly prominent positions every five to seven years. What does this mean for how we do our work? This gives me pause.

I gingerly broach the coronavirus subject, realizing that she is in an area where its effects have been especially widespread and ruthless. "The last eighteen months have been a string of daily small fires and crises. . . . It affected every single parishioner; everyone knew more than one person who died," she shares. Recalling Easter 2020, she says, "I was in a car, headed toward Trinity on this gorgeous Easter Day, and I looked out the window and saw an ambulance and two paramedics pulling a stretcher out," heading into a nearby hotel temporarily repurposed into a hospital. That scene made her wonder if *her* work mattered, reflecting, "I'm not a doctor, I'm not a chaplain, I'm not an essential worker." I get this deeply. I remember that not long before the pandemic, I was asked to play for a funeral about an hour away in a rural mission church with a small electric keyboard—no organ, no piano. It would require missing a staff meeting at the cathedral, so I asked the dean for permission. She replied, saying, "Do what you need to do." This wasn't a flippant remark but sincere, and it has stayed with me. Go do what needs to be done. Is this work necessary? If so, to whom?

One of the ways I've gotten to know Janet is through her advocacy of women composers. She and her friend Carolyn Craig have begun a number of initiatives. She says, "We realized we'd gone through a lot of years of excellent musical training while rarely, if ever, playing music by female composers, or for that matter, composers of color, so I felt like every time I wanted to find something, I was going back to square one." She shares that in the course of this work, they've debunked two myths: that there's simply not a lot of music composed by women, and that what does exist is not of substance. I wonder out loud about what the church's obligation is in supporting women composers and composers of color. She thinks about it briefly and says, "I think we are defining what it means to be an Episcopal church. . . . I think many of us . . . have a really deep love and appreciation for the Anglican tradition, and all that five hundred years has brought to us, and that's absolutely the bedrock of what we do. [But for the] American Episcopal tradition to reflect those who are in our pews, congregations, and choirs . . . that helps us glorify God in a more complete way."

Conversation with Daniel Jones

Daniel is the music intern—the Slater Fellow in Church Music, if we're being fussy about it—at St. Andrew's Cathedral in Jackson, Mississippi, where I serve as organist and choirmaster. He came to us to see whether he might like to pursue a career as a church musician after completing an undergraduate degree in music at one of the local universities. To the best of my understanding, a career in church music wasn't something he was deeply considering at the time, but he'd had some organ lessons, after being drawn to it by what he called a "mysterious allure." He had shown some aptitude and conveniently wasn't busy on Sundays. Daniel is in his early twenties and has a better-than-average theological vocabulary from growing up in an evangelical tradition. He has just recently discovered alternate harmonizations and Bruce Neswick's *Tomter* and seems to be enjoying himself thoroughly. Daniel is quietly intense, very deliberate, and thoughtful in speaking. He has a contemplative way about him; I think there's a little bit of a mystic streak forming. We speak on a Sunday afternoon after lunch, loitering at a table in the Thai restaurant where we ate following that morning's services.

I remember that Daniel began his internship at the beginning of the coronavirus-induced shutdowns. I couldn't promise him anything at first—I didn't know whether he'd even get to conduct or play services, or only be able to join our weekly choir gatherings via Zoom. I briefly explain Alec Wyton's formula. He absorbs that and reflects on his time so far, furrowing his brow a little bit and fidgeting with the buttons on his shirt. I think he's somehow intuited the role of music-making as a mode of pastoral care, even if he doesn't yet have that vocabulary. "Something I've noticed . . . ," he begins, "It was really evident to me," he continues, haltingly, "how much [the choir was] struggling without music. They were missing making music in a corporate sense." This is true—they were. In the earliest days of the pandemic, we would gather under an outside portico, masked and distanced, to sing hymns after church. It was the only communal music-making we could do here at the time and the best we could manage under the circumstances. He goes on, "To me, *if* there's a performative aspect, it's easy to say that that should be in service to God . . . but I like to think that [by virtue of] having this skill set that maybe God *likes* to listen to music? Maybe God likes interacting with artistic things like we do?" These statements all come out of his mouth as questions. "But I'm not sure how to balance all of it," he admits, recalling the original prompt.

What follows surprises me a bit. I ask Daniel, who is typically reserved, if he thought he might be called to this work—whether this might be God's will for his life. "May I be snarky?" I shrug. I didn't know you were supposed to ask permission. "I'm not really good at reading God's mind," he says wryly. This wasn't quite what I expected to hear from this evangelical-reared Gen Z person in the Deep South. He continues, "As a young person, you confront this sort of question pretty early on in our society—in high school, and then you have to go to college and know what you want to do. Purpose is a prevailing question in my life. . . . It has been for a long time." This is clearly something he's spent a lot of time with. "I grew up praying and asking for God's will, asking God to show [me what God wants me to do.] I know I'm young, but I've been doing that for years and have never reached any definitive conclusions. . . . God doesn't need to micromanage my life," he says, laughing. I like snarky Daniel. He goes on, "I think at this point, I can ask, 'What do I *want* to do, what do I *like* doing, what is something I can do *well* in service to God? I certainly think church music is something I *want* to do." I can affirm that he also seems to be able to do it well. I resist the urge to quote Frederick Buechner at him but make a note to buy him a copy of *Wishful Thinking*.[8]

Daniel has demonstrated a lot of curiosity about worship in the Anglican tradition, and we talk about his entry. "I think the pandemic allowed me to enter

---

8. "The place God calls you to is the place where your deep gladness and the world's deep hunger meet." Frederick Buechner, *Wishful Thinking: A Theological ABC* (New York: Harper & Row, 1973), 95.

slowly, so it wasn't so overwhelming," he recollects, remembering pared-down services in the early days of restriction. "Having the opportunity and the space to lose things that were no longer useful to me," as he begins to engage more deeply, "and to find things that were." I press him on that, asking if he can identify what it is he finds compelling. "I think I was searching for something like this—and a friend pointed something out that I thought was valuable. . . . She said that something *she* found valuable about the liturgy was the way it was about the Eucharist and felt more centered on Christ. In that respect, outside of the liturgy's beauty and deep meaning and tradition . . . there's something about the liturgy that takes me outside of myself, and I can just appreciate the mystery and wonder of God." He pauses for several seconds, opening his mouth a few times to say something and stopping. He's looking out the window behind me, and I can see the thought gelling in his eyes. "I always think about the hundreds of years that Christians have been doing all of this; [I think the] prayerbook traditions are really conscious of this connection we have with Christians across [and] through history, and especially in these pieces [of music] that have been passed down. But then there's also room for creativity and to really explore deeply—things that are 'good and true,' as the scriptures say." I ask if it's *just* the ritual aspect of it, or if there's something else. He says, "I think some of it is that these words that we use are deep and meaningful and written by people who think carefully about these things . . . but it's not just ritual for ritual's sake." I can tell his vocabulary hasn't quite yet caught up with his experience here, but he's getting warmer and warmer. "Do you think it's beautiful?" I ask. "Do you think beauty is pleasing to God?" He replies without hesitation, "Of course. I certainly do." He goes on, "Creation is beautiful, and that tells us something about God." He'd mentioned earlier that if he weren't a musician, he thinks he would've made a good philosopher, and I believe this. "God didn't have to make this creation beautiful, but they have. There are things that are beautiful for no other reason than they are. That tells us God values [beauty.]" We chat about human creativity, and I lead him a little bit, asking him if creating in community is important—why is it important that we make music *together*? He looks thoughtful for a moment, then muses, "Humans are communal by nature, and there's the whole community as the 'body of Christ' aspect of it. . . . If we try to do things by ourselves, then it's like a body with no arms and no legs. . . . It's incomplete when we're alone; we're made *together* in God's image . . . it requires community." This was a component of *imago Dei* with which I'd never really tangled—that it could be about something more than recognizing God in another individual. Where I've heard it used most often is as a part of admonitions to be kind to even those parishioners whose behavior can be somewhat less than ideal. It reminds me of something an alto in one of our choirs said on one of the first occasions we were allowed to sing again in (small, distanced, and masked) groups: "Finally. I feel like I'm back in my own body again," she sighed, with no small amount of relief.

I then ask him the question I dreaded at his age, and still dread now, "What's next for you?" I hope that what follows wasn't a response formulated in the interest of pleasing me. He thinks for a moment and says, "I think I'd like to go to seminary, not just for musical education, but for liturgical education. I feel like I'm only ever going to have a superficial understanding of the work—the liturgy and the things I'm participating in." I think Daniel is pursuing spiritual meaning through music in a deeply intentional way—in a way that I certainly didn't at his age. "I want to properly understand all this," he says, finishing his thought.

Conclusion

So back to my Abbott and Costello routine: Have our *what* and *how* changed? I believe that at its core, our *what* is holding up: we still make music to the glory of God in community and in the service of the church's worship. Alec Wyton's pastor-teacher-performer taxonomy is still accurate and useful, but we're living into those roles differently than we did a generation ago. Our *how* is changing along with the church. I'm not sure these conversations can be tied together neatly, but here are some things I've noticed that bear further consideration:

What does the church need and what do musicians have to give? The church needs musicians to lean more heavily into the teaching role—not only to disseminate musical knowledge, but to be about the business of Christian formation in our parishes. There are other modes of teaching as well. I don't think it's at all inaccurate to consider ourselves preachers, though we rarely do it from pulpits. I'm not going to make a tortured joke here, but we preach to our choirs when we stand in front of them in rehearsal, and we preach to congregations through our interpretation of scripture via hymnody and other music. Teaching also includes mentoring. A thread weaving its way through most of the above conversations is the presence of a mentor in addition to the musician's formal training. This is a person who has taught a younger musician by modeling, but more importantly, is someone who has shared platforms *with* them and created opportunities *for* them. Teaching also includes advocacy—not just for ourselves in our own contexts, but for the profession as a whole. Not long after beginning a new position, I once overheard a parishioner say to his spouse, "Hey, that's the new piano player." I resisted the urge to correct him in the interest of self-preservation, but was internally incensed. *Doesn't he know that I do more than that?* Well, no, he probably didn't. I am not suggesting we all overfunction to the point of burnout, but I think it's time to reconsider how we advocate for ourselves in the church. I think public relations people call this *branding*. We're not *just* anything. We need to tell people what we do and why it matters.

The church needs her musicians to be flexible. The construct of church being a primarily Sunday morning enterprise is being challenged and is changing the way people participate in the life of the church. This includes music-making.

While I would anticipate (and certainly hope) that our Sunday mornings are always filled with music made beautifully and offered to the glory of God, how must that vision expand? The church needs us to think of this work as missional, and we must not let the risk of failure deter us from developing new programs and trying new ways of making music in community. (We will all fail at something at some point. Fail spectacularly, then tell the rest of us what you learned from it.) Flexibility necessarily will require letting go of what no longer serves us well and will also require a certain amount of graciousness. To be clear, I am not suggesting that we no longer pursue excellence in music-making or let liturgy suffer in the interest of chasing needless innovation or eclecticism. What I *am* suggesting is that we shed unhealthy patterns—rigidity, territorial behavior, clinging to ways that, though comfortable, are toxic. I believe the center of sensibility will hold, even as we begin to explore new ways of going about our work.

The church needs us to "claim the high calling"[9] and acknowledge the Holy Spirit's work in our lives, however that call became apparent—whether discerned in childhood or actively avoided until it could be no longer. Articulating the Holy Spirit's work in my own life is often challenging, because I've so often heard the Holy Spirit invoked as some sort of good luck charm, cited for her aid in finding a parking spot or for the favor shown to a particular football team. The Holy Spirit is active in our lives and in all sorts of ways, but I think that perhaps her intentions are more cosmic than mundane. Claiming this calling is necessary, if for no other reason than to model for the church and the world that vocation is not synonymous with ordination. If we model that we understand this work to be a calling by being public about that and fully living into it, perhaps we will empower other laypeople to do the same.

One of the privileges of cathedral ministry is that we often get to host ordinations. By this point, I've heard a lot of ordination sermons, always well-crafted and beautifully preached. Most of these sermons include a mix of thoughtful scriptural explication and practical, pragmatic advice. But the best of these sermons include a charge to the ordinands—imperative instruction given to these new clergy from one with the benefit of wisdom and experience. It's more than advice or encouragement—it's direction. *You* must *do this.* Jane Borthwick's best-known hymn text "Come, labor on" is certainly of an era, a product of the time and place in which it was written, revealing a commitment to a work ethic not uncommon for 19th-century Scotland. Although the millennial understanding of the role of "work" in contemporary life is somewhat different, I still find within her text a charge fitting for musicians in these strange, liminal times:

---

9. "Come, Labor On," *The Hymnal 1982* (New York: Church Hymnal, 1982), hymn 541.

Come, labor on.
Claim the high calling angels cannot share;
to young and old the gospel gladness bear.
Redeem the time; its hours too swiftly fly.
The night draws nigh.

Come, labor on.
Cast off all gloomy doubt and faithless fear!
No arm so weak but may do service here.
Though feeble agents, may we all fulfill
God's righteous will.

> Jane Borthwick, adapted from *Thoughts for Thoughtful Hours*[10]

---

10. Jane Borthwick, *Thoughts for Thoughtful Hours: In Verse* (London: T. Nelson and Sons, Paternoster Row, 1859).

10

Musicians[1] in Bivocational Ministry

Jessica Nelson

Introduction

In my conversations about vocation, I was reminded time and time again of how many musicians serving Episcopal churches also have other employment, either out of desire or necessity, and I wanted to highlight this specifically. What follows is a semi-postscript to the conversations that precede it—bits and pieces of wisdom shared that I think are worth teasing out a little. *Bivocational* is a churchy buzzword these days, a sort of catchall term used in a number of different ways. In the ecclesiastical context, it's most often used to describe a typically nonstipendiary cleric who serves a parish (or two) alongside a full-time job in an unrelated field. I've seen this model employed more often in the last decade or so, often in rural communities or in areas where financial resources are stretched particularly thin. In my professional circles, "bivocational" is typically used to describe any musician who works more than one job, whether the two are in related fields or not.

Although there is precious little hard data with which to work, it's empirically observable that relatively few full-time positions for musicians exist in the Episcopal Church, with fewer every year as musicians retire from parish ministry, their positions reconfigured to meet shrinking budgets. As of this writing, the Association of Anglican Musicians' Placement Service job listings board contains eighteen postings for positions in parish ministry. Of those eighteen, three are advertisements for full-time positions.[2] This is not a statistical sample large enough to make sweeping generalizations, but I do think it reveals a trend. The

---

1. I'm tremendously grateful to the colleagues who took time to discuss their work with me: Jason Abel, Suzanne Daniel, Marissa Hall, Westley A. Hodges, Stephen Sollars, Taylor Sparks, and Dr. Henry Waters.

2. "Placement Listings," The Association of Anglican Musicians, accessed October 18, 2021, https://anglicanmusicians.org/members-area/placement-listing/.

Episcopal Church's Parochial Report indicates an increase in giving in parishes between 2016 and 2020 of 16 percent[3] but at the same time chronicles a decrease in active members. This figure doesn't account for the inflation rate and increased cost of living. The information is not included here to engender dread, but rather for a twofold purpose: to develop a realistic impression of the factors driving some of these employment trends, including the understanding that many aspiring church musicians will—at some point—likely be engaged in bivocational ministry, and to encourage professional organizations and denominational bodies to begin to capture this data in an effort to narrow the gap between clergy and lay compensation.

Prior to my current appointment, and with the exception of the years I was in seminary, the entirety of my career has been spent in bivocational ministry, whether it was simultaneously serving multiple church communities in different capacities or serving one parish alongside a number of other part-time positions. At most, I've juggled four part-time jobs simultaneously: a position in parish ministry, maintaining a private piano studio, and serving two different colleges as an adjunct professor. This is not at all uncommon among my colleagues. Did I feel called to each of those positions? Not exactly. But one or more additional sources of income has sometimes been required to support myself while living out the calling to parish ministry that I *did* feel.

From the conversations I've had with colleagues, I've identified three common configurations for bivocational ministry: musicians serving two or more parishes concurrently in different capacities; musicians working in two or more music-related fields, such as teaching music courses or doing other related work; and musicians engaged in two seemingly unrelated types of work, such as education administration alongside parish music ministry.

Musicians Serving Multiple Parishes Simultaneously

Marissa Hall is the Music and Worship Administrator at Trinity Church, Copley Square in Boston, Massachusetts. At Trinity, Marissa's position involves negotiating scheduling, organizing, and facilitating the goings-on of a large and busy program but little in the way of service playing or conducting. In addition to her full-time position, Marissa serves St. Peter's Episcopal Church in Cambridge as director of music and organist. Marissa is working to articulate a vocational identity that I'm not sure has been well-identified yet: there are plenty of musicians in parish ministry and plenty of skilled administrators, but she's at the center of the Venn diagram of people who possess remarkable skill in both areas and has a particular desire to put those to use in the service of the church and its music.

---

3. "Average Pledge by Province and Diocese: 2016–2020," 2020 Parochial Report Results: Average Pledge by Province and Diocese 2016-2020 Church, accessed February 17, 2022, https://extranet.generalconvention.org/staff/files/download/30694.

She's imagining a different way forward altogether: "At this time in my career, I am still gleaning as much experience and skill as I can [in both areas], in the hope that I might piece aspects of them together in the future to create something new. Both vocations are important to me, but I believe the best work I can do for the church happens within an intentional combination of the two." Marissa possesses an extremely high degree of self-awareness; she knows that she is incredibly organized—and that this is a highly desirable and sought-after skill. That impeccable organization in her primary role at Trinity allows her the bandwidth for her secondary role at St. Peter's.

Washington, DC–based musician Jason Abel's primary appointment is at historic Christ Church, Alexandria. His work there is full-time, but there are, perhaps, fewer organists in the area than necessary to meet the needs of nearby Virginia Theological Seminary's demanding schedule of chapel services, so he frequently accompanies services there as well. In addition to Christ Church and VTS, he regularly plays a Saturday vigil mass for a nearby Roman Catholic congregation. He's deeply aware that living in the DC area can be prohibitively expensive, and these additional income streams allow him more flexibility. "I'm well compensated at Christ Church, but this is also an expensive area to live in," he allows, "so the money I make from the extra gigs allows me to spend it on some fun things that my more budget-conscious self might not do otherwise."

Musicians Working in Closely Related Fields

Another configuration common to musicians working in parish ministry is the musician who holds multiple positions simultaneously in music-related fields, usually in the academy, entertainment, or in teaching privately. Suzanne Daniel is a versatile musician, skilled in woodwinds and keyboard instruments, among others. In addition to serving Grace Episcopal Church in Yorktown, Virginia, as director of music, she teaches music students at Christopher Newport University in Newport News and plays accordion at nearby Busch Gardens–Williamsburg. She also volunteers her time in a handful of area ensembles.

Westley A. Hodges is a musician in the Chicagoland area, serving St. Mark's Episcopal Church in Evanston in addition to teaching private music lessons and pursuing other income streams, such as piano tuning and other freelance work. "When I think of who I am, I see myself as more parish musician than anything," Westley says. I'm aware that Westley devotes a great deal of time and energy to educating others on issues related to LGBTQIA+ rights, so I wonder if a thread tying Westley's various other professional puzzle pieces together with parish ministry is a commitment to LGBTQIA+ advocacy. "I try . . . [to make] myself publicly vulnerable, by putting myself out there," Westley offers, no matter the arena—hoping to represent the LGBTQIA+ community as completely as possible whether in teaching or in the parish.

Dr. Henry Waters is the director of music at Plymouth Congregational church in Wichita, Kansas, and is an adjunct professor of music at nearby Butler Community College. Henry is an ardent supporter of diversity, equity, and inclusion in the classroom as well as the church. He has a well-articulated credo when it comes to diversity: "My vision contains music that is . . . reflective of both musicians and audience, and explores a wide variety of styles, languages, cultures, and backgrounds. . . . I am committed to [programming] works by less-known composers and underrepresented groups," he says, so that his students and members of his church choir will find themselves represented in the music they sing. Henry subscribes to a whole-person approach to music-making whether in an academic context or in the parish, working to create community and to recognize his singers as people first, with the musical output being secondary.

Musicians Working in Two (or More) Unrelated Fields

I'm especially curious about musicians who maintain positions in two (or more) seemingly unrelated fields, particularly if it's a field that seems incongruous—like finance or health care. Stephen Sollars is a musician in Columbus, Ohio, who, in addition to a part-time job in parish ministry, works a full-time job in health insurance administration. Though earning the majority of his living through nonchurch employment, he finds his primary identity in the parish and feels that offering his services to parishes that may only be able to afford a part-time musician is a calling of its own. He's clear that his work in insurance—though his primary source of income—is *not* his calling. He says, "For me, I view my full-time job as a *job*. It pays most of my bills, provides benefits, and will nearly always be what I consider my primary income. However, I do not feel like I was *called* to work in insurance administration. I do not feel like lives are enriched or changed by my activities in the corporate world. Working in parish ministry is a calling for me, and it gives me a sense of fulfillment."

Taylor Sparks is a musician in Tupelo, Mississippi, who "accidentally," as he describes it, began serving All Saints' Episcopal Church as choirmaster a few years ago. His primary job is as an elementary school assistant principal, and he's also in the process of completing a doctorate. Taylor describes himself as a "career educator" with a primary passion for education administration. Even though education is his primary calling, it often informs his work in the parish. "My job at the school reflects directly on the job I do with my choir. So much of the work of choral directing happens behind the scenes with preparation, assessing needs, logistics, handling interpersonal relationships, among many others," he says, and he attributes his success in one to success in the other.

Benefits of Bivocational Work

Because Suzanne Daniel's professional areas are so closely related, she's in more voice lessons every week than most voice majors or choral conductors will have over the course of their undergraduate education. "I feel like I get to be a sponge, continually learning," she says. "That influences the work I do with my choir at church and influences my own singing." The opportunities for cross-training that happen as musicians work simultaneously in multiple contexts are invaluable, even if they seem unrelated at first glance. I remember feeling I was getting free choral conducting lessons when I was accompanying college choirs at the University of North Alabama, but strangely enough, the most valuable byproduct of my time there was the skills in communication and classroom management I developed as an adjunct instructor. Because I was so regularly required to interact with students of widely varying ability—both music majors and non–music majors—I also gained experience in tailoring my teaching to accommodate a wide range of skill and learning styles, which has been useful in working with volunteer choristers. I learned how to create a lesson plan, how to plan for a semester at a time, and how to budget classroom time, all of which have come in remarkably handy in running a music program. Furthermore, at one time, my natural inclination was to be somewhat timid, somewhat prone to people-pleasing and often afraid to assert myself in the classroom or rehearsal room. This proclivity has been mostly cured by a few years of teaching. I was surprised to discover that the confidence I practiced managing a classroom full of eighteen-year-old college students was good practice for the assertiveness I needed to manage a room full of adult volunteer singers or my youngest children's choir choristers.

There are other benefits as well. Westley reminds me that teaching piano lessons on a parish's campus potentially increases the number of visitors to that parish, some of whom may never have another reason or opportunity to make a connection and that working in multiple arenas, particularly if they involve music and musicians, can widen the pool of available musicians to draw from when it comes time to hire instrumentalists or recruit new choir members. There are dozens of ways seemingly unrelated skill sets will interact with and cross-pollinate one another. "The administrative experience of handling payroll, ordering music, hiring instrumentalists, and creating bulletins gives me many points of reference for my work as a director of music and many resources that I otherwise would not be aware of," Marissa explains, continuing, "Likewise, my skills as a musician and choral director allow me to make informed decisions in my administrative role about different score editions, repertoire ideas, seating charts for the choir, and institutional knowledge from colleagues at different churches." Jason reminds me that seminary chapels often are laboratories for liturgical exploration and will employ new or developing resources. As a result, he's been exposed to a much wider variety of hymns and other congregational song than he might be otherwise.

Cross-pollination is not limited to musical activities. Taylor commented that his work in music ministry and educational administration are more closely related than one might suspect. "So much of the work of choral directing happens behind the scenes with preparation, assessing needs, logistics, handling interpersonal relationships. . . . If it weren't for being an assistant principal, I'm not sure how I would be as effective as a music director." Many of the musicians I spoke with cited musical training from an early age as central to their success in other arenas—practice habits ingrained in musicians from childhood can be helpful in learning to manage long-term, multistep projects. Accomplishing multistep tasks and projects incrementally (and with patience) is a handy skill to develop.

Concerns with Bivocational Work

I knew an organist years ago who served a downtown parish in a busy metropolitan area. He had a reserved parking spot. The sign read, "Reserved for the organist, twenty-four hours a day, seven days a week." I once commented to him that this seemed like a great perk. He responded dryly that it *was* a great perk but that the downside was that his parking spot was reserved twenty-four hours a day, seven days a week, meaning, he potentially could be at work at all hours. Now, he meant for this to be humorous, but it illustrates a larger point: so much of the work of parish ministry happens outside the nine-to-five workday on nights and weekends. Musicians juggling multiple positions often struggle with achieving and maintaining balance between their various roles, and this is of particular concern in a society in which busy-ness is a metric for success. I know many musicians who spend their office hours in the church grading papers and use free time in their other day jobs to Zoom into church staff meetings. Taylor underscores this point: "Brick-and-mortar structures go a long way in separating the two, but it is not uncommon for my mind to be occupied by either job while I am at the other." Scheduling issues also can be a frequent source of friction for the bivocational parish musician, often cited as a source of conflict between musicians and clergy, especially when a musician's schedule changes unexpectedly and without consultation.

Conclusion

How do we do this well—living an intentional life fulfilling *a* call to parish ministry, even if it's not our *only* call, or if we must do other work to enable us to live out our call? Suzanne tells me that the multiple positions she juggles are all so closely interwoven that she wonders if *bivocational* is the most accurate word to describe her. (I think "multivocational" or "omnivocational" would be more accurate—she seems to have a lot of irons in the fire.) "Rather than saying I'm a bivocational musician, I feel like I'm a pastoral musician and I just work in a bunch of different places. . . . I hope to be pastoral in all areas," she offers thoughtfully, whether that means teaching a class, accompanying lessons, dancing around a theme park with an accordion, or playing services on Sunday mornings. "Hopefully my relationships and interactions with [others] are informed by my being a pastoral musician," she concludes optimistically.

In the years since my peer group has achieved adulthood, I've noticed a preoccupation with professional identity. *Where are you working these days? What are you doing?* (Never mind all the unasked questions—*How much money are you making? What neighborhood do you live in? Where do your children go to school?*) It's a surface-level question. Knowing this information tells you just one thing about that person. But I've realized that with my closest friends—those with whom I'm most intimately acquainted—I cannot tell you what they do. I know their places of employment and titles and am vaguely aware of the basic functions of their work, but I can't tell you what they *do* with any degree of specificity. But I can tell you who they *are*. There's a difference. My friend Chelsea Marcantel is a Los Angeles–based playwright. She is funny and wise, and she writes compelling works of theater. (One recent piece of hers that's getting a lot of attention is *Airness*, a play about an air-guitar contest, of all things. Think '80s hair band meets the Van Cliburn International Piano Competition.[4]) Chelsea has been hustling for years and had a personal brand before any of us actually knew what that was. For years, the pithy bio she's used on her various social media outlets read simply, "Playwright/Actor/Person," or something very closely related. I think it's evolved over the years but has always ended with "person" or "human being." She says she can't take credit for it—that surely others have used some variation of it—but she's the person who introduced me to it, so I associate it with her. I've often been reminded of this little triad, not just because it makes me think of Alec Wyton's pastor-teacher-performer taxonomy discussed in the previous set of conversations, but also because it's such an economical and apt way to describe living a fulfilling life. The roles may evolve over time and the various puzzle pieces may shift around, but all of these parts come together to make a whole. It's the same way for us, I think—though the specifics may change from time to time, all of the various parts of our identities come together to make a person who they *are* and not just what they do.

4. Celia Wren, "Airness," *Washington Post*, November 19, 2019, https://www.washington-post.com/entertainment/theater_dance/in-airness-the-axes-are-invisible-but-the-play-is-loud/2019/11/19/5110923e-0a23-11ea-97ac-a7ccc8dd1ebc_story.html.

III

SERMONS

11

A Sermon Preached by The Rev. Erika Takacs at the Closing Eucharist of the 2013 Mississippi Conference on Church Music and Liturgy

St. Philip's Episcopal Church, Jackson, Mississippi
July 28, 2013
Proper 12

I wonder what Jesus looked like when he prayed. Did he stand or sit . . . or kneel? Did he face east or west, turn to the sun or to the sea? Did he walk about as he prayed, matching long strides to the pace of his prayer? Did he take off his shoes or cover his head? Did he hold himself still, or did he *daven* and silently move his lips? Did he chant or sing or hum? Did he close his eyes and bow his head? Did he smile, or frown, or weep? Did he begin his prayers in silence or with a sigh? Did he stretch his arms to heaven and say, "O Lord, hear my prayer, and let my cry come to you, in the name of the Father, and of me, and of the Holy Spirit?" No, perhaps not.

What did Jesus look like when he prayed? The gospels are fairly mute on the subject. There is, of course, the moment on the mount of transfiguration when Jesus's garments began to glow white like no amount of sunshine and Clorox could ever bleach them. But other than that one description of Jesus in prayer, the gospels leave us guessing. They do often tell us where Jesus prayed, that he liked to pray in places that were set apart and secluded—a mountain, the wilderness, places of privacy where the Holy Spirit had enough space to take wing. But what Jesus looked like when he prayed there? We are left only to imagine.

Today's gospel reading is equally silent on the subject. Luke tells us that Jesus is off praying "in a certain place," perhaps one of these deserted spots, away from the maddening crowds. But it seems that this particular "certain place" is not so very far away, because the disciples can clearly see him. And they are watching him closely. "Look!" they whisper to one another. "He's praying again. Just look at him. I wish I could pray like that. He looks like he is full of peace, full of beauty and holiness. I want to look just like that when I pray."

So when Jesus returns to the group, they ask him to show them how. "Lord, teach us to pray, they say, the way that John taught his disciples." Now scripture again has nothing to say about how John the Baptist prayed, but I would imagine that his prayer practices were as severe as his wardrobe. "Find a rocky spot in the desert," I can hear him saying, "and kneel there until you can feel the sharpness of your sin. If you are ever unsure of your need to repent, walk into the desert and sweat a while. Hairshirts are always helpful tools to keep you from being too comfortable with the riches of the flesh, and always, always remember to say grace before tucking into your locusts and wild honey."

Who knows what John the Baptist taught his disciples about prayer, and who knows what Jesus's are expecting when they ask him for some prayer instruction. But one thing is for sure—the disciples want to pray like Jesus. They want to look like him; they want to be like him. They want to be world-class pray-ers, Olympic athletes of supplication, Greek gods of petition. "Teach us to pray, Lord, so that we can be really good at this, as good as you are, beautiful and serene and holy, holy, holy, just like you."

Jesus, of course, knows what they are asking. He knows exactly what they are looking for. He knows what it is that they want from him, but he also knows what it is that they need from him. So instead of offering helpful hints about the seven habits of highly effective pray-ers, he just smiles and says okey dokey—or however you say "okey dokey" in Aramaic—this, my children, is how you pray.

Father. Hallowed be your name. And with those five simple words, Jesus changes everything. *Father. Hallowed be your name,* and instantly Jesus takes the focus away from the pray-er to the pray-ee. Because prayer, Jesus knows, is not primarily about our holiness; it is first and foremost about the holiness of God. God is the holy one, the numinous one. The disciples may have been asking about how to be holy themselves, but Jesus knows all holiness, all beauty, all prayer begins with God, the Holy One, the one whose very name is so holy it cannot be spoken, whose being is so holy it can only be expressed in the sound of sheer silence, whose presence is so holy that we cannot bear to look upon it. Take off your shoes, Jesus tells his disciples, for your God is holy, and the place of prayer is always holy ground.

But Jesus's teaching does not stop there, because he then goes on to show his disciples—including you and me, of course—that this holiness does not exist for its own sake. It is not a disembodied, disinterested holiness; it is holiness on your side, holiness for you. That holiness is your Father, your Mother. That holiness is closer to you than your own heart. That Holy God, Holy and Mighty, Holy Immortal One is extremely, intimately, inexhaustibly interested in you. And so ask, and your prayers will be answered. Ask for bread enough, for food enough, for patience and endurance and strength enough. Ask for whatever you need, ask again and again, ask and seek and knock, for our God is holy and righteous and will give you whatever you need, not because of your holiness, but because of his. God will give you whatever you need, not because you prayed well, or enough, or at the right time of day or in the right posture or with the right words, but because God is God and can do no other.

God can do no other—including giving us anything less than a good gift. Jesus promises us that God will respond to our prayers, but he does not promise that God will give us what we ask for in the form that we would prefer the very second we're looking for it. God actually knows better than that. God will not give us more stuff when what we need is more space. God will not give us a quick fix when what we need is a slow returning. God will not take us out of the wilderness when what we need is to see that he is in the wilderness with us. God will not even give us an instant cure when what we need is an enduring healing. This is good news, of course, but it is not always easy. It's difficult to lay aside our own expectations about what God's response will look like or when it will come. We can start to imagine that God has gone deaf and dumb, when really the problem is that while he's reaching out to offer fish and eggs, we're looking around for snakes and scorpions.

But the more we pray *Father, Hallowed be your name*, the better we get at seeing the gifts that God offers. The more we pray *Father, Hallowed be your name*, the more holiness we begin to see all around us. For the holiness of God cannot be contained. It spreads out and around, landing on everything like soft sunshine dripping down the soft leaves of summer. It is a saturating holiness that fills in the tiniest cracks and makes even the rests between the notes pregnant with the presence of the Almighty. It is a holiness that rubs off and rubs in, even into you and in me.

When we pray *Father, Hallowed be your name*, you and I actually become the holiness that we seek. When our eyes are pining for the beauty of God, when we turn our faces to the splendor of God's grace, we actually begin to look like heaven, begin to look like what we're looking for. "And every gentle heart," poet Robert Bridges writes, "that burns with true desire / Is lit from eyes that mirror part / Of that celestial fire." And that is what you look like when you pray. You look beautiful. You are beautiful when you pray. You are beautiful when you say *Father, Hallowed be your name*. You are beautiful when you join with angels and archangels to sing "Holy, Holy, Holy" with all the heavenly choirs. You are beautiful when you sing "Here, O my Lord, I see thee face to face," yes, even you in the back who thinks that God would probably rather you not sing in public. Let me tell you, you're wrong; God loves it when you sing, especially hymns out of *The Hymnal 1982*. When you sing, when you pray, you are so beautiful, filled with the holiness of God, afire with the light, the truth, the beauty that the world so pines to see. You are so beautiful that someone out there who is looking for a home or looking for a hope might just look at you and say, "Wow. I want to pray like she does. I want to look like that. Teach me how to do that." So tell them. *Father. Hallowed be your name.* Invite them to pray in the [beauty] of holiness. Alleluia, alleluia! Praise with us the God of grace.

12

A Sermon Preached by The Rev. Erika Takacs at the Closing Eucharist of the 2019 Annual Conference of the Association of Anglican Musicians[1]

Church of the Redeemer, Chestnut Hill, Boston, Massachusetts
Thursday, July 4
Independence Day

Twelve score and three years ago, our fathers brought forth on this continent, a new nation, conceived in Liberty, and dedicated to the proposition that all men are created equal. Or, should I say, twelve score, three years, and two days ago. For all the ado we make about July 4th, the only thing that really happened on that day in 1776 was that the Continental Congress made a few edits to the Declaration of Independence and sent it to the printer. The vote for independence, that thing that brought forth on this continent a new nation, had taken place two days earlier, prompting John Adams to predict, "The Second Day of July 1776 will be the most memorable [day] in the History of America. . . . It ought to be commemorated, as the Day of Deliverance by solemn Acts of Devotion to God Almighty. It ought to be solemnized with Pomp and Parade, with Shews, Games, Sports, Guns, Bells, Bonfires and Illuminations from one End of this Continent to the other from this Time forward forever more." And so we have done—some years with more tanks, I mean guns, than others—but always on the 4th, not the 2nd, the date on the parchment. (Adams really used the word *Epocha* not "day," but I've found that using archaic words is never particularly helpful in a sermon.)

So twelve score, three years, and two days ago our fathers . . . or should I say fathers and mothers, because women patriots were not just pacing in the waiting room while their husbands gave birth to this new nation. Adams's own thinking was considerably shaped by his prodigious and sometimes rather pointed

1. Reprinted with permission from the *Journal of the Association of Anglican Musicians* 28, no. 6 (August 2019): 17–18.

correspondence with his wife, Abigail, who once famously cautioned him to "remember the ladies" in his quest for independence. He didn't, but we sure can.

So twelve score, three years, and two days ago our fathers and mothers brought forth on this continent, a new nation, conceived in liberty, and dedicated to the proposition that all men are created equal. Or should I say all white men. Or should I say all literate white men. Or all literate white men of property. So twelve score, three years, and two days ago, our fathers and mostly-forgotten mothers brought forth on this continent a new nation, conceived in a fairly comprehensive idea of liberty, and dedicated to the proposition that some men who look exactly like each other are created equal. Our sentence might be more honest, but Lincoln's sure sounds better.

Lincoln, of course, knew that the first line of his address at Gettysburg was only partially true. This was, in fact, his point—that America had promised to be a nation where all men were created equal, but that four score and seven years later in the midst of a bloody civil war we were only just getting around to defining what we meant when we said men. Lincoln knew, as we know now, that this new nation was messy. He knew that our national rhetoric was always more aspirational than observational, and that while we hadn't exactly been lying about this thing called America, we hadn't exactly been telling the truth either. The truth is that we have always been a nation defined by what we haven't figured out yet. Who is free? Who counts? Who can come in and who can stay? Our answers to these questions have at times been courageous and at other times been cruel. Our leaders have inhibited justice as many times as they have inspired it. The great experiment begun all those years ago is still an experiment, a work in constant need of clarification and correction.

Not so different, it turns out, from that great experiment called the people of Israel. Here, too, was a new nation, conceived in liberty, whose attempts to live that liberty were at times excruciating. Here, too, was a new nation whose purpose was still aspirational, whose people could be cruel as often as they were courageous, who could be whiny and petulant as often as they were grateful and generous, who got it wrong as often as they got it right. Here was a nation that was messy, a nation that was sometimes disappointing, sometimes inspiring, and always deeply human.

And yet, despite their imperfections, God brought them to the promised land anyway. God bore them to the banks of the River Jordan, where Moses addressed them with a declaration of his own—a declaration of dependence on God. And in this declaration, which we call Deuteronomy, Moses told this fledgling, flawed nation that God was calling them to do something extraordinary. God was calling them—these people who had escaped from slavery, who were threatened by tribes and nations on every side, and who were holding on to each other by a thread—to reach out and risk loving the stranger. Just as their God loved the widow and the orphan, they, too, were to love those on the outside—the unfamiliar, the unseen, the unchosen. This is how God would help them to become the people God had always intended them to be—by not settling in but reaching out, by moving. God was calling them to be more than just a nation; God was calling them to be a movement.

We who today are offering our own solemn acts of Devotion to God Almighty are part of that same movement; we, too, are called not to just settle in, but to move. We are the Episcopal Branch of the Jesus Movement, as our presiding bishop faithfully reminds us, and we, too, are called to do what God called the people of Israel to do all those years ago—to move together into the margins; to welcome, serve, and bless those we find there; and to allow those encounters to shape us into the Church God has always longed for us to be.

The good news is that this movement is already happening in the Church in many, many ways. You who work in parishes across this country can testify to the ways the Jesus Movement is transforming the world by loving the stranger in our midst. But here is a little-recognized truth about movements, something the Church often forgets. Movements sing. Every movement in history has needed to sing—not just to reach out in compassion and mercy, not just to speak truth to power with love, but to sing. Every movement has had music at its core to inspire and to guide, to embolden and to comfort, and to connect its people to each other and to its purpose far more powerfully than any mission statement ever could.

Music is at the core of the Episcopal Branch of the Jesus Movement. Our movement loses strength and power when we forget this. Music is not tangential to the mission of the Church. Music is not simply adornment to cover our "real" work together; it is not entertainment while we catch our breath. No other movement would ever treat music in the way that we in the Church sometimes do. Imagine Black slaves choosing not to sing along with "Wade in the Water" because they just didn't consider themselves singers. Imagine Woody Guthrie telling American workers that it would be fine to just speak the words of "This Land Is Your Land" together in unison. Imagine Billie Holliday singing "Strange Fruit" as background music while waiters set the tables for dinner. Imagine cutting "We Shall Overcome" from a civil rights rally in 1960s Alabama because someone thought the money for the choir could be better spent elsewhere. What a waste when we treat the music of our own movement this way! Because just as with these anthems, every note we sing, every harmony we create, every voluntary you play has the potential to strengthen our movement and to change the world.

Now, I believe the spoken word can do this too; if I didn't, I would be in the wrong business. But I also believe that there are some issues too great for just speech. There are some injustices that are too grievous, some wrongs that are too vexing, some injuries that are too painful for just speech. Teenagers shot in school by young men wielding weapons of war is an issue too great for just speech. Children trapped in cages like animals at our nation's borders is an issue too great for just speech. Violence against Black men for just being Black men is an issue too great for just speech. Hatred of our Jewish neighbors is an issue too great for just speech. Abuse of women is an issue too great for just speech. But music—music can hold the pain of our wounds and the hope of our healing together in a way that speech strains to do. At this point in the sermon, I was going to try to describe how the music of [Ralph Vaughan Williams's] "Lord, Thou Hast Been our Refuge" does just this—but of course, I can't. And that's just the point. Music moves movements in ways that words simply cannot.

God has called us to be a movement, and God has called you to make this movement sing. Now, as some of your courageous conversations during this conference have demonstrated, at times in your history you have responded to this call with courage and at times with cruelty. Sometimes you have inspired justice in your ministry and sometimes you have inhibited it. You beautiful church musicians, sometimes you are a mess. But take it from this mess, God has called you anyway. God is calling you to help this movement sing, to proclaim a declaration not just of life, liberty, and the pursuit of happiness, but of eternal life, abundant freedom, and the discovery of true joy. God is calling you to help us sing so that we may make this into a land of promise for all people, a nation dedicated to the proposition that all human beings were created equal and beloved. God is calling you to help us sing so that we may become the movement God has always imagined us to be, bringing justice and love from one End of this Continent to the other from this Time forward forever more. O God, our help in ages past, our hope for years to come. You beautiful church musicians, have you ever thought that that help, that hope, might just be you? May God forever prosper your handiwork.

13

"The Two Calls": A Sermon Preached by The Rt. Rev. Eugene Taylor Sutton at the Opening Eucharist of the 2014 Annual Conference of the Association of Anglican Musicians[1]

St. Paul's Parish, K Street, Washington, DC
June 16, 2014

Now the eleven disciples went to Galilee, to the mountain to which Jesus had directed them. When they saw him, they worshiped him; but some doubted. And Jesus came and said to them, "All authority in heaven and on earth has been given to me. Go therefore and make disciples of all nations, baptizing them in the name of the Father and of the Son and of the Holy Spirit, and teaching them to obey everything that I have commanded you. And remember, I am with you always, to the end of the age."

Matthew 28:16–20

Core membership loss of over 8 percent. Uncertain leadership, with no strategic plan for growth. Loss of energy, lack of vision, with little basis for optimism in the face of a culture that appears to be increasingly hostile to the faith.

The Episcopal Church in the twenty-first century? No, I'm talking about the world of Jesus's disciples at the end of the gospel according to Matthew. In those days immediately following Jesus's resurrection, the Christian movement was at a very precarious stage, and it was not at all clear it was going to survive. How could it? Many of its followers and adherents had fallen away due to disillusionment, and religious and social pressures. The Twelve were now The Eleven due to the betrayal and suicide of Judas—representing the loss of 8.3 percent of

---

1. Reprinted with permission from the *Journal of the Association of Anglican Musicians* 23, no. 6 (July/August 2014) : 6–7.

its core members. The organization, such as it was, had no undisputed leader, no secure funding scheme, no sound administrative or board structure, and no strategic plan for the future—surely giving rise, I'm sure, to calls for "restructuring." Sound familiar?

It's in that context of spiritual and emotional malaise that Jesus gives his most famous farewell "charge" to his successors. The gospel lesson assigned for today is one of the best-known scriptural mandates for the mission of the church. It's called "The Great Commission," so named because it is when our Lord calls, or "commissions," his followers to go into all the world to make disciples, baptize them in the name of the Father and of the Son and of the Holy Spirit, and teach them to cling to everything that Jesus commanded them. The church has heard that call to mission very clearly, and while it has been sometimes misunderstood and abused as a basis for cultural, racial, and religious imperialism, it has also given rise to the spread of the good news of Jesus everywhere—as well as the establishment of schools, hospitals, and institutions promoting justice, reconciliation, and peace. Whenever the church forgets the Great Commission it does so at its peril, and it has served as a warning to the Church to not succumb to those inevitable self-serving tendencies to become nothing more than a religious social club for insiders.

But the call of the Great Commission contained in verses 18 through 20—the ones assigned for this day after the Feast of the Trinity—tell only part of the story. There were actually two calls given by Jesus on those final days to his disciples, and both calls are absolutely necessary for the health and growth of the Christian movement. Do you want to know what that other call is? You would have to go back a few verses to read the entire account of what our Lord directed his disciples at the close of Matthew's Gospel, beginning at [the sixteenth verse,] which reads: "Now the eleven disciples went to Galilee, to the mountain to which Jesus had directed them. When they saw him, they worshiped him; but some doubted."

The first call, then, of the resurrected Jesus was to go to Galilee, to go to the mountain. This call was first made to the women at the empty tomb; in verse ten Jesus tells them to "go tell my brothers to go to Galilee; there they will see me." In other words, the first obligation of the disciples of Christ was to go home and look for Jesus there. There, on the mountaintop—as has been true throughout the scriptures—is where God is always revealed in a significant way. It was true for Moses on Mt. Sinai, where he spent forty days and nights communing with the Lord before he was ready to receive the law to give to the Israelites. It was true for Elijah, who on the mountain had to listen to the "still small voice" of God to strengthen him for the hard journey below. It was true for Peter, James, and John, who could only see the full glory of the Lord on the face of Jesus on the Mount of Transfiguration before they could begin their mission of going into the towns and villages teaching, healing, driving out evil, and proclaiming the advent of the reign of God on earth.

And it was true for the disciples in today's lesson as well, serving as the prerequisite for hearing the Great Commission. In other words, before they could hear that second call to go and make disciples everywhere, they first had to hear his first call to go to the mountain and worship.

Is not this a crucial reminder for the Episcopal Church at this present time? Are we all that dissimilar to our spiritual ancestors in their moments of personal and/or communal weakness?

You're familiar with the figures, the numbers that seemingly tell a depressing story of a steady, deep, and continuing decline of the Church. But that story can and should be challenged at every opportunity. In April of last year, Dean Ian Markham, president of Virginia Theological Seminary, gave a much-noted address at the annual convention of the Diocese of Delaware in which he countered the conventional wisdom that the Episcopal Church has been in unbroken decline for the last fifty years, and that its future promises more of the same. He correctly points out that in the decade before 2002, the Episcopal Church actually grew in average Sunday attendance by 18,000 worshipers.

I remember well those days at the dawn of the 21st century when religious social scientists and church sociologists were openly talking about why was it that the Episcopal Church and the Evangelical Lutheran Church in America (ELCA) alone among the Mainline Protestant denominations was experiencing numerical growth—however slight—at least, not declining in worship attendance. The Diocese of Maryland was growing then, as well as the Dioceses of Washington, Virginia, Delaware, and several others.

The indications, of course, are that we grew then because we were known as the Church that worshiped well, emphasizing ancient prayers and rites, beautiful liturgies and music that lifts the soul out of the everyday into the glorified presence of a resurrected Lord. If the Episcopal Church was known for anything in those years, it was that.

But then something happened around 2002 and 2003 that changed the public's perception of the Episcopal Church. Do you remember? That was the period when the conflicts flared up in full force around the full inclusion in the church of all God's people, and in particular celebrating the gifts that gay and lesbian Christians bring to our common life. In 2003, my friend Gene Robinson was elected bishop of New Hampshire, which caused a firestorm in the church here and in the Anglican Communion. We began fighting, and many members—including substantial parts of four dioceses—left the Episcopal Church. Of course, we continued to gain new members, but that did not make up for the loss of those who left.

The point I'm making is that the Episcopal Church in the public's mind became more identified with conflicts, property disputes, fighting, and sex than it became known for its distinctive embodiment of worship. In short, in an era of sound bites, quick opinions, and superficial allegiances, the Episcopal Church lost its brand.

But there is good news here. Unlike many of our brothers and sisters in other Christian denominations, we Episcopalians are coming to the end of those troubles. Those members who are still unhappy with our church-wide stances on inclusion have already made the calculation that this is not the issue that is going to drive them away, and more importantly, their children are not at all likely to leave the Episcopal Church because of our openness to the presence and gifts of all people.

My brothers and sisters, I submit to you that repeated calls to "just focus on mission" is seriously missing the boat on what has been behind our institutional losses of membership and attendance. The "Go, therefore . . ." of the Great Commission is a very important call to the whole church—but it is the second call. The first call at the end of Matthew's Gospel is to go to the mountain, meet Jesus there, and worship him. Sadly, in the Episcopal Church at this present time, we hear very little about that first call.

This issue of the "first call" is very personal for me . . . it goes to the heart of the matter as to why I am an Episcopalian. I was born in this city of Washington, and my faith was nurtured at a large, Black, and vibrant congregation in the center of the Black community. What this means is that I sang, clapped, swayed, stomped, and shouted my way into the Christian faith—for which, of course, I am eternally grateful!

By my high school years, however, this way of worshiping no longer worked for me. Already by then, I was wary and weary of the constant demands for a highly charged emotional response on my part as the evidence that the Holy Spirit was present. I was tired of the anti-intellectualism, the easy answers to complex issues, the focus on individual gifts of performance rather than on the majesty of God, and the lack of a worshipful connection with the ancient past and the lives of our spiritual forbears in faith.

After a brief period of "atheism"—to the extent that a seventeen-year-old struggling with his faith could be an atheist—I came back to the faith. But where to worship? I literally went to dozens of churches, from storefronts to large sanctuaries, Protestant and Catholic Churches, Black and white, rich and poor. It wasn't, however, until I stepped into the Church of the Ascension and St. Agnes—that venerable downtown Anglo-Catholic parish—that I found my "home." I didn't understand much about what was going on liturgically at that morning's Mass; it was a whole new world for me. But I did know that what was happening there helped me to connect with the Holy One in a way that I had never experienced before—without having to check my mind at the door! Who said that a seventeen-year-old African American urban teenager can't be attracted to a tradition of liturgy and music that has stood the test of time for two thousand years?

My brothers and sisters, I believe that our parishes need to focus more on their community's worship as the vehicle for the kind of evangelism that works for us. The problem for the Episcopal Church is not that we are neurotically and unhelpfully fixated on music and liturgy. Rather, the problem for us from an evangelical and church growth stance is that we are not focused enough on our worship.

Good worship consists of its own "three-legged stool": music, liturgy, and preaching. Each leg of that stool is important, and if one of them is weak, then the other two will not be able to stand for long. The truth is no matter how earnestly a church may pour itself into serving its community (which, as I said earlier, is a good thing), if the preaching is uninspiring, the liturgy is sloppy, or the music is barely listenable, then that church will shrink and eventually may have to close its doors as a worshiping community.

This means that growing churches are going to have to spend more of their time, money, and other resources on having a good music program—not less. They are going to have to spend more time developing good liturgical practices for their services, not less. And they are going to have to insist that their clergy spend more time, effort, and training on becoming good preachers, not settling for mediocre preaching.

Ultimately, the reason for this turn, or return, to worship isn't to maintain market share. It's not to make us feel good or to achieve some vague spiritual high. The reason the Episcopal Church must focus on worship is to prepare itself to make disciples of all nations. It is to take seriously the first call of Jesus before the Great Commission to "go to the mountain, see Jesus there, and worship him."

To God be all honor, glory, and praise forever. Amen.

14

A Sermon Preached by The Rev. Canon Carl F. Turner at the 50th Anniversary Annual Conference of The Association of Anglican Musicians

St. John's Episcopal Church, Stamford, Connecticut
Monday, June 13, 2016

Marty Haugen, the American church musician, often talks about how music makes connections, but especially in the context of the liturgical life of the church. Speaking to a conference of Lutherans some years ago he said this:

> We sing to remember who and whose we are. The leader of prayer, the one who reads, and especially the one who sings, must know more than the notes. She must know the stories of our faith as well as the stories of her own community, and she must know how they are brought together in worship.[1]

She must know more than the notes.

The bringing of the hours of work into a performance that is liturgical is very different to that which is performed on a stage. Music in the Christian tradition is bound up with the telling of story and this, in turn, we have inherited from our origins in the Jewish faith where the saving works of God were celebrated in song in the temple, in the synagogue, and most especially in the singing of the psalms.

In our gospel reading today,[2] the Lord sends out seventy disciples, and they have a story to share. "Gospel," of course, means "Good News," and the news is that the kingdom of God has come very near. Paul reflects on this Good News, which is about the breaking down of division so that people can become dwelling places for God's presence. Only a few days ago we celebrated the feast day of St.

---

1. Marty Haugen, "Keeping the People's Song Alive" (lecture, Evangelical Lutheran Church in America, 1998).

2. The gospel appointed for that day was Luke 10:1–9.

Ephrem the Syrian—a deacon from the 4th century who was known as "the harp of the Holy Spirit." At a time of controversy and disagreement and the heady days of the first council of Nicaea, Ephrem knew that music could deepen the telling of story; over 1,600 years later we still have seventy-two of his hymns. As the ancient saying goes, "The one who sings, prays twice"[3]—music deepens the proclamation of the gospel and roots the story in the heart of the believer.

This is expressed through the coming together of various forms—rhythm, melody, and texture. The rhythm of music beats with the beating heart of God's love for the universe; his often-syncopated rhythm works beautifully around the rhythm of the created order even when humankind misses a beat. The melody is the storyline, which runs from the creation of the world, and which will find its finale in the consummation of all things at the end of time. Even when our human melodies selfishly drown out the principle theme of God's plan—God's story—his melodic line brings people back time and time again into unison. And the texture of God's music is the richness of the harmonies that he has created, weaving our stories with those of others in the past and anticipating those of the future. Even when men and women insert discordant and noisy passages into the world, God's harmonies are far richer and more sonorous, calling humankind into a new relationship with the Trinity. The Creator of the perfect fifth wants his sons and daughters to recognize that they are made in his image and can resonate with the frequency of his love or, as we sang in our psalm, to "worship the Lord in the beauty of holiness."

Significantly recorded in Psalm 137, we hear of the power of song but also how the powerful can silence song:

> By the waters of Babylon we sat down and wept : when we
>   remembered thee, O Sion.
> As for our harps, we hanged them up : upon the trees that are therein.
> For they that led us away captive required of us then a song, and melody,
> in our heaviness : Sing us one of the songs of Sion.
> How shall we sing the Lord's song : in a strange land?"
>
> Psalm 137:1–4 (Coverdale Psalter)

Silencing song also silences story. Traditional melodies are the means of passing on story from one generation to another; that is why folk melodies are so important to all cultures, for they bind up the story in the melodies handed down through many generations. To silence such melodies is to silence the telling of the story contained within them.

At the same time, melody and song can also be a means of protest and challenge; whole musical genres have developed out of the marginalization of people. From their desperation come melodies and musical forms from the past and deep

---

3. This quotation is attributed to St. Augustine.

within the soul: jazz, gospel, African American spirituals. These are but three examples of the way that songs can be of protest and also solidarity. (*How shall we sing the Lord's song in a strange land?*)

Our role as musicians in the liturgy is to aid the telling of the story of our faith but also to enter more deeply into the mystery of what we are singing. St. Augustine said that "we are an Easter People and Alleluia is our song." The Alleluia is the response to the greatest of all stories. Whereas many parts of the liturgy have had music composed for them to cover a particular liturgical action, the singing of the Alleluia before the gospel has always been sung as an end in itself. It is a response to what St. Paul proclaimed to be at the heart of our faith: "if we have died with Christ, we believe that we will also live with him" (Rom. 6:8). For this reason the Alleluia, for centuries, has included some of the most complex melodies and produced some of the most elaborate music. The groups of notes in plainsong notation—the *neums*—also have a special name when they are grouped together as in the Alleluia—they are known as the *jubilus*. They are not there to test the ability of the singer (or even the skill of the director of music to read them in the first place!); they are there to enable those singing, and those listening, to enter more fully into the mystery—entering so deeply into one syllable of a word so that the reality of the story takes root in our hearts:

Gradual Alleluia for the Mass of Easter Day
from the Liber Usualis of 1961, public domain

Sicardus of Cremona in the 12th century said, "The Alleluia is short in word and long in *neum*, because that joy is too great to be expressed in words." Or as Rupert of Deutz, another 12th-century Benedictine, said, "We rejoice rather than sing and prolong the *neums*, that the mind be surprised and filled with the joyful sound, and be carried thither where the saints rejoice in glory."

At the heart of Christian worship, then, is a community of faith retelling its story in many different ways but above all using the gifts of music, and of singing in particular, to engage the mind with the soul in order to proclaim that our lives are transformed by the power of God—which is to proclaim the gospel—the Good News. Our singing and our music-making reflect our life with God and our commitment to one another. We sing because we have a story to tell—a story of which we are a part and on which each of us needs to reflect. Our music takes us deeper into that story; that is why we lift our voices in joy and praise today because, as John Wesley put it so much better in "Love divine, all loves excelling," we sing to remember who and whose we are so that we may be:

> Changed from glory into glory,
> Till in Heav'n we take our place,
> Till we cast our crowns before Thee,
> Lost in wonder, love, and praise.

15

A Sermon Preached by The Rev. Dr. Katherine A. Grieb at the Funeral of Ray Glover

Immanuel Chapel at Virginia Theological Seminary
December 28, 2017
The Feast of the Holy Innocents

Please join me in this prayer of invocation from George Herbert: "Come, my way, my truth, my life; such a way as gives us breath; such a truth as ends all strife; such a life as killeth death." Amen.

I take as one of my texts, the words we heard from Psalm 139: "If I climb up to heaven, you are there; if I make the grave my bed, you are there also. If I take the wings of the morning and dwell in the uttermost parts of the sea, Even there your hand will lead me and your right hand hold me fast" (Ps. 139:7–9).

I say I take that as one of my texts because, as you will have noticed, Ray Glover gave us lots of texts—both biblical texts and hymnal texts—to ponder today, as we give thanks for his life among us and, reluctantly, give him back to the dust from which he and all of us come, as we remember solemnly every Ash Wednesday. And so this dust, this little pile of ashes, which we will soon commit to the earth, is an occasion for our thanksgiving for the many gifts he gave us; it is also an occasion for our songs of triumph because of Christ's triumph over Death; moreover, it is an occasion to reflect a bit about the resurrection from the dead; and, finally, it is an occasion of tenderness and gentleness toward one another and toward this very special little pile of ashes.

So first, to give thanks for at least some of the many gifts Ray gave us. In one sense that's easy; in another, it's impossible. This is what I mean. At the tomb of Sir Christopher Wren (1632–1723) the famous architect of St. Paul's Cathedral in London, is an epitaph in Latin: "Lector, si monumentum requires, circumspice," or "Reader, if you require a monument, look around you." When you look around, you see St. Paul's in all its splendor, but if you keep on look-ing around, you see dozens of other churches in London as well, all rebuilt by him after the great fire. Something of the same kind—in another key—is true of Ray Glover. We might say, "Singer, organist, church musician, music scholar, if you require a monument, open the blue book in front of you, open [*The Hymnal 1982*]." And when we do that, when we open it, we see a great richness of quality, of diversity, of tradition preserved, of newness celebrated, of depth and weight in those German chorales, and also lightness and dancing in those French Advent hymns, of Anglican staples, and of newly discovered gems from around the Anglican Communion and from our ecumenical partners. It's amazing that it all fits between the covers of one book.

But then when we look around further, we see the four-volume *1982 Hymnal Companion*, a massive work of scholarly interpretation; we see many years of teaching here at this seminary by a man who "delighted" in his students (there's really no other word for how Ray taught); we also see the AAM, the Association of Anglican Musicians, which Ray helped to found under another name in 1966. We see almost fifty-six years of marriage to Joyce MacDonald Glover until her death in 2013 (you'll notice that it's her translation of "Ubi caritas" that we sing today. (Ray was careful to include that.) And their daughters, Margaret and Kathryn, and a lovely group of grandchildren. If we keep looking, we also see the Leadership Program for Musicians Serving Small Congregations—that would be the 95 percent of church musicians who are not serving in cathedrals or tall steepled parishes—Ray helped to found that too. We would also see many enduring friendships, conversations that were too good to stop, people who remember feasts of the kind that Isaiah 25 describes—rich food, well-aged wines—to celebrate life, because God will destroy the shroud that hangs over the people; God will swallow up Death forever!

We still haven't exhausted all that we want to give thanks for or listed all of the gifts that Ray Glover has given to us, but that's my cue to move on to the next point: this is an occasion for our songs of triumph because of the victory that Jesus Christ has won over Death. At the Lamb's High Feast (Easter) we sing! Of course, we sing—"praise to our victorious king—praise we Christ, whose blood was shed, Paschal victim, Paschal bread—now no more can Death appall, now no more the grave enthrall; thou hast opened Paradise, and in Thee thy saints shall rise!"[1]

That's why "All [our] hope on God is founded." Ray Glover, our DJ for today, knew exactly what he was doing theologically. This hymn is in here not only because, as Bill Roberts says, "Michael" is the most beautiful tune in the [*The Hymnal 1982*], but also because it's some of the best theology in the hymnal, and the last verse calls us to praise and to trust:

---

1. "At the Lamb's high feast we sing," *The Hymnal 1982* (New York: Church Hymnal, 1982), hymn 174.

Still from earth to God eternal sacrifice of praise be done,
High above all praises praising for the gift of Christ, his son.
Christ doth call one and all: ye who follow shall not fall.[2]

We need to be reminded that God is trustworthy because it is the hardest thing Christians are called to do: to place the body or the cremated remains of a loved one into the ground and trust God to raise it from the dead again. All the evidence of our senses, all the history that we personally have experienced, and all the history we have heard about before us, gives us no grounds to expect much to happen after that. But even at the grave we make our song: Alleluia, alleluia, alleluia. Why?

Well, this is where we need to hear from St. Paul and perhaps also from George Frederick Händel (1685–1759). When I travel to the [American Academy of Religion and Society of Biblical Literature meeting] once a year, if there is no youth hostel, I stay in a hotel, and because travel is usually stressful, I'm tired, but I want to get to the first session on time, so in addition to the alarm clock I carry with me, I usually ask the front desk to give me a wakeup call—and they do: the phone rings, and I make my session. Well, Ray, the good news for you—and for all of us—is that there is no way we will miss the wakeup call. The trumpet shall sound! "The trumpet shall sound, and the dead shall be raised incorruptible, and we shall all be changed. For this corruptible must put on incorruption, and this mortal must put on immortality" (1 Cor. 15:52, KJV). Händel choreographed that as an air for the bass in his *Messiah*. But it is punctuated by the brilliant sound of the trumpet.

I'm thinking on that day it will be an angel who sounds something like Wynton Marsalis—clear, crisp, well-defined notes that ring out the joyful summons to resurrection. On that first note, people will jump out of their graves. It's the greatest wakeup call ever.

It's not clear from the New Testament whether those who die in the Lord will sleep a long time or a short time: in 1 Corinthians 15, as we heard, Paul talks about the difference between the physical body that we put into the ground and the spiritual body that God raises from the dead. The analogy he uses is that it's like planting corn: we put into the ground a small, square, yellow thing, but God raises a long, tall, green leafy thing from that. It's different from what we knew. This is supported by every single resurrection story in the Gospels where people who had known Jesus well, worked with him, traveled with him, listened to him, for several years didn't recognize him at first. But Paul's analogy in 1 Corinthians seems to imply a long time and an end time in which the whole creation—all the dead from the past—will be raised at once on the last day. The trumpet shall

---

2. "All my hope on God is founded," *The Hymnal 1982* (New York: Church Hymnal, 1982), hymn 665.

sound! The dialogue we heard from John 11 between Jesus and Martha about her brother, Lazarus, seems to assume the same thing: Martha says, "I know that he will rise again on the last day."

But in Luke's Gospel, Jesus says to one of the thieves on the cross next to his, "Today you will be with me in Paradise." And Paul, in Philippians, wonders whether he will get out of that prison alive and says to the church, "I would rather depart and be with the Lord," as if it were almost all one action, not much time lapse at all. So even Paul himself is inconsistent on this point, and you can't really blame him—he didn't know how it would be. Like all theologians, he's wondering and imagining how it must be or how it might be. One of my favorite cartoons shows a man standing in front of the heavenly gate. We see St. Peter writing in the book and behind him is God, who says, "A theologian, huh? You guys are always fun." My point here is that we don't know any more than Paul or Luke or John or Isaiah or the psalmist knew about exactly what will happen after death. We are called to trust God and we are free, we are even invited to wonder creatively about how God will welcome those whom we have loved and lost, how they will be reunited with those they have loved and lost, and how we will be reunited with them in God's good time, whether the time is long or short, whether time, as we understand it here, is anything like what it is in the presence of God. We don't know, but God knows, and we trust God.

That brings me to my final point, that today is an occasion for tenderness, for gentleness, as we entrust to God this little pile of ashes for safekeeping in the meantime. Ray Glover and I team-taught a course on Johann Sebastian Bach's (1685–1750) *St. Matthew Passion*. Naturally, we did it in the spring of the Matthew lectionary year and tied it to Reilly Lewis's Washington Bach Consort. I think we did it three times, over a period of nine years, and each time was significantly different. One famous year, the class as a whole decided to stage a mini-version of the passion for the VTS community. Jay Chadwick rescored it for horns and invited some horn players to help play the orchestral parts; others sang their favorite solo pieces, and we all sang the choruses. Needless to say, I learned a lot from Ray about Bach and the *St. Matthew Passion*. There were many parts of it he loved, but he was especially taken by the opening double chorus, where the daughters of Jerusalem are asked to help tell the story, juxtaposed to a chorale about the sacrifice of the sinless Lamb of God for our sins. And he also especially loved the ending, the chorus at the very end of the passion, which is a kind of lullaby.

It is sung, again, with the help of the daughters of Jerusalem, to the body of Jesus. I couldn't help thinking of it as I prepared this sermon, so I share these words with all of you, but Ray, I speak them to you.

Wir setzen uns mit träner nieder und rufen dir im Grabe zu:
Ruhe sanfte, sanfte ruh; ruhe sanfte, sanfte ruh.

We sit down with tears and we call to you in the grave:
Rest softly, softly rest; rest softly, softly rest.

Ruhe sanfte, Ray, *sanfte ruh*, and thank you for a life well lived,
   a life full of love and hope and laughter.

16

A Sermon Preached in Two Parts by The Rev. Andrew Mead and The Rev. Canon John Andrew at the Requiem Eucharist for Gerre Hancock[1]

St. Thomas Church, New York City
February 5, 2012
This is a sermon with two parts by two preachers.

Part I: Fr. Andrew

In the Name of the true and living God, Father Son, and Holy Spirit. Amen.

"O God, my heart is ready, my heart is ready; I will sing and give praise with the best member that I have" (Ps. 108:1).

I have chosen this verse from the Psalms not merely because it is the motto of this Church of Saint Thomas, but because it encapsulates the character of the great man whose soul we commend to God today. His musical genius flowed from that ready heart of his. His amazing capacity for improvisation at the organ stemmed from it, restless for perfection in the fingers he used to produce heavenly sounds, restless for perfection in the voices of the many generations in the Choir School he encouraged and inspired, restless for perfection in the miracles of their blending in the worship of the Lord he loved. He never stopped. He never gave in. Physical weakness and pain never cowed his priestliness. Yes: priestliness. Around him like a cloak was his priestly readiness to spend himself—and his expectation that others in his care and guidance would honor his Lord by their readiness to give more than they imagined they could ever give in worship.

Uncle Gerre, as generations would call him, had a ready heart for friendship of the committed souls who shared his vision, leading often to the robust loyalty of professional disciples who caught his spirit. He showed them something of the music of heaven, as a priest should. He knew what he was talking about, and he

---

1. Reprinted with permission from the *Journal of the Association of Anglican Musicians* 21, no. 3 (March 2012): 11–13.

talked a lot about it. Blend this readiness of heart with a lightness of spirit and an earthiness of Texan humor, and you can see a portrait emerging of a genius musician who loved his Lord, and laughed. He gladdened our hearts with the funny things he could come out with. One Easter Eve, as we were giving pots of flowers from around the Pascal Candle to the children and Gerre was improvising gently during the distribution, my ear caught a distinct rendering of the song the "Easter Parade." I can still recall the laughter. Such was the partnership: twenty-five happy years of it. I submitted to his authority always when I would rehearse the priest's part of the Versicles and Responses set for that day's evensong. I needed to. As a former chorister myself, when I went off key, he would require me to put it right.

In all those twenty-five years of musical partnership—and social friendship—we only had one scalding row, and it was within my first six weeks as rector, just around Christmas time. A young Australian diplomat at the UN, a devout Anglican and knowledgable with church music, came with his future wife of Spanish descent to discuss the musical details of their forthcoming wedding. His preferences and hopes were very impressive and persuasive. When he had finished, I turned to his future wife and said, "Wonderful suggestions. Now do you have any?" "Oh, Father," she said, "I would love 'Ave Maria'" and hummed the tune. "Wonderful!"—And then I saw Gerre's face. Pea green with fury. "I am appalled, sir. This is no real church music! This is prostituting the boys' voices." His upper lip came out. And he protested more. I listened, and then my patience was exhausted. "Go down and learn the darn thing!"—and exit Gerre.

There was silence in heaven from the music office for two days. On the third day the voice of Gerre was on the phone, with all the happy chirpiness I knew.

"May I come up, sir?"

"Delighted, my dear Gerre."

He stood at my office door. "You won't believe this, Father, but the little so-and-so's learned the blessed thing in twelve minutes."

We cut a record-disc, our first recording together, the next month. The first number was the "Ave Maria": a smash hit. Gerre hit the jackpot with our first recording, as he subsequently did in the settings he composed and are sung worldwide.

So began a quarter-century partnership, enriched by our beloved Judy. Full of hilarity, full of worship's sublime moments, which the sufferings he had to go through never diminished; his ready heart surmounted the depletion of his health. His ready heart of devotion to his wife and daughters never flagged.

Through our tears we know that Gerre, our beloved friend and God's ready servant, in heaven prays for us as he casts a critical eye on the angel choir, for now he sees everything with a clarity of eyes that have seen God.

Part II: Fr. Mead

When I succeeded Father Andrew as rector in 1996, Dr. Hancock catechized me early on concerning a most vital matter. Gerre told me the story of his call to Saint Thomas as organist and master of choristers in 1971. The task of finding the successor to William Self had been delegated to a lay leader who told Gerre that the Choir School would probably close but that Gerre's preeminence as an improviser would provide Saint Thomas with a new musical signature. "Well," said Gerre, "I had run a little men's and boys' choir in Cincinnati, and I thought I'd be—darned—if I'd lie down and play dead and let that school be gone with the wind."

Gerre had not known when he began here in 1971 that the retiring rector, Dr. Morris, would be succeeded by John Andrew, a priest who celebrated liturgies demanding choral music in the Anglican tradition—justifying and calling for the treble voices that the Choir School could produce. And so from 1972 forward, the vision of our Choir School's founder, Dr. Noble, was revived with transformative power by the new young partnership of the rector and director of music. What had seemed in the turbulent decade of the 1960s to be an anachronism from the Middle Ages—a boarding school for boy choristers—was recovered and polished by that dynamic duo as the jewel of our heritage and the key to future success—success in an era when the mainline churches have on so many fronts been challenged by secularity and decline.

Saint Thomas simply would not be what it is today without Gerre Hancock. Attendance, buoyed by his enthusiasm and talent, soared. Between the time our website announcement about Gerre appeared at 10:00 p.m. on the day he died and that midnight, there were 960 hits (and many thousands since)—so much that we have added extra capacity to the site for the webcast of this Requiem lest it crash from overload. Churches around the country—from our mother Trinity Church, Wall Street to Tennessee to California and around the world—have paid special tribute to Gerre since hearing of his death. His influence among church musicians is immense.

Gerre's ashes were privately interred yesterday beneath the chancel pavement, near where the choir director conducts—a permanent tribute to Dr. Hancock's place in our history. Dr. Scott is not quite standing on the spot (you can see and read the inscription on that side), but he is standing on the legacy of his predecessor.

Judith, Gerre's beloved wife, was also his best friend and partner at the organ and in the chancel. For some years she left Saint Thomas to be a director of music in her own right. Gerre clearly missed her, and early on in my time I suggested he ask her back—I thought it would strengthen Gerre's tenure, especially as he contended with physical pain stemming from heart and other surgical procedures. When Judy rejoined him and once more became his associate organist, I saw their love and devotion to each other. Judith was Gerre's great mainstay and support. And as we think of the challenges that children of church musicians face (for example, no Sundays together, at least not much), we admire the love evident in the Hancock family, love reflected by Debbie and Lisa, cherished daughters of this musical superstar couple.

Gerre mentored many other children over generations—the alumni of the Choir School, and they are grieving a paternal loss too. Their families, like Hannah with the boy Samuel in the Bible (1 Sam. 1:28), "lent them to the Lord" as boarding choristers. But Gerre, together with Mr. Clem, their longtime headmaster during those years, helped turn those boys into men, including some outstanding musicians, priests, and other professionals and leaders of accomplishment. It is good to see so many of them; they are family.

We all know Gerre could be very, very funny. Once I told him a young woman in the congregation, who became a seminarian and whom Saint Thomas sponsored for ordination, worked at Radio City Music Hall as one of the dressers for the Rockettes. Gerre deadpanned, Did I know if she was looking for an assistant? In a different life Gerre could have been a musical comedian like Victor Borge. His sidesplitting humor and keyboard mastery, his genius—animated by the rich timbre of his voice resonating from Lubbock, Texas—could find its way (as we have heard) into the Saint Thomas sanctuary. And why shouldn't church be and include fun? The sacrifice of Jesus Christ is, yes, heartbreaking; but his resurrection means that, after all, the Christian life is a divine comedy.

In one of my first Christmas seasons at Saint Thomas there was a service of lessons and carols in the midweek. It's popular and attracts a crowd. Off went the procession from the ambulatory with Gerre at the console playing a magnificent intro to "Hark the Herald Angels Sing." The problem was, the first hymn as printed in the leaflet was "O Come All Ye Faithful." I didn't catch it at first, but the headmaster, Mr. Roland-Adams, did, and keeping his alarm under control whispered the mistake to Gerre on the organ bench as the solemn train behind the processional cross and candles was leaving the station. Not missing a beat, Gerre leaned into an improvisation that then led to a medley of various carol tunes and at last we landed at "O Come All Ye Faithful." It was like a great trailer truck, a lorry juggernaut, backing into a garage from a New York side street—I am amazed how they do it. Walking up to me after the service, Gerre said with a grin, "Father, it's been a great pleasure working for you."

Gerre told the story—it was published in *The Diapason*—of how that brilliant improvising started. As a youngster he had practiced hard and done well for a big piano recital. When he got home his father said, "Gerre, it's time to practice." "Surely not," he replied, "not today." "Yes, we practice every day," said his father. So Gerre deliberately played some notes wrong, and from the other room his father chastised him on the unusual mistake. But Gerre kept on in the same mode, making something out of it. "I enjoyed the rise I got out of my father," said Gerre, "and you can make whatever Freudian sense of it that you will, but that began my love of improvisation." And you know, although Father Andrew and I certainly remember Judith at the console practicing, we can't recall seeing Gerre there for that purpose! He seemed to sit at the console only to play for services!

At a pre-evensong rehearsal in the chancel Gerre once relieved me of a great anxiety as the officiant. I couldn't complete a phrase in a collect because I ran out of breath. With a gentle smile, Gerre said, "Father, whatever is wrong with taking a breath? Just chant, breathe, and continue." With gratitude for that kind moment of instruction, I see Gerre's face every time I chant with the choir.

As we have heard, Gerre was a man of real faith and devotion, with real sympathy for the work of priesthood. The sacred texts of the repertoire moved him, but more than that, the Lord himself was at the center of Gerre's life. Gerre was tough and worked hard, but his faith also enabled him to persevere, with courage and tenacity, over the years. He said his prayers. His work was utterly his vocation from God. He loved Judith and his two "girls." He broke the records and outlived his doctors' predictions. It was an honor to work with him. The young man from Lubbock became a New York Yankee, and he was received back by the University of Texas with distinction—they created a department in the Butler School of Music for Gerre and Judith to develop a degree program in organ and sacred music.

I last saw Gerre at our midnight Mass this past Christmas, where we reserved a front pew on the gospel side of the center aisle for him and Judith. As the grand procession began its way down the center I looked at him, but he had his eyes closed and was looking up, singing heartily, what else—"O Come All Ye Faithful." When I got back from my post-Christmas break, waiting for me was a beautiful note from Gerre. But I did not know that he was so infirm by that time that he may not have seen my reply. Judith told me that by then he was asking for texts by John Donne—one of which is our offertory anthem in this Requiem. Judith, Deborah, and Lisa were there with him. Gerre died in Judith's arms. God is great and good, and his servant is in his unveiled presence now, a presence most certainly including music. As we said in the beginning: "O God my heart is ready!" His soul, delivered now from "the burden of the flesh," is in joy and felicity; and may he rise with Christ in glory.

As for the heritage to which Gerre devoted his life to secure for our beloved Saint Thomas Church and Choir School, to borrow his phrase: "Long may we wave."

In the Name of God the Father, God the Son, and God the Holy Ghost. Amen.

Contributors

The Rev. Jennifer M. Deaton is rector of St. Stephen's Episcopal Church, Indianola and vicar of St. John's Episcopal Church, Leland, both of which are in the Mississippi Delta. She is a retreat leader, writer, and an avid and accomplished knitter.

David Sinden is organist and director of music of St. Peter's Episcopal Church in Ladue, Missouri, a suburb of St. Louis. He is a cohost of the podcast *All Things Rite and Musical*, a frequent blogger, and has an active social media presence.

The Rt. Rev. Deon Johnson is a native of Barbados and is the eleventh bishop of the Episcopal Diocese of Missouri. He and his husband are the parents of two children.

Singer-songwriter, composer, and arranger Keith Tan is minister of music, missions, and outreach at Christ Church, Episcopal in Richmond, Virginia. Working with a number of choral groups, Keith is a sought-after collaborator and frequently speaks at retreats and workshops.

Beauregard, Alabama, native Michael Smith is minister of music to St. Thomas, Whitemarsh, an historic Episcopal church in suburban Philadelphia. Prior to that appointment, he held positions at The Shipley School as well as Groton School.

The Rev. Rita Teschner Powell is the Episcopal chaplain to Harvard University. Her work has taken her to the Black Hills of South Dakota as well as the Taizé community in France.

C. Ellis Reyes Montes is a lifelong Episcopalian and versatile musician who has held a number of leadership positions in service to the Episcopal Church, including work with the Standing Commission on Liturgy and Music and Integrity USA.

CPSIA information can be obtained
at www.ICGtesting.com
Printed in the USA
JSHW052003220522
26021JS00004B/5

9 781640 654440